Adjudicating Fa

While there are many books on Islamic family law, the literature on its enforcement is scarce. This book focuses on how Islamic family law is interpreted and applied by judges in a range of Muslim countries — Sunni and Shi'a, as well as Arab and non-Arab. It thereby aids the understanding of shari'a law in practice in a number of different cultural and political settings. It shows how the existence of differing views of what shari'a is, as well as the presence of a vast body of legal material that judges can refer to, make it possible for courts to interpret Islamic law in creative and innovative ways.

Elisa Giunchi is an assistant professor of History and Institutions of Muslim Countries at the University of Milan, Italy.

Durham Modern Middle East and Islamic World Series

Series Editor: Anoushiravan Ehteshami, University of Durham

Adjudicating Family Law in Muslim Courts

Edited by
Elisa Giunchi

LONDON AND NEW YORK

First published 2014
by Routledge
2 Park Square, Milton Park, Abingdon, Oxfordshire OX14 4RN

and by Routledge
711 Third Avenue, New York, NY 10017

First issued in paperback 2016

Routledge is an imprint of the Taylor & Francis Group, an informa business

British Library Cataloguing in Publication Data
A catalogue record for this book is available from the British Library

Library of Congress Cataloging-in-Publication Data
Adjudicating family law in Muslim courts : cases from the contemporary Muslim world / [edited by] Elisa Giunchi.

pages cm - - (Durham modern Middle East and Islamic world series)

Summary: "While there are many books on Islamic family law, the literature on its enforcement is scarce. This book focuses on how Islamic family law is interpreted and applied by judges in a range of Muslim countries - - Sunni and Shi'a, as well as Arab and non-Arab. It thereby aids the understanding of shari'a law in practice in a number of different cultural and political settings. It shows how the existence of differing views of what shari'a is, as well as the presence of a vast body of legal material which judges can refer to, make it possible for courts to interpret Islamic law in creative and innovative ways"- - Provided by publisher.

Includes bibliographical references and index.

1. Domestic relations (Islamic law) 2. Domestic relations- -Islamic countries.
I. Giunchi, Elisa.

KPB540.3.A35 2013
346'.167015- -dc23

2013019621

ISBN 13: 978-1-138-68738-7 (pbk)
ISBN 13: 978-0-415-81185-9 (hbk)

Typeset in Perpetua
by Taylor & Francis Books

Contents

Acknowledgements

This volume is a product of a longstanding interest in the interpretation of shariʿa and its gender implications in the contemporary world, beginning when, as a PhD student in the mid-1990s, I looked into the enforcement of the 1979 Zina Ordinance by Pakistani courts. Soon it became evident how sexual offences are strictly interconnected with the family structure and its internal asymmetries, and court documents enabled me to have a valuable vantage point on a whole range of legal, religious, political and sociological issues connected to the private domain.

In all these years I have had the fortune to have colleagues who have shared my passion for ideas and stimulated my thinking on a wide range of issues. My family has always supported me and my boys have put up with a mother whose mind is often in faraway places. I am grateful to them all.

Specifically for this book, I wish to thank Werner Menski, Prakash Shah and Philip Ostien for their support in the initial phase of the project, Peter Sowden of Routledge for patiently answering all my queries, Helena Hurd for her editorial assistance, the copyeditor Janet Macmillan for her professionalism, the production editor Ruth Bradley and the authors of the case studies for enriching me with their essays.

Notes on Contributors

Nausheen Ahmed is an accredited mediator and master trainer with the Karachi Centre for Dispute Resolution and has long been a researcher on gender and law. Her research work includes studies on honour killings, law enforcement and gender, and women's property rights in Pakistan.

Nathalie Bernard-Maugiron is a senior researcher at the Institute of Research for Development (IRD) and co-director of the Institute of Islamic Studies and Muslim World Societies (IISMM/EHESS) in Paris. She works on the judiciary, personal status laws and the process of democratic transition in Egypt and in other Arab countries.

Morgan Clarke is university lecturer in social anthropology and Fellow of Keble College at the University of Oxford. His research focuses on Islamic law and its relationship to positive law, secular ethics and the civil state. His most recent work is on Lebanese shari'a courts and their relationship to non-state Islamic institutions.

Elisa Giunchi teaches history and institutions of Islamic countries at the University of Milan, Italy. She is senior research fellow at the Italian Institute for International Political Studies (ISPI), where she co-ordinates the programme on South Asia. Her research focuses on Islamic law and gender in Pakistan.

Monika Lindbekk is a doctoral research fellow at the Faculty of Law at the University of Oslo, Norway. Her PhD research focuses on divorce law in Egypt before and after the Egyptian revolution in 2011.

Fatima Sadiqi is Professor of Linguistics and Gender Studies at the University of Fez, Morocco, and Founding Director of the Isis Centre for Women and Development. She is also a UN gender expert and an active member of numerous international bodies and projects that deal with language, women and gender issues.

Anna Vanzan teaches Arabic culture at the University of Milan and is a visiting lecturer at the European Master M.I.M. Ca' Foscari University where she teaches gender and Islamic thought. Her research focuses on Iranian women and gender in Islam.

Sylvia Vatuk is Professor Emerita of Anthropology at the University of Illinois at Chicago, USA. She has extensively studied kinship and social organization in India.

Her most recent research focuses on Muslim Personal Law and the impact of India's pluralistic legal system upon Muslim women.

Ihsan Yilmaz is Associate Professor of Political Science at Fatih University, Istanbul, Turkey. He is the editor-in-chief of the *European Journal of Economic and Political Studies* (EJEPS) and the editor of *Turkish Journal of Politics* (TJP). Islamic revivalist movements, Muslim legal pluralism and neo-*ijtihad* are among his main research interests.

List of Abbreviations

ADR	alternative dispute resolution
AIMPLB	All India Muslim Personal Law Board
APWA	All Pakistan Women's Association
CrPC	Criminal Procedure Code (India)
DMMA	Dissolution of Muslim Marriages Act 1939 (India)
FCA	Family Courts Act 1984 (India)
FSC	Federal Shariat Court (Pakistan)
HRLN	Human Rights Law Network (India)
IPC	Indian Penal Code
MENA	Middle East and North Africa
MPL	Muslim personal law
MWA	Muslim Women (Protection of Rights on Divorce) Act 1986 (India)
MWVA	Mussalman Wakf Validating Act (India)
OLFR	Ottoman Law of Family Rights
PCMA	Prohibition of Child Marriage Act 2006 (India)
PIL	Public Interest Litigation
RCR	Restitution of Conjugal Rights
SAA	Muslim Personal Law (Shariat) Application Act 1937 (India)
SCC	Supreme Constitutional Court (Egypt)
SIS	State Institute of Statistics (Turkey)
SPO	State Planning Organization (Turkey)
UCC	Uniform Civil Code

Preface

Great attention has been paid in the academic literature to Islamic rules pertaining to marriage and divorce, particularly those that are most at odds with Western legal systems and are seen as discriminating against women, such as polygyny, repudiation and inheritance rules. This might be a product of the persisting Orientalist fascination with Muslim women and their subordinate role and of the awareness that the locus of either change or maintenance of the status quo is the family. In the Muslim world itself, scholars, whatever their ideological inclinations, have long focused on the family as the microcosm of the ideal society and on women as the heart of that microcosm.

While countless books and articles have been produced on classical Islamic law and modern-day legislation on personal status, the actual interpretation and implementation of those statutes has received little scholarly attention until recently. This text-centric approach is integral to what Hallaq calls 'the invented narrative of Islamic legal studies' (Hallaq 2009: 10), reflecting the pervasive idea that to understand Islam and its legal system one has to study texts rather than social and legal practices, an idea based on the assumption that Islamic law is an entity divorced from historical and sociological processes. For a long time, Western academic study of Islam focused on religious texts, preventing scholars from fully grasping the historical evolution and local variations of Islamic law. Partly as a consequence of this distorted image, European intellectuals and colonial officials alike, who partook of the same positivist and Orientalist assumptions, saw shari'a courts as peripheral institutions in the development of Islamic law, where law was applied mechanically and administered by qadis (judges) whose integrity and competence was increasingly questioned. Whether irrelevant or corrupt, or both, shari'a courts did not seem to constitute a useful field of study.[1]

Contributing to the idea of the courts' irrelevance has been the scarcity of documents on their working, particularly concerning judgments given by qadis' in pre-modern times, in contrast to the wealth of fatwas (religious decrees) and fiqh (jurisprudence) literature. For the pre-eighteenth-century period we, therefore, have access mainly to normative works telling us what principles should guide the judge rather than how the judge came to a decision. Court registers, when available, contained decisions that may not have been actually applied, as they could be revoked for a number of reasons. As to travellers' diaries recounting instances of judicial rulings, they were coloured by preconceptions and an incomplete understanding of the legal and social context. To make things more complex, a great part of adjudication remained outside the scope of official courts, particularly in private matters involving family honour.

A further factor explaining why court practice has long been neglected might be that its study falls between different disciplines – social history, legal anthropology, and legal history – which until recently have mostly worked in isolation. Practical hurdles may have also been in the way: studying court documents or observing court practice implies mastering non-Western languages (with the exception of countries where court documents are written in the language of their former colonial masters) and familiarity with legal and religious discourse; court observation requires anthropological sensitivities; and both courts and collections of court records might not be easily accessible or, as in Afghanistan, might have been largely lost in the course of decades of destruction and neglect.

In the second half of the twentieth century earlier court practice in the Muslim world was the object of several studies that reflected a growing interdisciplinary approach and interest in 'law in action' and the deconstruction of Orientalist prejudices. Court records – particularly of courts under Ottoman and Mamluk rulers and in al-Andalus (the Iberian peninsula and Septimania that were under Muslim rule between the eighth and fifteenth centuries) – were increasingly analysed and offered a wealth of information which from the late 1960s onwards led to several publications. In the following decades, particularly since the 1990s, present-day shariʿa courts have received increasing attention.[2] However, to date very little has been written on non-shariʿa official courts that in the contemporary Muslim world apply personal status norms that are inspired by Islamic law – what we might call, following Arabi (2001: 193), 'state Islamic law' or, in the words of Welchman (2004: 6), 'state law-led new shariʿa'.[3] In particular, existing studies on courts in the Muslim world – whether shariʿa or not – do not focus on the religious discourse of judges.

What may have hindered research on this specific issue is the assumption that, nowadays, courts – particularly non-shariʿa ones – simply apply codified law (cf., e.g. Zubaida 2003: 160), as the non-religious background of lay judges coupled with the rigid format of codified prescriptions do not leave great scope for discretion and interpretative creativity. It is also often assumed that legal codes in Muslim countries do not have much to do with Islam, being the product of Westernized elites who copied European legal systems, adding a veneer of authenticity to them in the form of religious references that are socially meaningful.

And yet, I would argue, Muslim codes on personal status are much more than this: they constitute an act of delicate balancing between the wish to preserve ingrained values and beliefs while responding to new circumstances and sensibilities, and are effected through a mixture of traditional methodologies that allow for flexibility and innovation, as well as novel concepts linked to the values and objectives of religion. Far from being a cosmetic adjustment, reforms have mostly occurred within an Islamic methodological and conceptual framework, albeit reshaped and accompanied by concepts and procedures of external origin.

As to the attitudes of judges, even a cursory look at contemporary court practice tells us that, far from simply being 'legal technicians' (Coulson 1969) who adhere strictly to the letter of the law, in several contexts judges, both religious and lay, interpret the statutes with great latitude by referring to external sources, including uncodified religious precepts, encouraged in doing so by the references within the codes themselves to specific *madhhabs* (religious schools), the *fiqh* of which is often turned into the residual law and interpretative framework of positive law, and to *ijtihad* (interpretation of primary sources). This religiously inspired judicial activism raises a number of questions: what are the judges' sources, other than codified norms? What guides their decisions when the religious sources available to them are composite and, at times, contradictory? Is reference to Islamic law used to substantiate, to expand or to contradict codified law? Are religious customs that violate codified law accommodated? The analysis of court practice, through documents and direct observations, can help us answer these important and under-researched questions.

There are many other reasons why studying court practice is important. Court documents indicate to what extent judges adjust the laws and religious discourse to changing social realities, and how they fill legislative gaps and ambiguities. In some cases, they may, de facto, exercise a semi-legislative task that all too important in countries where the parliament and the executive are unable, or unwilling, to reform the law. It needs to be stressed here that reform is particularly sensitive, and therefore politically dangerous, when it pertains to a contested and vital symbol such as the family and women's role within the family. By validating or challenging prevailing discourses, judges, particularly at the highest levels of the judiciary where controversial doctrinal points are most discussed, also take sides in the struggle between competing narratives and imperatives, and in so doing they contribute to wider doctrinal debates. By echoing different definitions and interpretations of Islamic law, court practice also reminds us of a heterogeneity that was central to classical Islamic law and that is often forgotten by simplistic visions of a standard, unified Islam and by calls to enforce it. As devout Muslims in several countries call for the application of shari'a, and in Western societies they strive to see it recognized by the official legal system, what Islamic law is according to Muslim judges, rather than in the abstract prescriptions contained in doctrinal works, is of extreme relevance, though the authority of the rulings of those judges may be contested on religious grounds.

Court documents are also a valuable 'window' on the judges' inclinations, shedding light on the contextual issues that affect their interpretations – primarily their relationship with power and their socio-economic and regional background. Despite being a synopsis rather than a verbatim transcript or account, court documents also contain rich social data and reflect the context where disputes arise, thereby providing insights into society, family and how power is distributed among groups and institutions. While informal adjudication has long been a focus for anthropologists, it is only in the last decades that it has become clear that, in Rosen's words, 'in the Islamic world, as in many other places, the world of formal courts offers a stage – as intense a ritual, as demonstrative as war, through which a society reveals itself' (Rosen 2000: 37).

Particularly interesting aspects include whether women petition the courts, to what extent their demands and expectations are redressed, and what are their strategies to counter legal asymmetries and restrictive customs. While there is now a wide literature on the gender aspects of court practice, particularly in the Ottoman era, the gender implications of religiously inspired judicial activism have not been as well studied. Some of the questions arising are: are uncodified sources referred to by judges used to expand or to limit women's rights as contained in the codes and practiced in society? Are there some sources that more than others can be used to further women's interests?

The aim of the present volume is to contribute to filling a gap in the literature on the practical implementation of law by examining how courts in contemporary Muslim countries interpret and apply Islamic law in matters related to personal status. The reason why the book focuses on family law is that this is the domain of law that has remained most anchored to classical religious prescriptions. It is here, then, that it is easier to see what is the interplay between 'state Islamic law' and classical Islamic law.[4]

The collection of case studies in this volume brings together a number of scholars from different disciplines; most of them base their writings on recent field research focused on court documents, interviews and, in some cases, court observation. With one exception (India), the countries analysed are inhabited by a population the majority of which is Muslim. To avoid the common tendency to equate the Muslim world with the Arab Sunni Middle East, we have included non-Arab states (Turkey, Pakistan, India) and states that are predominantly Shi'a (Iran and Lebanon). The case studies share some characteristics but are different in some respects: all the countries analysed have a plurality of family legal systems that allow recognized religious minorities to follow their own laws, with Lebanon going as far as to provide for distinct laws and courts for Sunnis and Shi'a. Family law is, at least in part, codified, and absorbs classical Islamic principles. One notable exception is Turkey, where shari'a has been replaced altogether by a secular code. Codes on personal status, particularly in the first phase of codification, have been mostly imposed from above, with little or no public debate, reflecting – with the exception of post-Pahlavi Iran – a modernist minority view that has been increasingly contested by neo-traditionalist and Islamist groups. In some cases state intervention through codification has been minimal (Lebanon, India), leaving classical Islamic law almost untouched, while in others, state-directed reform has been far-reaching and detailed (Morocco, Egypt, Iran), with Pakistan at mid-way, implementing limited reforms that are less extensive and courageous than those enacted elsewhere.

The countries analysed have different political systems and institutional settings. References in the constitution to shari'a as a source of law also vary from country to country, as well as references within the codes to a specific *madhhab* as the residual law and to extra-legal sources such as customs. The courts analysed are in some cases shari'a courts, staffed by religious figures (Iran, Lebanon), while in others they have a mixed composition (the Federal Shariat Court in Pakistan) or are staffed by lay judges only (Morocco, Egypt, Turkey, India, family courts and High Courts in Pakistan).

An introductory chapter provides some terminological and conceptual background for those who are not experts in Islamic law and, by drawing on existing literature, as well as on the case studies in this book, delves, on a general level, into modern-day court practice and its religious sources. We then proceed with the case studies, starting with countries that are characterized by a pronounced legislative passivity, before moving on to those that have codified family law in greater detail and reformed it more recently.

The first case study is of Lebanon, where Islamic family law is applied by *shaykhs* with a religious training and within courts that have exclusive jurisdiction over Muslims. In this country Islamic law concerning personal status is still mostly anchored to the Ottoman Law of Family Rights (OLFR), which in 1917 was the first comprehensive codification of family law in the Muslim world. The OLFR expanded women's rights within the family by combining the precepts of different legal schools, but was surpassed by more progressive norms in the countries emerging from the Ottoman Empire, with the partial exception of Palestine and Lebanon. Another peculiarity of Lebanese family law is that there is no unified code for Muslims: while Sunni judges apply the OLFR, but can refer to Hanafi law in residual cases, Shi'i courts can adjudicate according to the Ja'fari doctrine and, where it is in harmony with Ja'fari doctrine, to the OLFR. This is, as we will see, quite a crucial difference, which gives rise to differing practical solutions to family disputes and different rights for women. The OLFR, which draws from different *madhhabs* in fact gives women more rights, particularly with regard to divorce, than Ja'fari *fiqh*. The lack of recent reforms, coupled with the legislated reference to uncodified sources, makes Lebanon potentially open to a great degree of judicial activism. Whether this is the case or not is the subject of Clarke's chapter. In his study, he analyses, on the basis of extended anthropological fieldwork in Beirut in 2003–04 and 2007–08 that focused on initial courts and appeals courts, the functioning of shari'a courts and the family law they apply, and points to the differences between Sunni and Shi'i courts in terms of structure, sources they refer to and rulings.

Legislative passivity on Islamic family law also characterizes India, where Muslims, who constitute a minority, though a conspicuous one, are entitled to follow their religious norms. The family law by which they are governed – known as Muslim personal law – is based upon shari'a as interpreted and modified by British colonial and post-independence Indian courts, and remains largely uncodified. As a consequence, and as in Lebanon, some of the checks and restrictions imposed on men's prerogatives in most other Muslim countries in the last decades do not exist. On the basis of interviews and case files consulted during various field trips – in 1998–99 in Chennai, in 2001 in Hyderabad and in 2005–06 in Delhi and Hyderabad, Sylvia Vatuk reviews the way in which legal pluralism operates in India with respect to some of the key issues of Muslim personal law, both in the state courts (regular civil courts or, in large cities, specialized family courts) and in non-official dispute-settlement venues, where the majority of Muslims take their family disputes. Attention is also given to the changes that Muslim personal law has undergone recently through judicial interventions in cases relating to marriage and its dissolution, indicating that Indian courts, which are staffed by lay judges who are not necessarily Muslim, have at times upheld women's rights in the name of shari'a, thus making up for the lack of legislative reforms.

In neighbouring Pakistan, family law is governed by British enactments dating back to the colonial era and by the Muslim Family Laws Ordinance (MFLO) promulgated in 1961, which expanded women's rights by referring to different *madhhabs*. Since the late 1970s the country underwent a process of Islamization of the legal system and the judiciary, and calls to abrogate or amend the MFLO multiplied. The MFLO was not amended, but constitutional references to the primacy of shari'a were evoked since 1980 by the lay High Courts and the Islamic appeal courts to challenge some of its clauses. In particular, the clauses on registration of marriage and repudiation were not abided by and in their place uncodified norms and principles drawn from a variety of religious sources were applied (Giunchi 1994, 2013). Nausheen Ahmed reviews in her chapter the history of codification of personal status law in Pakistan and investigates how the MFLO has been interpreted by family and superior courts since 1961.

The following two chapters deal with Egypt. Since the 1920s, Egyptian personal status laws have been adopted in a piecemeal manner and have included elements from different legal schools, especially Malikism for issues pertaining to divorce initiated by women. Civil courts, which in 1956 replaced shari'a courts, while called to apply statutory norms drawn from various *madhhabs* are expected to rely on the predominant Hanafi school in the absence of statutory provisions. In 1980, renewed attention to religion resulted in the decision to amend the Constitution so as to turn shari'a into 'the principal source of legislation' (Article 2), but this has not stemmed progressive reforms, the most controversial of which is the 2000 '*khul'* law'. After reviewing the development of Egyptian personal status codes, Monika Lindbekk focuses on their enforcement, using her analysis of judicial decisions from the Supreme Constitutional Court, Court of Cassation, Cairo Appeal Court and family courts in Cairo in the period 2008–10, with some reference to earlier cases. The final section of her chapter looks at prospective changes in family law in the aftermath of the Arab Spring. Nathalie Bernard-Maugiron narrows the investigation of Egyptian court practice by analysing court decisions dealing with judicial divorce for *shiqaq* and polygamy; the cases analysed concern decisions taken after the 1970s by the Court of Cassation, the Supreme Constitutional Court, appeal courts, courts of first instance (until 2004) and family courts (after 2004). Her chapter ends with a discussion of the arguments used by the Supreme Constitutional Court to hold that Egyptian legislation on personal status is in conformity with Article 2 of the Constitution.

The next chapter turns to Morocco. Legislation on personal status in this country is very comprehensive, has been the object of recent reform and is considered one of the most advanced in the Muslim world. Its first codification of family law, the Code of Personal Status, commonly known as *Mudawana*, was enacted soon after independence, in 1957–58, and reformulated the precepts of Maliki jurisprudence so as to expand women's rights and constrain husbands' prerogatives, though retaining the asymmetrical family structure that characterizes classical Islamic law. The Code was the object of minor reforms in 1993 and was replaced by a new *Mudawana al-usra* (Code of the Family) in 2004 that further improved women's status within the family.

The changes introduced in Morocco, in 2004, including the principle of equality of men and women as joint heads of the household and the abolition of the requirement of wife's obedience, were justified by the right of the king, in his position as Commander of the Faithful, to practice *ijtihad*. The new law provided that for issues not addressed by the Code, judges may refer not only to the Malikite school, as prescribed by the previous *Mudawana*, but also to *ijtihad*, in order to 'strive to fulfil and enhance Islamic values, notably justice, equality and amicable social relations'. Clear-cut prescriptions were thus accompanied by the possibility for the judges to resort to uncodified religious sources and even to surpass the rules of classical *fiqh*, leaving great scope for judicial innovation. Fatima Sadiqi reviews the codification of Muslim family law in Morocco since independence and then discusses, on the basis of her fieldwork in the region of Fez-Boulmane and other related material, some cases adjudicated between 2006 and 2012, with the aim of assessing how Moroccan courts today practice *ijtihad* when deciding on cases of divorce for discord (*shiqaq*) and what factors make judges more or less likely to resort to *ijtihad*.

A very different case is that of Iran. In the 1930s, and to a much greater extent in 1967 and 1975 under Reza Shah Pahlavi, Iran widened women's rights within the family and restricted male privileges. In the late 1970s–early 1980s, following the Revolution, the country embarked on a process of Islamization of the legal system that, like Pakistan's Islamization, was primarily focused on women's status and criminal law. One of the first steps taken by Khomeini upon his return to Tehran was to suspend previous family law. Special civil courts, staffed by religious figures, were given the task of judging family law matters on the basis of the Ja'fari school as defined by incremental laws, which coexisted with pre-existing legal concepts and procedures. Family law reforms in subsequent decades led to a reinstatement of some of the pre-Revolution laws and even expanded some women's protections, which was partly a result of the pressure from women's groups and activists. Codified family law, which since 1999 is administered by family courts, has however retained a strongly asymmetrical gender structure, with the clerics controlling the legislation and the judges applying it reluctant to exercise *ijtihad* to further women's rights, despite the reference in the Constitution to the need for the 'continuous *ijtihad* of the *fuqaha*' (jurists)'. Anna Vanzan examines Iranian family law under the Pahlavi, its changes since the onset of the Islamic Revolution, the attempts by women's organizations to press for further legal ameliorations and the way female scholars have furthered new interpretations of shari'a and female litigants have used the courts to expand the rights available to them. As a scholar of Islamic feminism in Iran, she does not analyse court practice, the subject of Mir-Hosseini's seminal work (1993), but focuses on the attempts by women's groups to revise the legal doctrine on the basis of a gender-sensitive reading of the primary sources.

The concluding chapter is devoted to a Muslim country – Turkey – that is a unique case. Under Mustafa Kemal, in the 1920s, Islamic law and shari'a courts were dismantled, and the OFLR was replaced with a code of European inspiration, mostly drawn form Swiss law. Religious customs in the field of family law have continued to survive, however, particularly in rural areas. Ihsan Yilmaz raises the issue of the interaction between the Turkish secular legal system and surviving customs rooted in Islam, focusing on the differences between living and codified law in issues pertaining to the solemnization of marriage, marriage age and polygyny and the ways in which judges address customary behaviours not sanctioned by codified norms, and that are typically brought to their knowledge when the parties want to obtain official recognition of marriage for reasons linked to inheritance or insurance matters or when they are unable to settle a dispute out of court.

The contributions in this volume are no doubt micro-accounts, with no ambition to form a grand narrative valid for the whole Muslim world or to analyse all aspects arising from court practice. However, some interesting elements appear from our limited picture that, hopefully, can shed some light on the complexities of present-day adjudication in the Muslim world and contribute to the growing field of law in action.

Elisa Giunchi
Milano, January 2013,

***

Note on transliteration

To make the volume accessible to non-specialists, a simplified transliteration has been adopted, without diacritical marks; for chapters on non-Arab countries, the spelling chosen by the authors and closer to the local pronunciation has been retained. Thus some inconsistencies will appear, with the same word appearing in different forms of transcription, such as *shari'a* for the Arabic, and *shariat* for the Urdu. A glossary is provided at the end of the book. To indicate plurals the Arabic singular is pluralized according to the English language, by adding a final 's', with the exception of plurals which are commonly used in Western texts, such as *fuqaha'* (pl. of *faqih*) and *'ulama'* (pl. of *'alim*). The article 'al-' and the letters 'hamza' and 'ayn' are disregarded in the alphabetical ordering in the bibliography and index.

Notes

1 Also, contemporary scholars see the *qadis'* role in developing Islamic law as peripheral vis-à-vis that of *muftis* and jurists: cf. for example Hallaq (1994: 55). Many authors also hold a disparaging view of shari'a courts. Lev for example, writing on Indonesia, observed that '[t]here is little question that Islamic courts, nearly everywhere they exist, do not stand out as institutions of great influence, integrity, and innovative sparkle' (Lev 1972: x).
2 Among the few books on shari'a courts adjudicating family law that were published before the 1990s are: Layish (1971 and 1975) on the occupied Palestinian territories of Israel; Djamour (1962) on Singapore; Lev (1972) on Indonesia; for the following period, see among others: Fluehr-Lobban (1987) on the Sudan in the late 1970s; Mir-Hosseini (1993) on Iran and Morocco; Shaham (1997) on Egyptian shari'a courts before they were abolished in 1955; Welchman (2000) on the West Bank; Hassan and Cederroth (1997) on Malaysia; Nurlaelawati (2010), Butt (1999), Bowen (2003 and 2007) on Indonesia; Peletz (2002) on Malaysia; Nasir (2007) on Nigeria; Rosen (2000) on Morocco; Hirsch (1998) on Kenya; Hussain (2007) on India.
3 Among the exceptions are Monsoor (1999) on Bangladesh and some articles that are mentioned in the bibliographies included in this book, such as those by Bernard-Maugiron and Dupret (2008), Sonneveld (2011) and Dupret (2006) on Egypt.
4 A clarification of terminology is required here: with 'Islamic law' I mean, in the Preface and first chapter, classical doctrine that is considered orthodox; by 'state Islamic law' I mean the classical doctrine as reinterpreted by contemporary legislators and found in codes; with 'Muslim law' I indicate law as concretely applied.

1 From Jurists' *Ijtihad* to Judicial Neo-*Ijtihad*

Some introductory observations

Elisa Giunchi

The origins of Islamic legal doctrine

Shari'a is often evoked – by the general public and academics, as well as within judicial proceedings, by litigants and judges alike – to indicate different things. Usually translated as Islamic law, it is often meant as much more than that, i.e. as a 'total discourse' reflecting religion, morality, economics and justice in Islam, or as a set of ethics, governing the every day behaviour of Muslims. When it is considered in its legal aspect only, it is sometimes taken to mean the entire normative edifice of Islam as built in the seventh–eleventh centuries, comprising the prescriptions contained in the sacred sources (the Qur'an and the Sunna, as an embodiment of God's will) and in human, and therefore contestable, legal constructions (*fiqh*, or jurisprudence), thus conflating absolute truth and fallible human reasoning, abstraction and concrete understanding. At other times, shari'a is identified only with the legal component of the Qur'an and Sunna, or even with that of the Qur'an alone. Whether in its limited or expanded legal sense, shari'a is often described as a code. And yet, the legal prescriptions in the Qur'an – only a fraction of the whole text – are often broad or ambiguous enough to tolerate different readings. The *hadiths* (words and deeds of the Prophet) that compose the Sunna are highly contextualized, and there is no total agreement, even among Muslim scholars, on their authenticity. As to the jurisprudence that developed in the centuries after Muhammad's death, it includes divergent opinions, all of them, as we will see, equally legitimate. Thus, despite oft-claimed to the contrary, by no stretch of imagination can shari'a, or *fiqh*, be considered as a code, in the sense of a systematic set of ready-made judiciable prescriptions.

Etymologically, shari'a is the 'path' indicated by God through the revelation and the Sunna. In order to unfold the path, so as to understand it and apply it in concrete situations, in the centuries after Muhammad's death an exegesis of the Qur'an developed and the *hadiths* were collected and screened; those considered as authoritative were validated and incorporated in canonical compilations in the mid-late-ninth century and came to be considered a 'divine scripture' alongside the Qur'an, though of lesser status. The compilations considered most authoritative by the Shi'a appeared slightly later, from the first half of the tenth century to the first half of the following century. To address new

2 Elisa Giunchi

circumstances as the Islamic empire expanded to new geographical areas and ruled increasingly complex societies, these sources were complemented by others; thus Islamic law incorporated mechanisms that ensured its adaptability to new circumstances, the main one being *ijtihad* (individual interpretation of the primary sources), which was practiced by scholars (*mujtahids*) who possessed specific qualifications mainly linked to their scholarly competence.[1]

According to the doctrine of *usul al-fiqh* (the roots of jurisprudence) that emerged in the Sunni world around the ninth–tenth centuries,[2] and is usually, albeit not fully correctly associated with the work of Muhammad b. Idris al-Shafi'i (d. 820),[3] the secondary sources of law are the consensus (*ijma'*) of qualified jurists on a specific legal issue or interpretation, and analogy (*qiyas*) – actually a method to arrive at a norm rather than a source – which was the derivation of rules by analogical extension of rules already established. While several *ijtihads* could converge in consensus, analogy was a restricted form of *ijtihad*, and expressed a compromise between supporters of *ra'y* (individual reasoning) and those who wished to restrict it.

Consensus was often established by the absence of dissenting opinions on a particular legal issue; several factors limited its potential as a method to formulate new legal rules, *in primis* the fact that it needed to have some basis in the Qur'an or Sunna, and that disagreement, once visible and known, could not, according to the majority of classical scholars, be replaced by a later consensus. In some cases *ijma'* was actually at variance with the Qur'an. The caliph Umar for example introduced stoning for adultery, which became for all *fiqh* the standard penalty, though, while found in several *hadiths* attributed to the Prophet, it contradicts the Quranic text, which prescribes flogging (24: 2) as the penalty for sexual crimes, and house confinement for unspecified forms of 'indecency' (4: 15–16). *Ijma'* also validated the 'triple *talaq*', a form of repudiation that immediately dissolves marriage, though this practice is not recognized by the Qur'an. Whether some issues were or were not subject to *ijma'* was actually contentious: for example, while the Hanafi school considered the triple *talaq* as validated by *ijma'*, Hanbali jurists pointed to the contradictory practice reported in the Sunna and to the differing opinions of early scholars and thus rejected any claim of *ijma'*. This takes us to an important point: in matters of substantive law, *ijma'* was considered as a valid source if it was carried out within recognized schools, an issue to which we will return.

Other sources of law and methods of deriving norms from existing sources played a role in the development of *fiqh* to address issues that were not mentioned in scriptural sources, to adapt existing norms to changed circumstances and to accommodate human needs: customs that did not expressly contradict the Qur'an, Sunna and *ijma'* were incorporated in *fiqh*; juristic preference (*istihsan*) motivated by the common good (*maslaha*) was referred to by Hanafis and Hanbalis, often to overcome a stricture of *qiyas*; among the Malikis a similar principle was that of *istislah* (to seek the social good); considerations of *maslaha* and necessity (*darura*), which developed particularly in the context of the discussion on the aims of the law (*maqasid al-shari'a*) in the fourteenth century, also influenced *fiqh* and would be emphasized, as we will see, by reformists in the nineteenth century and onwards.

These methods and sources, or rather, as Abou El Fadl calls them, 'aids to textual interpretation' (Abou El Fadl 2001: 35), contributed to a highly sophisticated and diversified jurisprudence that left wide margins of discretion to the *mufti* (the scholar qualified to issue *fatwas*, i.e. religious decrees) and to the *qadi* (judge). Doctrinal variations, often emerging from distinct cultural and socio-economic circumstances, were streamlined, starting in the eight century, in different bodies of doctrines, resulting in the mid-ninth to early tenth centuries in structured regional schools (*madhhabs*). These schools, named after a leading scholar of that time who putatively founded them, gradually became limited in number, with the Hanafiyya becoming the largest in terms of the total of its adherents. The other Sunni *madhhabs* that survived beyond the eleventh century are the Shafi'iyya, Hanbaliyya and Malikiyya. These schools differed from one another on hermeneutical points and on the relative weight given to various sources, particularly *qiyas* and Sunna, and thus arrived at different rules on virtually every subject, thereby giving rise to a vast body of literature on *ikhtilaf* (difference) that illustrated the variations between *madhhabs* and within each one. Although the Sunni *madhhabs* formed their main identity and structure around the tenth century, subsequent scholars built upon the school's juristic tradition, forming a cumulative body of law that remained very diverse. Differences persisted also within each school, and were pronounced especially within the Hanafiyya.

Far from being the product of irrational thinking, as is often presumed by Western audiences, *ikhtilaf* was grounded in reasoning: prescriptions revealed in the Qur'an and exemplified by the Sunna were the basis for a framework for thinking, under which differing solutions to human problems could be found and new circumstances could be addressed. *Fiqh* indicated how to arrive at an authoritative definition of practice that accommodated time and space rather than a once and for all definition. Past opinions were not to be replicated but were intended to be heuristic examples of a mode of thinking, an epistemological and methodological framework, and an ethical discourse (Wheeler 1996: 239; Vikør 2005: 30). Some opinions were considered stronger than others, in the sense of better argued and based on more solid scriptural grounds, and therefore were agreed upon by a greater number of scholars, but even weaker opinions, as long as discussed within a given framework, were valid, as only God knew the right interpretation. Jurists would be compensated in the hereafter for the *ijtihadi* efforts, and *qadis* for their concrete choice of opinion from those available to them, as long as they made an attempt (*jihad*) to unfold the shari'a to the best of their abilities and without violating express prescriptions laid down in the primary sources and the general values and objectives of religion. All judges could do was to rule on the basis of appearances – the exterior (*zahir*) – thus remaining within the realm of probability: what they provided was a 'probable, but fallible interpretation of infallible texts' (Johansen 1999: 37). This interpretation was based on the knowledge of the litigants and facts, which changed from case to case. A verdict, as a consequence, did not have validity beyond the specific circumstance in which it was expressed. The common law's doctrine of precedent was thus totally foreign to Islamic law, and the appeals system was accepted up to a point: two judgments based on *ijtihad* did not invalidate each other, and *ijtihad* could be reversed only if it departed, according to most jurists, from a clear text of Qur'an, Sunna or explicit *ijma'* or, according to others, if it contradicted *ijma'* (Kamali 1993: 72–73). Qadis could differ not only among themselves, but also with their prior judgments, and did not have to abide by *fatwas* unless they felt they were unable to perform *ijtihad*.[4]

Alongside *qadis'* courts, informal channels of adjudication, as well as *siyasa* courts, linked to the rulers' interests, functioned. The division between profane and religious was permeable: decrees by political authorities were framed in a religious discourse and developed alternative rules and punishments rather than invalidating those mandated by Islamic law, while religious matters were adjudicated also with reference to external factors such as *'urf* (Gerber 1999: 61–63). Issues that were the object of *fiqh* and part of the realm of *qadis*, particularly those issues involving criminal law, were adjudicated by non-shari'a courts in several regions. Even when decided by *qadis*, punishments and evidence requirements were often not in accordance with Islamic law.

Flexibility at the adjudication level was compounded by what Hallaq calls 'a socially embedded system inspired by judicial relativism' (Hallaq 2009a: 165). The judge, who was part and parcel of the community where he served, knew and took into consideration the context in which the parties lived and used this knowledge to mediate and search for compromise. His overarching aim was to ensure social harmony, which meant preserving the status quo while checking abuses and protecting the weakest elements of society from excessive hardship. Judith Tucker, who examined Ottoman Syria and Palestine, found, for example, that *muftis* and *qadis* used a selection of sources and interpretations to enable a flexible interpretation of the law that would best serve the stability of community and the interests of justice (Tucker 1999: 181–82). Kristen Stilt in her study of the *muhtasib* (inspector of public spaces) in Mamluk Egypt similarly observed that the rules of *fiqh* were not predictive of decisions and many contextual factors influenced jurists as well as public officers (Stilt 2011). The attempt to avoid excessive hardship meant that the worst abuses against women were corrected by bringing gender relations within their shari'a limits or even, in some cases, expanding the limits outside the bounds of *fiqh*. Also *fatwas*, which were consulted by jurists when compiling treatises and by judges applying the law, reflected gender imbalances while checking abuses. While Hallaq may go too far when stating that women were afforded 'plenty of agency' (Hallaq 2009a: 196), there is no doubt that the judge often offered them a sympathetic ear. Many studies on the Ottoman Empire show that women easily approached the courts, often saw their grievances redressed, were assertive in presenting their case, and developed strategies to maximize the rights they enjoyed (Peirce 2003; Meriwether 1996; Zilfi 1997).

The flexibility described above might induce the reader to imagine Islamic legal doctrine as haphazard and court practice as totally arbitrary, as an Orientalist interpretation of Islam has suggested.[5] Judges, however, shared certain principles and sources, did not question unequivocal divine texts and substantive rules on which a solid *ijma'* existed and acted within a given ethical, methodological and epistemological framework. Those who did not conform to this framework were excluded from orthodoxy and prevented from participating in the development of Islamic law, thus condemned to marginality or extinction. It was to escape this fate, according to some scholars, that the mainstream Shi'a adopted an *usul al-fiqh* that conformed to the Sunni legal doctrine (Stewart 1998).

The Shi'i body of law and methodologies, which became a distinct legal theory in the tenth century, continued to develop its doctrine on secondary sources in the following centuries and perfected its methodology after the establishment of the Safavid state in the early sixteenth century. Despite its similarities to Sunni doctrine, Shi'i legal thought has some peculiarities. As the Twelvers (or *Ithna'Ashari*), who follow the Ja'fari *fiqh* and form the main Shi'a group, did not refer to a living *imam* after the ninth century, the *hadiths* of past *imams* became central to them. They thus developed their own compilations of Sunna based on narrations of the *imams*, which had authority alongside the *hadiths* referring to the Prophet's example as recounted by the *imams* themselves. *Ijma'*, usually not referred by that name, was accepted with some reservation and increasingly obscured by the role of the living *mujtahid*. *Qiyas* was rejected and replaced with the evidence of reason, *dalil al-'aql*. The *imams* inherited some functions of Muhammad and, in turn, according to a later doctrinal development, the twelfth *imam* after his occultation transmitted those functions to the higher religious scholars, enabling the knowledge of God's will to continue after the end of revelation. *Ijtihad*, generally accepted in the thirteenth and early-fourteenth centuries, was assigned to *mujtahids* who were required to hold qualifications similar to those of their Sunni counterparts, with laymen allowed to choose which one they would follow. In theory, *ijtihad* aimed to find what the twelfth *imam* would have decided had he been present, which implied a good dose of caution was needed. As a consequence, freedom to practice *ijtihad* was de facto limited, and most later *mujtahids* confirmed what previous jurists had said (Gleave 2005: 133–34; Clarke 2001: 63). The concept of a *marjia' al-taqlid* – the ultimate source of emulation, which although rooted in earlier times was fully explicated in the nineteenth century – would further limit innovation and excessive doctrinal heterogeneity.[6]

The door of *ijtihad* becomes ajar

In the mid-twentieth century it became quite common among Western scholars to write that around the ninth–tenth century the dynamism of the formative period had ended within the Sunni fold. According to this thinking, usually attributed to Schacht (1964), but shared by many others, in that period Sunni jurists agreed that the *ijma'* of previous jurists should be followed (*taqlid*), and new interpretations avoided. This decision, which was accompanied by a growing diffidence to external philosophical inputs, called *bid'a*, was referred to as 'the closing of the door of *ijtihad*' and was seen as prompted to a large extent by the fragmentation and decline of the Abbasid dynasty and its eventual collapse in 1258. Since the 1980s, scholarship, in particular that of Wael Hallaq, has questioned this idea, concluding that *ijtihad* never stopped, either in theory or in practice, despite increasing limits to its scope (Hallaq 1984; see also Gerber 1999).

These limits aimed to create a canon. From the beginning, Islamic religious and legal doctrine became increasingly systematized, following a pattern of rationalization that has characterized all major religions. The writing down of the Qur'an, the emergence of the theory of abrogation and the selection of authentic *hadiths* were early attempts to define orthodoxy, thereby limiting whim (*hawa'*) – which was considered as contrary to justice – as well as political contestation. As *fiqh* grew, displaying increasing internal variations, further mechanisms were devised to control innovation and limit discretion at the adjudication level. The ethos of diversity, exemplified by *ikhtilaf*, came to coexist with the ethos of structure, stability and unity (Abou El Fadl 2001: 11). Thinking outside the recognized *madhhabs* became increasingly difficult: while scholars continued to develop the legal doctrine, their opinions were mainstreamed into the main existing schools. Interpretations outside those schools came to be considered as heterodox, eventually disappeared or, as with Twelver Shi'ism, felt compelled to conform in order to escape this fate and to contribute to wider doctrinal debates. Within the main *madhhabs*, with the partial exception of the Hanbali school, the practice of following past rulings grew stronger, limiting the scope of fresh *ijtihad*, and scholars who had purportedly founded a *madhhab* became the ultimate source of authority. The development of an internal hierarchy resulted in the compilation of abridged manuals (*mukhtasar*), which included the most authoritative rules of legal schools. This allowed the *madhhabs*, and particularly the Hanafiyya, the most heterogeneous one and therefore the one that most needed to be systematized, to become more homogeneous. The development of a hierarchy was particularly evident among the Twelver Shi'a, and culminated in the nineteenth century in the decision to have a *marja-e taqlid*, or source of emulation with the greatest doctrinal authority, at the apex of that hierarchy.

As a parallel development, to address a doctrine that had become very sophisticated, *ijtihad* came to be practised to different degrees by '*ulama*' according to the level of their qualifications and expertise. What we may call 'total *ijtihad*' – as practised by someone who has mastered all of legal science – became the preserve of a smaller number of specialists and eventually was considered by most scholars as no longer possible. When the Hanafi, Maliki and some Shafi'i jurists claimed that there was no scholar around who could claim the status of *mujtahid*, by this they meant an 'independent' *mujtahid* who could give a fresh interpretation of the scriptures with regard to any legal issue and was cognizant of all of *fiqh*. Less senior and less capable *mujtahids*, who could practice *ijtihad* within the methodology of their own school or formulate subsidiary rules using *qiyas*, continued to exist. This meant that *taqlid* became diffused, with virtually all *mujtahids* practising it on some issues, and coexisted with *ijtihad*.

It is important to emphasize that scholars from all schools continued to contribute to their *madhhab* through commentaries on the opinions of their predecessors and through *fatwas* (Johansen 1993; Wheeler 1996: 236). *Mukhtasars*, which synthesized the development of law, were themselves the object of further commentaries and elaboration. Some schools, primarily the Hanbali one, used *ijtihad* more freely than others, with Ibn Taymiyya (d. 1328) going as far as to hold that even a lay person may practise *ijtihad* and that it should be used in each specific case. Also, al-Mawardi (d. 1058), a renowned *faqih* (jurist) and himself a *qadi*, thought that a judge should not be bound to adhere to a specific *madhhab* unless his *ijtihad* led him in that direction.

Islamic legal doctrine thus continued through a cumulative and dialectical process to be 'an ongoing argument' (Messick 1993: 33), with previous authority refined, questioned and occasionally supplemented by new opinions. While the teaching of law remained within its *madhhab* traditions, thus maintaining the unity of the legal system, other literary genres, such as the commentaries and *fatwas*, provided new solutions, adding new material to the existing legal treaties (Johansen 1993: 30–31). *Qadis* themselves, by selecting some opinions and ignoring others, continued to adapt *fiqh* to new circumstances, sometimes even dissenting from *fatwas*. When an innovating decision by an established scholar acting as a judge was repeated, an 'established custom' emerged that was incorporated into the law by *fatwas* and legal literature, and inserted in the appropriate shar'i framework and argumentation, thus contributing to ongoing *ijtihad* (Hoexter 2007: 72–73).

The modern state and social control

The search for uniformity accelerated with the formation of centralized systems of governance under the Ottoman, Mughal and Qajar empires. As strong and modern states were built, rulers tried to unify and control the application of the law by promoting a single school over others. Thus the Ottomans for example enjoined the *qadis* administering Hanafi fiqh, their 'official school', to follow the most authoritative opinions of the Hanafiyya and when, in the beginning of the sixteenth century, they conquered large parts of the Arab Middle East, where other *madhhabs* existed, they displayed an increasing pro-Hanafi bias. Indeterminacy was also fought, and control exercised, by way of *fatwas* issued by the chief *mufti* of the empire. The *fatwas* were particularly effective when accompanied by a sultanic decree addressed to all *qadis* of the empire (Hoexter 2007: 78–79). In the second half of the seventeenth century the Emperor Aurangzeb in Mughal India similarly insisted on Hanafi law and simplified the legal doctrine by ordering the compilation of *fatwas* belonging to this school, resulting in the *Fatawa-e-Alamgiri*. Despite the fact that this work contained contradictory material, leaving some scope for discretion, the fact that the Ottomans did not completely prohibit judges' recourse to different schools, and the fact that everywhere the reach of officialdom was mainly limited to urban areas, the tendency towards top-down homogenization and away from flexibility was incontrovertible.

Together with the attempt to promote consistency came procedural changes. Writing was increasingly introduced as a means of control and as a sign of modernity, and adjudication became part of a growing state apparatus. In some parts of the Ottoman Empire, for example, the requirement that marriages be recorded was introduced, court documents were removed from the private domain of judges, courts were given a physical site – a public courtroom – and the single *qadi*, who had been part of the community where he served, became a salaried official and was replaced by a number of judges often originating from other areas. Thus judges became removed from the litigants' milieu, turning what had been a personalized adjudication process into a more impersonal one. Their allegiance became divided between the state – their employer and, increasingly, the source of legislation on matters lying outside the private sphere – and God, the ultimate lawmaker.

This trend was bolstered by the reformists' search, from Ibn 'Abd al-Wahhab (d. 1787) and Shah Waliallah (d. 1782) onwards, for an 'authentic' Islam, away from human 'deviations' and back to the scriptures, so as to deter internal decay and foreign encroachments. As part of this return to the original message, the diversity of *fiqh* was negated in favour of a simplified and cohesive legal framework. In the nineteenth century the search for authenticity bifurcated between traditionalists and modernists, with the latter relativizing the Qur'an and Sunna to time and space and focusing on their broad principles, and the former more anchored to a literal reading of the primary sources. However, both emphasized an original Islam represented by the Qur'an and Sunna as the ideal to go back to, thereby devaluing *fiqh* and implicitly making religious scholars redundant; in the meantime lay people were called to directly access the primary sources and could do so thanks to advances in schooling. *Taqlid* was increasingly challenged: reforms were invoked, by Jamal al-Din al-Afghani (d. 1897) and Muhammad 'Abduh

(d. 1905) onwards, under the right to exercise *ijtihad*, while the role of *ijma'* was increasingly limited (Kerr 1966).

Under the deconstruction of traditional Islam, *madhhab* identification also weakened considerably among religious scholars, and the boundaries between schools started to blur, as an analysis of *fatwas* shows (Messick 2005: 162–74). Inter- and intra-*madhhab* heterogeneity was an uncomfortable feature, particularly for reformists who, whether modernist or not, saw systematicity and coherence as the hallmarks of modernity. Thus calls for *takhayyur* (the choosing of a legal opinion outside one's own school) and *talfiq* (fusing of different legal opinions), debated since the seventeenth century, multiplied as they were seen as means to bring about reforms that would suit modern conditions while preserving Islamic values (Krawietz 2002). Reformers also emphasized *maslaha* as a means to adapt shari'a to new situations but transformed it: while originally it had been strictly linked to textual sources, now it became a subjective evaluation of human benefit, linked to the 'spirit' of revelation and its social goals, and at times contradicting both *ijma'* and Sunna.

The search for uniformity, which emerged as an autochthonous quest, became irreversible with the contact with colonialism and, through it, with the ideas of coherence that informed Europe's legal developments in the nineteenth century. Colonial officers were confronted with juristic disagreement, conflicting practices and, in general, a flexibility that they were not familiar with and that appeared to them as a mere caprice and arbitrariness associated with an irrational Orient. This prompted them to 'rationalize' the law of their subjects, which meant reducing its richness and sophistication. Although colonial powers differed in the degree to which they recognized shari'a and local customs and the extent to which they replaced them, they all tended to interfere with the local legal system by introducing new legislation. Legislation greatly simplified the complexity of local law: some opinions were retained and others ignored from the huge body of *fiqh* that had developed through the centuries, leaving nuances and subtleties behind when they could not easily fit into judiciable norms. What was retained was severed from its commentarial tradition, adapted to colonial sensitivities and interests and delinked from it local context. Traditionally, the judge had attempted to adapt religious ideals to the need to preserve communal harmony while protecting the weak, and to this end facilitated compromises between the parties. Now an all-or-nothing approach was introduced where, at the end of the judicial process, there was a winner and a loser and no room for mediation. A hierarchical judicial structure was introduced, dispensing with the idea that a *qadi*'s *ijtihad* could not be overruled. The jurisdiction of shari'a courts was increasingly narrowed and ultimately limited to family matters, while *muftis* were increasingly marginalized from the legal process.

As Hallaq notes (2009b: 105): 'Ironically, the machinery and tools of the modern state were called upon by both the colonizers and the colonized, for through these modern governing instruments the colonizers aimed to colonize, whereas the colonized wanted, at most to decolonize.' Reforms were not only aimed at resisting foreign encroachments, but, as we have seen, were attempts to form centralized, efficient states that responded to the interests of the authorities and merged with the pre-existing trend in Muslim history towards coherence and authenticity. The reforms were also an expression of the colonized elites' fascination with novel ideas associated with modernity. Steeped in European culture, they believed in the centrality of the state and of positive law and wanted, through state-directed legislation, to shake off the remains of what they perceived as backwardness.

It is indicative that efforts at homogenizing the law and restructuring the legal system along modern lines were made also by Muslim states that were not colonized. During the nineteenth century, as we have seen, the Ottoman rulers increasingly imposed top-down control and supervision of the judiciary and introduced modern codes as part of the reorganization (*Tanzimat*) of the Empire. The word *Tanzimat* significantly comes from *nizam*, order, the leitmotif of reforms: their aim was to tame a *fiqh* that had become to the elites' eyes 'problematically vast, difficult to assess, and ... inappropriate for the times' (Messick 1993: 54). Thus a number of codes, most importantly the Mecelle (1873) that dealt mainly with economic and procedural matters, were introduced, where precepts, distilled from *fiqh* through *takhayyur*, were set out in numbered articles that were short and clear cut and did not leave room for the nuances and intricacies of *fiqh*. A similar process was attempted in Afghanistan under King Amanullah in the first half of the twentieth century, though it was much slower and more limited, and eventually the conservative nature of the Afghan society and foreign interferences caused a backlash.

Although metamorphosed through the introduction of new administrative and procedural techniques, the substance of family law was long spared by colonial powers that did not want to interfere with a very sensitive sector and, in any case, considered it irrelevant to their political and economic interests. Non-colonized countries were similarly reluctant to reform this area. The first attempt to introduce a comprehensive codification of family law occurred only in 1917, with the Ottoman Law of Family Rights (OLFR), which was the springboard for similar reforms throughout the Middle East in subsequent decades. To understand the changes introduced by the OLFR and subsequent laws we must outline some of the basic features of classical Islamic family law.

Some elements of classical family law

Although there are considerable variations between and within *madhhabs*,[7] it can be said that Islamic law provides that men and women of sound mind who have reached puberty are eligible for marriage if no legal obstacles exist. Such obstacles are described in great detail in the doctrine and include marriage within the prohibited degrees and to a woman who is not a *kitabiyya* (i.e. in today's world, a woman who is not Muslim, Christian or Jew). *Fiqh*, particularly within the Hanbali *madhhab*, allows stipulations that modify marital rights and duties, including those that safeguard or ameliorate women's condition, as long as they do not run counter to the objectives and main ingredients of marriage. Sunnis agree that the presence of witnesses is essential to ensure publicity and distinguish between lawful intercourse and *zina*, which carries heavy penalties. The woman contracts her marriage through a male agnate *wali* (guardian), usually her father, though the Hanafi school believes that if she has already attained puberty this requirement can be dispensed with.[8] The *wali* can, in any case, dissolve the marriage if the groom is not equal to the woman's family under the doctrine of *kafa'a* (equality). There must be equality in religion and, according to most *madhhabs*, in social standing, by which is actually meant that man should be equal or superior to the wife's father in social status.[9] *Kafa'a* is important not only because it constitutes a ground for dissolving marriage, but also because *nafaqa* (maintenance) by the husband must be proportionate to what the wife was accustomed to in her own family. The Hanafi also believe that a woman given in marriage by her *wali* can rescind the union upon attaining puberty if the marriage has not been consummated and provided that the *wali* was not her father or paternal grandfather (the so-called option of puberty). Consummation has other legal implications: for example, if marriage is dissolved before consummation the woman is entitled to only part of the *mahr* (dower). Sexual intercourse also prevents divorce for impotence and creates kin prohibitions.

The *mahr*, not to be confused with the 'bride-price' that is customary in many Muslim countries, is an amount of money, an object or property given by the groom to the bride and has to be specified in the contract. Prompt dower is payable upon marriage, and the deferred portion has to be paid upon divorce or upon death of the husband and constitutes a deterrent to easy repudiations. If the amount of *mahr* is not specified in the contract, the marriage is valid but the proper dower (*mahr al-mithl*) becomes due, calculated on the basis of the sum agreed for women of similar social standing and other female members of the wife's family. The wife solely owns her dower and any other property she acquires before and after the marriage.

Only the Shi'a recognize a marriage limited in time (*mut'a*), ensuing from a contract that establishes the date when the marriage will end. Mut'a does away with some characteristics of other kinds of marriage, such as the requirement of financial support and the women's rights of inheritance.

Marriage can be polygynous: men can have up to four wives simultaneously and, according to classical doctrine, an unlimited number of concubines. Wives are expected to be obedient, though what this means exactly is subject to interpretation, and in return they receive maintenance during the duration of the marriage and in the *'idda*, the waiting period of three months (four months and 10 days for widows) following divorce. Divorced women and widows are entitled to *mahr* until delivery if they are pregnant. Maintenance includes food, clothing and lodging, and depends on the social and economic status of the wife's family.

The husband is entitled to divorce by *talaq*, a unilateral declaration that does not require any good cause and that, according to the Sunnis, does not need any witnesses, nor the wife's consent; according to most classical jurists, it is valid even if she is not notified. In the 'revocable *talaq*' the husband utters a single pronouncement and can revoke it during the *'idda* without any formalities, even if the wife opposes its revocation; when the *'idda* has ended, if no reconciliation has taken place the *talaq* becomes final, though the couple can remarry. Repudiation can occur up to three times. If the wife is repudiated for the third time, the *talaq* becomes absolute and the couple can remarry only if an intervening marriage occurs, is consummated and then rescinded by divorce or widowhood. The Hanafis approve *talaqs* that are unintentional, contrary to other schools that reject such repudiations. Shi'a rules for *talaq* are more stringent and require two trustworthy male witnesses and unambiguous statements that include the term *talaq* or one of its derivatives. A common method of *talaq* is 'triple *talaq*', or *talaq* al-bid'a (innovatory *talaq*), which is three pronouncements at one time and has the same effect as the third *talaq*. This kind of repudiation becomes effective immediately and irrevocably severs the marriage. The triple repudiation is considered invalid by the Shi'a, while most Sunni jurists consider it as reprehensible but nonetheless valid.

Women can obtain divorce in the following circumstances: if the husband delegates to her the power of divorce (*talaq al-tafwid*) or if he consents to it, in exchange for some form of compensation (*khul'*); if both spouses seek dissolution of the marriage, the process is known as *mubara'* and does not require the wife's forfeiture of financial rights other than the return of her dower. If these avenues are not open to the wife, she has to go to court to obtain judicial dissolution (*tafriq*) or annulment (*faskh*) if there is some irregularity in the marriage contract or in the characteristics of the parties contracting marriage. Available grounds vary considerably from school to school. The valid grounds that the Hanafi recognize for a judicial divorce are mainly apostasy and impotence, while the Maliki, on the opposite side of the spectrum, allow a wide array of grounds for judicial divorce, including failure to provide maintenance, prolonged absence, harm or ill-treatment (*darar*) which can be even a single wrongful act.[10] The Twelvers allow judicial divorce only in the event of the husband's impotence, provided that the wife did not know about it at the time of divorce, or of his apostasy.

Males inherit double the portion of females. For all *madhhabs*, the divorced wife has no right to financial support after the *'idda* other than the deferred part of the dower and she keeps the custody (*hadana*) of her children only for a certain number of years, which varies from school to school. She loses the right of custody if she remarries outside the husband's family, if she changes her religion or proves to be immoral. The father must maintain his children even after divorce until they reach a certain age and must pay the ex-wife for the *hadana* – a sort of caretaker wage. Only in some rare circumstances can the wife obtain guardianship (*wilaya*), which means taking all major decisions concerning the children.[11]

The codification of family law

The OLFR introduced some changes that were foreign to the *fiqh* rules described above: for instance, it made registration of marriage and divorce compulsory and set a minimum age of majority, though the *qadi* could approve marriage below the prescribed age. On some points it drew from *madhhabs* other than the official Hanafi school: for example, relying on Hanbalism, it established that stipulations limiting men's prerogatives could be inserted in a marriage contract, providing, for example, that a man could not take an additional wife; adopting the Hanbali view, recourse to *talaq* was restricted in that it was invalid if pronounced without intent, for example, under intoxication or compulsion; drawing from Maliki norms, the OLFR recognized various situations in which a woman could sue for divorce, including absence of the husband, incurable defects and diseases hindering conjugal relations, and discord (*shiqaq*).[12]

The first major reforms after the OLFR were introduced in Egypt in the 1920s, expanding the grounds for divorce available to women, restricting polygamy and *talaq* and raising the minimum age for marriage. In India, in 1929 the British fixed a minimum age of marriage, and ten years later they established, by referring to the Maliki *madhhab*, additional grounds for divorce initiated by women. In 1926, Turkey adopted a code that eliminated all reference to shari'a, thus doing away with the most distinctive features of the Islamic marriage, such as polygamy and *talaq*. Limited reforms were undertaken in the 1930s by Iran; in the same decade, the Sudan extended the period of child custody, outlawed triple *talaq* and regulated other forms of repudiation.

Family law reform spread after Muslim countries acquired independence. Introducing prescriptions similar to those of the OLFR, Jordan enacted its family law in 1951, Syria in 1953, Morocco in 1957–58, Tunisia in 1956, Iraq in 1959, Pakistan in 1961, South Yemen and Indonesia in 1974 and Somalia in 1975. In Iran, Reza Shah Pahlavi introduced new legislation on family law in 1967, and extended it in 1975. The Sudan expanded its reforms in 1973 and 1977; Afghanistan promulgated a civil code in 1971 and reformed it in 1977.[13] As these reforms ameliorating women's status within the domestic sphere were being adopted, a renewed interest in religion started in Muslim countries, resulting in the emergence of Islamist parties and neo-traditionalist movements that called for the amendment or abrogation of existing legislation so as to bring it in conformity with 'authentic' Islam.

This Islamic surge did not result in the abrogation of previous legislation on personal status and did not deter further improvements called for by women activists. In Egypt a new law was introduced in 1979 under Sadat's rule, repealed in 1984 on procedural grounds and replaced in 1985 under Mubarak by a new law that incorporated many of the elements of the 1979 law, in particular, limiting polygyny, introducing divorce for discord and providing new financial rights for repudiated women. In 2000 a law allowed women to divorce, with or without the husband's agreement, in exchange for any money, good or property he had given her upon their marriage and provided she forwent all remaining financial rights. In Iran, soon after the Revolution the Khomeinist regime suspended previous family law, but in subsequent decades some norms were introduced to relax post-revolutionary legislation.

The first decade of the twenty-first century saw further reforms. Morocco introduced minor reforms to its Mudawana in 1993, followed by a new radical Mudawana in 2004 that increased the age of marriage, abolished the legal requirement of wife's obedience, required judicial authorization to take a second wife and placed *talaq* under judicial oversight. New forms of divorce were also introduced, including divorce for irreconcilable differences. Legislation on personal status was also adopted in the United Arab Emirates (UAE), which in 2005 codified a family law with a more traditionalist approach.

Some countries were not touched by the second and third phases of codification, and as a consequence have lagged behind social and legal developments. Legislative passivity has been particularly pronounced in India where Muslims are still governed by Islamic law as interpreted by colonial laws and post-independence Indian courts. In Pakistan and Bangladesh, which on its independence inherited Pakistan's legal system, family law is still mostly regulated by colonial enactments and by the 1961 Muslim Family Laws Ordinance (MFLO), with minor amendments in Bangladesh. In Lebanon, Islamic family law remains anchored to the OFLR, which has long been replaced by other countries in the region. Person status is also mostly based on the OFLR in Palestine, though reforms introduced mainly by Israeli authorities have contributed to a pronounced heterogeneity of laws and jurisdiction dividing Gaza, the West Bank and East Jerusalem. Saudi Arabia has not codified its family law, and traditionally-trained judges resort to Hanbali fiqh books and occasionally to other *madhhabs* when administering the law. It may be interesting to note that the Saudi experience is in stark contrast to that of post-revolutionary Iran, which, despite being ruled by religious scholars, has chosen to depart from classical Islam by making the judge dependent on codes that on some points are at variance with Ja'fari *fiqh*.

Where it occurred, the process of codification presented distinctive features in different countries. Some reforms were more radical than others – Tunisia for example did away with polygamy and *talaq*, while most other countries simply restricted these practices, subordinating them to controls and conditions. Some reforms, as in Egypt, were piecemeal, addressing particular matters in subsequent laws. But, despite differences, some common elements are discernible: all countries that codified their family law, with the exception of Turkey and the partial exception of Tunisia, incorporated the distinctive features of Islamic family law in their legislation, preserving men's prerogatives while at the same time limiting them. The limits and controls imposed on these practices were similar: polygyny and unilateral repudiation were constrained to varying extents and put under judicial supervision; in most countries, legislators outlawed the triple *talaq*; the mother's right to child custody was widened; registration of marriages and divorce was introduced to avoid *zina* cases and facilitate integration of children into the family unit; *wali*'s prerogatives were eroded; and a wife's access to judicial divorce was considerably extended. These changes were mitigated by the fact that punishments for non-compliance were light and that outlawed actions, such as under-age and unregistered marriages, were not in many cases considered invalid.

Some reforms were justified by the fact that they were not explicitly forbidden by Islamic law (for example, the requirement for registration of marriages and divorces); most, however, were legitimized by recourse to the traditional mechanisms of flexibility offered by *fiqh*. In most cases, legislators took advantage of differences between and within *madhhabs*. Takhayyur and *talfiq* were prevailing features of all codification efforts – no code relied on just one school. These were traditional mechanisms (particularly in the Hanafi and Hanbali schools), but were emphasized and refashioned: while traditionally *takhayyur* had been mostly restricted to the dominant opinions of other *madhhabs*, now even minority positions were accepted.

In some cases the *madhhabs*' constraints were bypassed by recourse to *ijtihad*, with legislators referring to the revelation, and particularly to its general principles and 'intentions' as had been advocated by nineteenth-century reformists. Tunisia, for example, prohibited polygamy arguing on the basis of a combination of various Qur'anic verses that the man was allowed to marry up to four wives *only if* he were just and fair to all of them, something that the Qur'an itself deemed not possible for human beings (4: 2–3 and 4: 129). The 2004 Mudawana introduces some of its main changes in the name of *ijtihad*. For example, the introduction of divorce by *shiqaq* has been justified by recourse to verse 4:35. Another example of a drastic change to a traditional norm justified by recourse to the Quranic text and to *ikhtilaf* is the law of *khul'* in Egypt. While *fiqh* is nearly unanimous in establishing that *khul'* necessitates the husband's consent, the law I/2000 makes is possible for wives to obtain a judicial divorce even if their husbands oppose it, thus bringing divorce law closer to no-fault divorce.[14]

We should perhaps use the term neo-ijtihad, as some of the traditional features of *ijtihad* are considerably altered. The most obvious alteration is that the legislators are not *mujtahids*. With the possible exception of Iran, where legislation is dependent on Islamic review by an external body partly staffed by religious experts, legislators – whether kings assisted by commissions, national elected assemblies or presidents in undemocratic systems – are not qualified according to traditional parameters to practice *ijtihad*. We should also add that *ijtihad*, which traditionally was excluded for matters covered by *ijma'* and referred to specific textual prescriptions, is now evoked and often used for issues on which there is a consensus and is justified at times by resorting to modern and contemporary scholars and to very general references to Quranic principles.

Reform, whether by *takhayyur* or *ijtihad*, has not covered all aspects of family law. The precepts regulated by clear and unambiguous textual prescription and on which a solid *ijma'* exists have been more difficult to reform, particularly when they touch ingrained economic interests. Thus inheritance rules, which, through complicated rules detailed in the Qur'an, provide that females inherit half of what male heirs in a similar position inherit, have been mostly untouched by codifications.

Islamic review of family law

While pressure from Islamist groups since the 1970s has neither resulted in the repeal of family law legislation, nor prevented further reform, in some countries the constitution has been amended to give enhanced importance to the shari'a as a source of law. In Egypt the 1971 constitution established that 'Islamic shari'a is *a* principal source of legislation'. This clause was considered descriptive and did not prompt attempts to Islamize the laws or to challenge them in court. Things changed when a 1980 amendment turned shari'a into '*the* principal source of legislation' (Art. 2), with the Supreme Constitutional Court (SCC), composed of lay judges not well versed in Islamic doctrine, paradoxically vested with the function of Islamic review. The SCC has in turn confirmed the lay members of the People's Assembly as capable and qualified to perform *ijtihad* and laid down a method through which lower lay courts can establish whether or not Egyptian law conforms to the shari'a. The constitution adopted in 2012 after the ousting of Mubarak reaffirms that shari'a is the principle source of legislation, adding that 'Al-Azhar senior scholars are to be consulted in matters pertaining to Islamic law' (Art. 4). The role of the association of senior scholars of al-Azhar, which was reconstituted in 2012 and comprise '*ulama*' representing the four Sunni *madhhabs*, is not defined in detail, but many believe that its decisions, albeit not binding, will carry great moral weight and may eventually strip the parliament and the judiciary of their powers.

In Pakistan the 'repugnancy clause', included since 1956 in the country's constitutions, established that all laws must be brought into conformity with 'the injunctions of Islam as laid down in the holy Qur'an and Sunna' and that no laws must be enacted that contradict such injunctions; however, that clause long remained dormant because until 1980 no court existed that was entitled to review the Islamicity of laws. As in Egypt, a shift occurred in the 1980s. In 1980 the Federal Shariat Court (FSC), composed of lay judges and '*ulama*', was entrusted with reviewing the Islamicity of laws and regulations and recommending to the government whether to amend or repeal un-Islamic laws. In addition, the FSC was to hear appeals arising from the Hudud Ordinances. Five years later, a constitutional amendment made the 1949 Objectives Resolution, until then the preamble of the country's constitution, a substantive part of the constitution, thereby establishing that steps should be taken to enable Muslims to live 'in accordance with the teachings and requirements of Islam as set out in the Holy Qur'an and Sunna' (Art. 2A). In 1991 the Enforcement of Shari'a Act stated that the shari'a shall be 'the supreme law of Pakistan' and established that when interpreting statutes the courts' interpretation should be consistent with 'the Islamic principles and jurisprudence', though it added that the rights of women 'as guaranteed by the constitution shall not be affected'.

The 1979 Iranian constitution prescribes that legislation must be subject to Islamic review before entering into force, and entrusts the Council of Guardians, composed of both clerics and lay persons, with the evaluation of proposed laws before they are voted on in the Majles. The members of the council are nominated, directly or indirectly, by the Supreme Guide, making him the ultimate safeguard for the Islamic nature of national legislation. In Afghanistan, the 2004 constitution has a clause prescribing that no statute can contradict 'the beliefs and rulings' of Islam, though it is not clear yet whether or not this is meant to be a justiciable norm or what the means are to make it operative. In Morocco, the constitution adopted in 2011, while establishing that Islam is the state religion and emphasizing '[l]a prééminence accordée à la religion musulmane dans ceréférentiel national' (preamble), does not mention Islam as a legal entity. The king, in his capacity as *amir al-muminin*, 'veille au respect de l'Islam' and as such '[i]l préside le conseil supérioeur des Oulémas', which is 'la seule instance habilitée à prononcer les consultations religieuses (fatwas) officiellment agréés' (Art. 41). The composition of this council is fixed by royal decree. It is quite obvious that the correct interpretation is in the hands of the king and cannot be easily challenged, contrary to what happens in other countries where the executive and bodies vested with Islamic review can be (and have been in some cases) at odds when deciding what does or does not conform to Islam. That this is an important point does not need to be emphasized: 'Who controls the symbols, and who controls the shari'a, is – as Vikør observes – both a result of and a factor for the relationship of power in society' (Vikør 2005: 256–57).

Irrespective of *who* decides, giving the shari'a a specific content is no easy task, for reasons that the previous pages have made obvious. To overcome the problem of doctrinal heterogeneity, and to appease all, constitutional references to Islamic legal doctrine are vaguely worded. While using different terms ('Islamic injunctions', 'shari'a', 'beliefs and rulings of Islam', and so on), they either do not specify the sources of reference, or refer to quite wide entities, such as the Qur'an and Sunna, without going into hermeneutical details. The 2012 Egyptian constitution attempts to address this problem by specifying that 'the principles of Islamic shari'a … include general evidence, foundational rules, rules of jurisprudence, and credible sources accepted in Sunni doctrines and by the larger community' (Art. 219).[15] These references are vague, however, and no criteria for selection are provided.

No consensus on questions of interpretative methodology has emerged so far. In Egypt the SCC has interpreted Art. 2 to mean that all legislation passed after 1980 must respect some broad principles identified as 'fundamental' by the shari'a, which are found in the Qur'an and have been accepted by the community of scholars over the years. Once these principles have been identified, the (civic) judge must extrapolate their social goals and determine whether the contested norm promotes or hinders such goals. While fundamental principles cannot be subject to *ijtihad*, and cannot be contradicted by legislation, relative ones evolve in time and space, give rise to different interpretations and adapt to changing circumstances and needs (Lombardi 1998). In Pakistan, the FSC has stressed that all sources of law are subordinate to the Qur'an and Sunna, and that *ijtihad* can be applied only where there is no injunction in these sources. In specific cases brought to its attention the FSC has frequently invoked both primary sources and *fiqh*, though since the 1990s it has increasingly referred to general principles of justice and equality rather than identifying concrete provisions of the Qur'an and Sunna to be applied.

Neo-traditionalist and Islamist groups in Egypt and Pakistan have referred to constitutional clauses on the prominence of shari'a when asking the government to repeal 'un-Islamic' laws – some on personal matters – but to no avail. In Egypt, since 1993 a number of Art. 2 cases have been brought before the SCC, and in almost all cases the Court has upheld legislation.[16] The Court has tended to take a middle path between the competing positions of religious conservatives, Islamists and feminists, refusing to overhaul statutory norms. In Pakistan, constitutional references to Islamic law have been used by Islamists and traditionalists when demanding the repeal of the MFLO. The FSC for a while considered itself formally restrained by a constitutional norm prescribing that its jurisdiction did not extend to 'Muslim personal law'. The High Courts, particularly since the mid-1980s, declared some of the MFLO norms as un-Islamic and replaced them with precepts that are more consonant with their vision of shari'a, supporting these decisions with the argument that Art. 2A controlled all other laws rather than constituting a mere principle of policy. In 1988 the FSC ruled that after the introduction of Art. 2A no law could prevail over Islamic precepts and that the areas excluded from its competence, such as family law, could be judged by the High Courts and Supreme Court and in such cases their interpretations would be binding on the FSC. The religion-oriented activism of the High Courts was finally reined in (but not altogether ended) when in the early 1990s the Supreme Court, expressing the fear that the very constitutional foundations of the state would 'yield to nebulous, undefined, controversial juristic concepts of Islamic *fiqh*',[17] ruled that no court other than the FSC could review the Islamicity of laws and that statutes could be amended only by the competent legislative bodies. The Objectives Resolution could not be considered as a supra-constitutional document nor was it self-executory, but it could, at most, inspire new legislation, though it was admitted by the Supreme Court that courts could directly apply Islamic precepts in relation to matters not covered by statutory law.

In the 1980s, the FSC increasingly referred to uncodified shari'a principles in *zina* cases, which intersect in many ways with family law. The FSC's involvement in family law increased when the Supreme Court clarified in 1994 that 'Muslim personal law' meant the particular interpretation of personal law by each sect and not the existing legislation on personal status. While not going so far as to declare the MFLO un-Islamic, the FSC has advocated the right to fill legal loopholes by referring to Islamic law and has stressed that some of the precepts of the Ordinance, such as those on registration of marriages and of *talaq*, are not mandatory as they are not prescribed by Islam, but are optional procedures that are not forbidden either. Thus Art. 2A has been referred to not just to uphold legislation, as in Egypt, but also to add new more authoritative rules to codified norms, thereby creating parallel legal 'texts', and to cover areas of law that are not addressed by statutory norms. Some scholars have observed that Art. 2A has been increasingly used to safeguard and even expand constitutionally mandated human rights (Lau 2010: 401–2). On the effects of Art. 2A, however, the FSC and the Supreme Court have remained somewhat ambiguous, as shown in the well-known 1993 case *Zaheeruddin v. The State*, when the majority view of the Supreme Court in a case on the legislated restrictions on the Ahmadis held that 'the legal provisions and principles of law, as embodied in the Objectives Resolution, have become effective and operative' with the effect of superseding even fundamental rights that might violate the Islamic injunctions.[18]

Court practice

We may wonder at this point whether *ijtihad*, *takhayyur* and *talfiq*, which have inspired legislation on family law, have entered judicial practice, and, if so, what are their implications for women. Existing publications, as well as the chapters in this volume, indicate that courts in the contemporary Muslim world, albeit formally constrained by the norms of positive law, retain some of their traditional elasticity. While in some countries, courts deciding on family disputes tend to apply the letter of the law with minimal resort to extra-codified religious sources, in others judges refer to either uncodified *fiqh* or to *ijtihad*, or both, to legitimize, expand or restrict state law. Neither is judicial activism necessarily a characteristic of countries were family law has not undergone recent reform or is not codified in a systematic and detailed manner, as might be expected, nor are religious judges more prone to deviate from statute books in the name of religion than lay judges.

Although the information available does not allow us to generalize, it seems that religious judges, in fact, tend not to stray from codified law in the name of Islam and, while often referring to the predominant *madhhab*, as allowed by the law, they are more reluctant to look outside of their *madhhab* through *takhayyur* and *talfiq* and to exercise *ijtihad* as compared to lay judges.

In Lebanon, for example, as Clarke observes in his chapter, *shaykhs* working as judges refer to a great extent to their *madhhab*, as permitted by the law. Shi'i judges tend to rule according to the Ja'fari school and cite contemporary leading Shi'i jurists, particularly the late *marja'* Abu al-Qasim al-Khu'i (d. 1992) and his pupil 'Ali al-Sistani. In the Sunni courts, rulings that make reference to Hanafi doctrine often cite Ibn 'Abidin's nineteenth century *Radd al-Muhtar*, which is one of the most comprehensive and authoritative compilations of the Hanafi school. Religious reference is important to a degree, however, because at the appeal level court rulings eschew references to *fiqh*, and procedural rules seem to take the precedence over learned discussions on religious law.

As for Iran, another country where family law is adjudicated by religious figures, the constitution prescribes that in the absence of a clear written norm on a specific issue, judges must reach their judgments in accordance with their *ijtihad*; if unable to provide independent reasoning, they must follow authorities that they recognize and accept. Court observation indicates that judges tend not to deviate from statute books and when confronted with issues not covered by the law they mostly refer to compilations by contemporary Shi'i scholars and by the late Khomeini. In Saudi Arabia, religious judges are expected to apply Hanbali law or, if deemed preferable, other Sunni *madhhabs*. Although the lack of codification and Wahhabism's favourable view of 'free *ijtihad*' unconnected to a specific *madhhab*, might have prompted innovative rulings, judges mainly refer to Hanbali jurisprudence and refrain from *ijtihad* (Vogel 2000). In Indonesia, religious judges also tend to apply the written law, though they deviate occasionally by referring to the predominant school, i.e. Shafi'i *fiqh* (Nurlaelawati 2010: 143–44).

Lay judges seem more prone to resort to *talfiq* and to practise *ijtihad*, despite not, in theory, having the qualifications to do so. However, comparing cases is made difficult by the fact that different meanings are given to technical terms, such as *ijtihad*, by both judges and scholars and significant variations seem to exist within each country. In Pakistan, lay judges of the High Courts – and to a lesser extent the FSC – have referred, particularly in the 1980s, to uncodified religious principles in order to clarify vague or ambiguous statutory norms, and as mentioned above, have gone as far as replacing in some cases codified norms with uncodified Islamic norms. A wide variety of religious sources are referred to, often within the same case: Quranic verses, relevant *hadiths* from one or other of the Sunna collections, *fiqh* treaties, in particular the twelfth-century *Hedaya* and the seventeenth-century *Fatawa-e-Alamgiri* (the two traditional Hanafi texts in use in the subcontinent), reference books and manuals written by Indian and British judges in colonial times, precedents in British and colonial India's courts, and texts written by contemporary Muslim scholars, both in the subcontinent and outside. When referring to *fiqh* sources, the judges resort to *talfiq*, often within the same case, and make use of different hermeneutical approaches (Giunchi 1994). As a result, judgments are often contradictory. One example is the FSC's 1980 ruling that the stoning penalty for illegal sexual intercourse prescribed by the 1979 Zina Ordinance was illegal because it was not prescribed by the Qur'an. The argument was that the Sunna, even when absorbed by subsequent *ijma'*, cannot supersede the Quranic text. The military regime headed by Zia promptly enacted a new law giving the FSC the power to review its own judgments, changed its composition and filed a review petition against the FSC decision. In 1982 the reconstituted court, which comprised more pliant judges, annulled the previous judgment and religiously sanctioned the punishments prescribed by the Hudood Ordinances.

In neighbouring India there are no official religious courts. Judges who rule on family disputes between Muslims generally lack a detailed knowledge of shari'a and are rarely Muslim. As Vatuk tells us in this book, judges in the lower courts, when confronted with a 'Muslim personal law' case, tend to refer to one of the standard Indian textbooks or manuals compiled during or shortly after the end of the colonial period. Some of the judges at the higher levels of the judiciary have greater erudition on

Islamic law and in their judgments they cite relevant passages from the Qur'an, translated into English, quote from some pre-colonial Indian legal texts and compilations such as the Hanafi *Fatawa-e-Alamgiri* and on occasion, from prominent contemporary Muslim scholars.

Dupret has written that in Egyptian courts 'references to Islamic law are conspicuous for their paucity' and that when judges refer to compilations of Hanafi fiqh they do so through the provisions of Egyptian law, as eventually interpreted by the Court of Cassation, and so as to substantiate positive law (Dupret 2012: 121–33), though other authors have observed the growing tendency under Mubarak to refer to uncodified shari'a, partly in defiance of the government (Vikør 2005: 242). In their chapters, Bernard-Maugiron and Lindbekk, while agreeing that judges mostly adhere to the letter of the law, observe that they exercise a significant degree of discretion, particularly when assessing the nature and extent of harm. Moroccan judges often refer to the spirit of the Qur'an and the objectives of the shari'a in order to uphold statutory norms and even extend them in women's favour, as Sadiqi tells us in her chapter.

In the main, lay judges, who are trained in modern faculties of law and have no detailed grounding in Islamic sciences, refer mostly to primary sources. The reason might be that, whether progressive or Islamist-oriented, they are imbued with a discourse centred on religion that has became pervasive in their societies since the 1970s. While Islam becomes thus an inescapable reference, the religious sources they have access to are limited: as they are not well versed in *fiqh*, they cannot refer to an intricate jurisprudence they are not familiar with. Lack of knowledge of *takhlif* and of the traditional methodological discourse, in particular, limits their capacity to draw from different opinions. *Fiqh*, in any case, with its intricate rules, would not comply with their vision of Islam as a systematic code-like law.

Although judicial activism has resulted in some cases, for example in Pakistan, in a challenge to existing legislation, we should remember that statutes themselves leave the door open to extrajudicial sources. Most legislation on family law establishes that in cases not covered by the law, judges should refer to one particular school: in Egypt according to a 2000 law, reproducing a clause in decree 78 of 1931, the residual law is 'the dominant opinion' of the Hanafi school. The 1962 Law of the Shari'a Courts in Lebanon establishes that Sunni judges issue their rulings 'according to the preponderant statements of the school of Abu Hanifa, except in those cases where the [Ottoman] Law of Family Rights ... speaks'. Shi'i courts can issue their rulings according to the Ja'fari *madhhab* and, where the decisions are in harmony with this school, according to the OLFR's rulings. References to a specific *madhhab* are found also in recent legal reforms: in Afghanistan, the 2004 constitution establishes that if no relevant law is found, the Hanafi school is to be utilized for Sunnis, and the Ja'fari *madhhab* for issues of personal status involving Shi'as. The 2009 code of personal status of Shi'i Afghans specifies that Ja'fari law is to be found in the writings of its *marja'-e taqlid*. The 2004 Mudawana states that: 'For all issues not addressed by a text in the present code, reference may be made to the Malikite School of Jurisprudence and to ijtihad ... which strive to fulfil and enhance Islamic values, notably justice, equality and amicable social relations'. The 2005 code on family law in the UAE prescribes that if no rule can be found in codified form, judges should apply Maliki and Hanbali fiqh or, in absence of norms in these sources, other Sunni *madhhabs*.

These provisions are in line with previous experiences, like those of the Ottoman Empire, where the central authorities identified the prevailing *madhhab* and supplemented it with imperial decrees. What is different now is that codes, while mentioning one *madhhab* as the residual law, draw their rules from various schools. This puts judges in a peculiar position: for example, Egyptian judges in divorce cases apply norms that are largely taken from the Maliki school, but they are also instructed that, in the absence of statutory provisions on particular points, they should rely on the most prevalent opinion within the Hanafi school. Thus 'madhhab-surfing' by judges, while not explicitly allowed by the law, is made inevitable by the *talfiq* nature of legislation. Whether reference to a school should in theory preclude *madhhab*-surfing is actually subject to debate. In Morocco, in particular, it has been discussed whether the *ijtihad* mentioned in the Mudawana is autonomous, and might thus refer to *madhhabs* others than the Maliki one and to other sources, including international law, or must occur within the framework of Malikism (Benradi *et al.* 2007: 185–86). This debate is not new: in the history of Islam the issue of whether when exerting *ijtihad* the jurists could go out of their *madhhab* has always been contentious (Gerber 1999: 80).

It is particularly through loopholes in the codes that legislators leave ample room for judicial discretion, allowing judges to look for unwritten sources. For example, in Egypt, requests for divorce by a woman because of injury or polygamy require the court to assess the nature and degree of harm suffered by her, an assessment that, without a detailed description in the code of what constitutes injury, leaves ample room for discretion (Bernard-Maugiron in this book; see also Shaham 1997: 234 for pre-1955 shari'a courts in Egypt). In Morocco, the arbitrariness of the judges is compounded by the vagueness of the concept of *shiqaq* in the codified law (Sadiqi in this book). In Pakistan, no definition of valid marriages is given in the MFLO, and no mention is made of the legal consequences – on the validity of marriage – of the failure to provide notification of *talaq*. Similarly, the text of the 1979 Zina Ordinance left vague the criminal implications of pregnancy when the woman is either unmarried or did not cohabit with her husband at the time of conception, the definition and consequences of irregular marriages and the legal consequences of self-exculpatory statements by alleged victims of rape (Giunchi 2013). It is, significantly, mainly to fill these loopholes that Pakistani judges have referred to uncodified religious sources.

Gender implications of judicial activism

Existing research on court practice in family disputes indicates that, in general, judges, including religious ones, tend to be sympathetic to women's marital problems and receptive to their claims, debunking the conventional view that women are powerless under Islamic law. Both Lindbekk and Bernard-Maugiron confirm previous research on pre-1955 shari'a courts in Egypt pointing to the judges' sympathetic approach to women (Shaham 1997: 234). Lindbekk notes that in cases on divorce due to discord, judges do often rule in the wife's favour. Bernard-Maugiron shows how judges interpret injury broadly thus facilitating divorce and, in general, are quite open towards divorce requests brought by women, though they discriminate against lower-class women, who are expected to put up with greater harm than their well-off fellow citizens. In Pakistan the Supreme Court and the FSC have often taken a stand in favour of women, particularly in cases concerning divorce initiated by women, honour killings, women's marriage without the *wali's* consent (Yefet 2012) and custody, though their approach has not extended to other judicial matters (Ahmed in this book). The language employed by judges in marital disputes reveals, according to some, a sympathetic attitude to the plight of women locked in unhappy marriages (Yefet 2012), but Ahmed notices that it also upholds women's subordination, their role as mothers and a traditional view of the family. In *zina* cases disparaging language is often used when addressing women who do not conform to expectations. Women's autonomy is often perceived as an act of insubordination and even gossip about their behaviour can be considered as evidence of their 'loose character' and invalidate their testimony (Giunchi 1994).

In India, as Vatuk observes in this book, the Higher Courts and the Supreme Court are sensitive to gender imbalances in society; expressions of sympathy for the plight of Muslim women under particular provisions of family law appear frequently in their judgments and are reflected in their decisions on important cases involving unilateral divorce, polygamy and maintenance, though lower courts have not followed suit. In Iran Mir-Hosseini (1993) found that women could manipulate statutory law to their advantage to press for more rights and to see their grievances redressed, and that courts were receptive to their claims. Lev observed that in Indonesia in the 1960s, Islamic courts improved women's situation 'slightly' and an increasing number of women brought their cases to court as they found them sympathetic (Lev 1972: 179, 126–28). In a more recent study, Bowen found that in most cases in rural Aceh judges ruled in women's favour (Bowen 2003). Courts in the Sudan also tend to leniency when women are the petitioners (Fleuhr-Lobban 1987: 91). In Algeria, research on court practice after the promulgation of the 1984 code reveals an inconsistency in judgments, though in cases of men-initiated divorce quite often the judge decided in favour of the wife, granting her damages for the harm (*darar*) she had suffered (Mitchell 1997: 200–02). Analysing court practice in Israel, Reiter observed that some judges are more liberal than others, without a consistent pattern emerging (Reiter 1997). Hirsch found in her ethnographic analysis of Kenyan Islamic courts that women have some success in the legal processes, though the language they use in court reinforces their image as subordinate to men (Hirsch 1998).

There is, thus, consensus that judges tend to lend a sympathetic ear to women's plight and to redress the worst gender inequalities ingrained in society and reflected in statutes, though the reasoning and the language used in court often betray ingrained stereotypes. However, we do not know much about the gender implications of religiously inspired judicial activism: does reference to uncodified religious sources penalize or advantage women?

Case analysis shows that by referring to uncodified Islamic law, judges can do either, depending on the sources they refer to, the interpretation they give to these sources, and the contingent situation in which the verdicts are given. Sadiqi observes that Moroccan judges use *ijtihad* in a progressive sense in a wide variety of cases when they feel justice would not be done through strict application of the law, and do so by referring to specific Qur'anic verses and to a greater extent to the more evanescent 'spirit' or 'goals' of shari'a. In Egypt, Lindbekk notes, reference to uncodified rules gives rise to contradicting verdicts: applying the preponderant Hanafi opinion, most judges have held that an adult woman has the right to get married without the intervention of a guardian. Some judges, however, have at times required that a woman's guardian concludes the marriage on her behalf even if she has reached puberty. As for Pakistan, in some cases the judiciary has interpreted Islamic law in a manner that enhances women's rights; by referring to the Qur'an's letter and spirit, and stressing the principles of justice and equality, they have departed from traditional *fiqh* interpretations of *khul'*, allowing women to divorce without consent of their husband, and have condemned honour killings (Yefet 2012: 557; Rehman 2007). In cases pertaining to registration of *nikah* and *talaq*, judges in the Supreme Court and FSC, by neglecting the norms of the MFLO and replacing them with *fiqh* norms have helped women escape the criminal consequences of *zina* charges, where adhering to the text of the law would have penalized them. Similarly, in cases related to the *wali's* consent, an issue on which the law is silent, the judges of the Supreme Court and FSC have consistently upheld the Hanafi rule that after puberty such consent is not mandatory, protecting from criminal prosecution adult women who choose their spouse against the will of their family members (Giunchi 1994 and forthcoming).[19] It is, however, important to stress that court rulings have not been consistent, and that in numerous cases the High Courts and FSC have interpreted Islamic law in a manner that penalizes women. For example, the pregnancy of an unmarried woman has often been considered, on the basis of the Maliki school, as evidence of *zina*, thereby leading to the conviction of the alleged *zaniya*. More generally, the reference to uncodified Islamic law has often confirmed and perpetuated a patriarchal structure and ingrained stereotypes about women's proper role (Giunchi 1994).

Studies on adjudication in Bangladesh indicate that judicial activism in this country, as compared to traditional constructions of shari'a and state law, tend to ameliorate women's conditions (Hoque and Khan 2007), though the most courageous interpretations have been overruled in the name of a traditional understanding of Islamic law, particularly with regard to economic empowerment of women (Rahman 2008). In India, superior courts have decided in favour of women in cases of maintenance, polygamy and *talaq*, bending statutory laws so as to benefit women, at times by referring to the Qur'an and other religious sources (Vatuk, in this book).

What sources are used, according to which hermeneutical approach and whether or not discretion results in favour of women ultimately depend on the personal inclinations of, and therefore on the background of, judges, the composition and priorities of the government, and the autonomy, or lack thereof, that judges enjoy vis-à-vis the government, an issue that is connected to the pattern of recruitment – a theme on which there is unfortunately almost no research. It is worth emphasizing here that the fact that lay judges are products of modern faculties modelled along Western lines does not necessarily mean that their rulings will be progressive. For example, in several countries, primarily Pakistan, since the 1970s law faculties have been greatly influenced by Islamism. Thus, while the Supreme Court is composed of older judges with modernist backgrounds, younger judges in the High Courts are more influenced by Islamism, though the composition of the Supreme Court and the FSC is also changing. In

Egypt, Islamists have similarly made inroads into the judiciary, first at the lower level, and now in appeals courts. It has been noted that there is a relationship between Islamism and the expansion of university education to a greater number of people, with the bar, and then the judiciary, increasingly including people from geographic areas and social strata that were traditionally excluded from elite professions, with the consequence that an increasing number of lawyers and judges come from sections of society that are less Westernized and have economic grudges against the secular elites (Lombardi 1998, n. 114: 119).

As some researchers seem to indicate that female judges are more gender-sensitive (Sidiqi, Vanzan in this book), it is relevant that in the first decade of the twenty-first century the judiciary has opened to women, as the contributors to this volume tell us. Just to give some examples, in Iran, the Majles decided in 1994 that women could become legal consultants in the special civil courts and in the administrative justice courts. In Egypt the SCC appointed its first woman in 2003. Since 2007, women have also been sitting in ordinary courts. In Pakistan, in 2002, a law allowing female judges to be appointed in the family courts was passed. In 2010 the Malaysian government agreed to appoint women as judges in shari'a courts.

Whether the executive reflects Islamist tendencies and selects the higher judiciary is also relevant: in Egypt, under Mubarak, security forces made security inquiries on all law students who were applying for judicial positions, and those from a low socio-economic background, or with an Islamist, communist or criminal family background did not stand much chance of being appointed. This screening ensured that judges were recruited from socially conservative but politically liberal strata, the values of which coincided with those of the authorities and highest echelons of the army (Bernard-Maugiron 2012/3: 11). This may be one of the reasons why attempts to Islamize the law and reverse progressive norms through recourse to Art. 2 of the constitution have been resisted by the SCC, which is staffed by liberals. In Pakistan, state-sponsored Islamization has increased the Islamists' presence in the institutions, including the ministry of justice and that of education. In some cases, where the FSC has decided against the Islamicity of state-enacted norms, its composition has been changed by the executive, as in the case of stoning mentioned above, or disregarded, as in the case of *riba* (interest), leaving no doubt as to where real power sits.

Adjudication and context

The issue of judges' attitudes to women is linked to another characteristic of modern-day courts: judges, whether religious or not, seem to retain the interest in the context of litigation that characterized traditional *qadis*, despite having lost the personal day-to-day connection to their community. Often, today's judicial practice appears driven by the attempt to compromise and to avoid excessive hardship, and to understand the character of the litigants, their trustworthiness and their position in society (Rosen 2000: 14; also cf. the Chapters in this book).

It could be argued that this contextuality is not a peculiarity of the Muslim world: judges everywhere strive to make the law and social life fit each other. In the contemporary Muslim world, however, these efforts may be more visible than elsewhere as social reality and codes, particularly in urban areas, are clearly at odds with each other. Increasingly, particularly among urban middle-class families, many factors contradict the ideal family structure that is reaffirmed through the requirement of the wife's obedience and other male prerogatives that have been reproduced in the codes: the weakening of kinship bonds, the increasing number of women entering the job market and contributing to the household income, increasing female literacy rates and increasing exposure to alternative social mores through old and new media.

These societal changes are reflected in court cases. For example, Lindbekk observes that dower, which has to be included in the standardized marriage contract, is considered meaningless among some higher middle-class couples in view of women's increasing education and economic independence. In several countries inflation has caused soaring *mahr* costs, delaying men's marriage (Fluehr-Lobban 1987; Mir-Hosseini 1993). Clarke, in this volume, observes that in Lebanon the hyperinflation of the civil war period rendered many women's *mahr* worthless and prompted some judges to argue in favour index-linking the dower.

In some countries, including Pakistan (Giunchi 1994), court documents also reveal the extent to which extrajudicial forms of conflict resolution persist, with family members, village elders, or other authoritative figures acting as arbitrators. The formal court process may be used by the litigants as a tactic and is often the final stage in a long-standing dispute that has many ramifications, some of which are not recorded in court files. In some cases, litigants find informal courts more sympathetic to them, easier to access, cheaper and more expeditious. Vatuk tells us how in India women activists, believing that female mediation bodies can better meet women's needs, have recently promoted the formation of so-called women's courts. Poor women find it easier to narrate their marital problems before an audience of their own sex and background and find these bodies more attentive to their needs than state courts or other alternative dispute resolution (ADR) bodies, such as caste *pancayats* and shari'a courts. The judge himself often explicitly enjoins litigants to sort out their problems extrajudicially. Analysis of cases in Pakistan shows, for example, that in the course of the trial the families involved in *zina* cases try to settle the case by arriving at a compromise, which often results in an exchange marriage, in the marriage between the *zaniya* and the *zani*, or in monetary compensation. In some cases the FSC has held that such compromises are against the principle that *hudud* crimes are not compoundable, while in others it has held compromises to be acceptable if made before a *hadd* offence is reported to the authorities (Giunchi 1994).

Although several codes direct the judge to refer to custom,[20] there is no doubt that in rural and tribal areas it is local usages that are the main hurdle to gender equality and are often more restrictive than *fiqh*. For example, rural women are often deprived, particularly in South Asia, of their legal share of an inheritance from their parents and not given the deferred portion of the *mahr* in the event of divorce. They are also usually not allowed, once they have reached puberty, to choose their own partner without the *wali*'s consent. What are, we may ask, the judges' attitudes towards '*urf*? Often, in cases pertaining to family matters, customs that violate the law and reflect a traditional interpretation of Islamic law are validated in court and result in lenient penalties or no penalty at all. Even in secular Turkey, as Yilmaz tells us in his chapter, judges accommodate religious customs that contradict state law with regard to solemnization of marriage and polygamy. In Egypt, in a concession to 'urfi marriage, which is often resorted to in order to avoid the costs of wedding ceremonies and circumvent legal requirements, the law prescribes that a claim to judicial divorce or dissolution shall be accepted if marriage is established 'by any document'. Lindbekk tells us in her chapter that higher courts have been willing to consider unregistered marriages as valid, though they are less keen to accommodate the entrenched practice of marriage among minors. Also in Pakistan, irregular marriages are often considered as valid, particularly in *zina* cases (Giunchi 1994). In all these instances, the rationale seems to be that by recognizing de facto marriages, the courts can facilitate the integration of out-of-wedlock children in the family unit, prevent criminal charges, guarantee state benefits to irregularly married women and their offspring, and protect their interests in disputes related to divorce, maintenance and *hadana*.

Patterns and challenges

We have seen that, contrary to the common image of shari'a as a 'textual entity' made of fixed judiciable norms that we find in Western perceptions and Islamist ideology, the traditional flexibility of Muslim courts is still alive and animates, in particular, lay judges, who take advantage of the space for manoeuvre and room for discretion left open by state legislation to advance their ideas of an ideal society.

The reality of court practice in the contemporary Muslim world is much more nuanced, flexible, contextual than is often imagined and can liberate as well as oppress. The gender implications of judicial activism are mixed, but certainly contradict commonly held opinions that applying shari'a always goes against the amelioration of women's rights. It may be argued that in countries where consuetudinary gender restrictions are pervasive and profound, the reference in normative texts and judicial fora to *fiqh*, particularly through the use of *talfiq*, may protect women from consuetudinary abuses and be more effective than the replacement of religious norms with secular ones or the use of minority modernist interpretations. Improving women's conditions is, however, different from guaranteeing gender equality. Whether referring to the wealth of opinions and approaches in classical tradition is sufficient to redress and ultimately overhaul gender imbalances is doubtful unless *ijtihad* is used to a greater extent and is guided by a modernist exegesis and a progressive agenda.

Whereas complete equality may be reached within a religious framework, this might not be likely in the current political climate. The Arab 'springs', despite their message of freedom from oppression, in fact pose new challenges to the personal status law codes: in Egypt, the ousting of Mubarak fed women's hopes of empowerment that were then shattered by calls from various groups to amend personal status norms considered not in conformity with Islam; in Tunisia, the proposal to introduce a clause stating that women are complementary to men was interpreted by many as a first move towards a reform of one of the most advanced personal status law in the Middle East. The introduction of democracy, as Iraqi and Afghani women know all too well, might not signify women's empowerment, at least in the short and medium term. Those who have studied women's involvement in decolonization movements will see a familiar pattern here, with women contributing to a global discourse on liberation and human rights, yet not benefitting from it (Moghadam 1994). In countries with traditionalist or Islamist-dominated governments, or with secular-oriented executives but strong societal pressures to Islamize, we might witness an increasingly difficult coexistence between traditionalist and Islamist sectors on one side, and a shrinking, modernist higher judiciary on the other. The SCC's interpretation of Art. 2 in Egypt may not continue to uphold legislation, and the FSC and Supreme Court in Pakistan may not continue to check the High Courts' activism. Ultimately, existing codes on personal status might be amended to respond to societal pressures, particularly under religion-oriented governments; or, they may be surpassed by uncodified references to religious authenticity that restrict women's rights as the composition of the judiciary changes. Either way, in Egypt, as in Pakistan, the immediate priority for women's groups is to preserve hard-won gains rather than pushing for further rights. Religion, however, is unlikely to totally overrule political considerations: as Khomeini reminded us in the only theocracy of the contemporary world, state interests have primacy over Islam (Crone 2006). Economic considerations too, in countries dependent on Western aid, may hinder the overhaul of existing family laws.

The lay judges who refer to *ikhtilaf* and resort to *ijtihad* to complement, integrate and in some cases contradict positive law, represent the apex of a process of marginalization of the *ulama* and transfer of religious authority to the common man that had started in the nineteenth century: *ijtihad* authority has passed from the *mufti* and jurist to the judge, even the lay judge who is not grounded in traditional legal discourse. True, neo-*ijtihad* is practised without the sophisticated textual evidence and argumentation followed by classical *mujtahids*, and *talfiq* is limited by a superficial knowledge of *ihkilaf* literature. As a consequence, Islamic law as it is interpreted and applied today is much less rigorous than it used to be, appearing to some scholars as a set of poorly justified new rules devoid of a sound methodology and divorced from the intellectual discourse that accompanied traditional *fiqh* – an 'unabashedly result-oriented and disingenuously selective' practice (Abou El Fadl 2001: 171). But, being less constrained by previous authority and by *ijma'* than traditional *fiqh*, neo-*ijtihad* allows much more innovation while keeping alive a tradition of flexibility and attention to both the context and the ultimate goals of shari'a.

The practice of *talfiq* is not found only in codes and in judicial practice: the blurring of *madhhab* boundaries, as widely advocated by reformists since the nineteenth century, is today magnified through Internet *fatwas* and the practice of 'surfing' across doctrinal lines by lay believers. These developments, besides challenging traditional forms of authority, constitute a counterweight to the executive's authority and its unresponsiveness to societal pressures, as well as a challenge to the modern state and its attempt to control society. The uniformity of the subject, which is the aim of state-directed codification, is countered by judicial activism and the parallel atomization of neo-*ijtihad* as amplified by the new media. These developments are part of a wider deconstruction of the state, towards more globalized networks where differences do not disappear, but follow transnational paths rather than geographical boundaries. As countries fragment along multiple cultural and social lines, these fragments are reproduced in court as well as in cyberspace, contributing to new doctrinal developments.

Notes

1 There was no consensus about what these competences were, though scholars tended to agree on knowledge of the Qur'an and Sunna, familiarity with the Arabic language, and with the principles of *usul al-fiqh*. Often considered as essential characteristics of *mujtahid* were justice, majority of age and, according to some, male gender.

2 Some scholars hold that the elaboration of *usul al-fiqh* dates to the ninth century (cf. for example, Hallaq 1993), while others hold that it occurred in the subsequent century (cf. for example Stewart 1998: 31–37).

3 On Shafi'i's role in developing the *usul al–fiqh*, see Hallaq 1993.

4 For the history of adjudication in the Islamic world, the evolution of courts, doctrine and procedure, see Masud, Peters and Powers 2005; Zubaida 2003; Tyan 1960.

5 The Islamic judicial process appears to Lev, for example, as inconsistent, unable to arrive at the truth and following a haphazard procedure (Lev 1972: 128–29). More famous espousers of this idea were Joseph Schacht and Max Weber, whose expression *kadijustiz* has come to epitomize the arbitrariness of the *qadi*.

6 On the emergence of the *marja'* in the nineteenth century, see Moussavi 1996. Other scholars have emphasized that this concept dates back to the early eleventh century and is not exclusively Shi'a (Stewart 1998: 230).

7 For a thorough discussion of family law in classical *fiqh*, see Pearl and Menski 1998 who focus on the subcontinent.

8 The Shi'a also accept that a divorcee or a widow does not require a *wali*.

9 As on other issues, there is a difference between *madhhabs*, and within them, as to the exact definition of equality, with the Shi'a confining it to religion only, while the Hanafi interpret it in an extensive way, probably a by-product of the lesser importance of the *wali* for this school as compared to other *madhhabs*.

10 Apostasy was mainly considered as a ground for *ipso facto* annulment, with no need of judicial intervention. Other traditional forms of repudiation, such as by *li'an* (mutual imprecation), are not discussed here as they have not generally been incorporated into present-day codification. Dissolution of irregular contracts is also not discussed here as judicial practice on this issue is not analysed in this volume.

11 Inheritance rules are very complex and are not mentioned here as the case studies do not look at this aspect. In general, they are based on Quranic injunctions and on customary rule, with the Sunnis privileging the agnatic side of the family, and the Shi'i dividing the inheritance that is left over after the Quranic shares are divided proportionally on the basis of genealogical distance from the deceased.

12 Judicial divorce on similar grounds had already been introduced in the Sudan in 1915–16. The OLFR remained in force in Syria until 1953 and in Jordan until 1951. It was an important basis for decision-making by Jordan and Egypt when administering, respectively, the West Bank and Gaza and has been utilized as a non-binding source of law in Bosnia Herzegovina. Today it is in force in Lebanon, as Clarke explains in his chapter, for both Sunni and, to a lesser extent, Shi'i.

13 For more details on these reforms, see Otto 2010 and Welchman 2007. Legislation on family law left intact the legal status of recognized religious minorities, who were allowed to apply their distinct laws to personal status and often made use of their own courts. In Morocco, for example, the Jewish minority can be governed by its own laws. In Egypt, Jews and Christians are similarly exempt from the enforcement of national laws in family matters. In Lebanon, Christians and Druzes have their own courts to deal with such matters.

14 Jordan and Algeria also allow for *khul'* without the husband's consent. In the UEA a 2005 law allowed it in particular circumstances. In Pakistan, since the end of the 1950s, the courts have also departed form the traditional understanding of *khul'*, allowing women to divorce under *khul'* even without the husband' consent. In the Sudan, a similar concept is enshrined in the divorce by *fidiya* (ransom).

15 This in an unofficial translation of the 2012 constitution, which is available online at www.egyptindependent.com/news/egypt-s-draft-constitution-translated. No official version is available yet at the time this book goes into print.

16 In the only exception, the law that was struck down was found to violate several constitutional provisions and not just Art. 2. For a 1994 case involving child support, see Lombardi 1998: 102–06.

17 *Hakim Khan v. Government of Pakistan* (PLD 1991 SC 595) and *Mst. Kaneez Fatima v. Wali Muhammad and another* (PLD 1993 SC 901). See Lau (2003): 197–202.

18 1993 SCMR 1718.

19 This is less relevant after the Protection of Women Act 2006 provided that for a woman to avoid a *zina* conviction it is sufficient for her to believe that she is validly married.

20 The 2004 Mudawana, for example, established that among the factors to take into account while fixing maintenance are 'the customs and traditions prevailing in the locality where maintenance is awarded'.

Bibliography

Abou El Fadl, K. (2001) *Speaking in God's Name. Islamic Law, Authority and Women*, Oxford: Oneworld.

Arabi, O. (2001) *Studies in Modern Islamic Jurisprudence*, The Hague: Kluwer Law International.

Benradi, M., M'chichi, H.A., Ounnir, A., Mouqit, M., Boukaissi, F.Z., and Zeidguy, R. (eds) (2007) *Le code de la famille. Perceptions et pratique judiciarie*, Fez: Friedrich Ebert Stiftung.

Bernard-Maugiron, N. (2012/3) 'Les juges et les elections dansl'Egypte post Moubarak: acterursou victims du politique?', *Confluences Méditerranéè*, 82: 117–32.

Bowen, J.R. (2003) *Islam, Law and Equality in Indonesia. An Anthropology of Public Reasoning*, Cambridge: Cambridge University Press.

Clarke, L. (2001) 'The Shi'ī construction of taqlīd', *Journal of Islamic Studies*, 12(1): 40–64.

Coulson, N.J. (1969) *Conflicts and Tensions in Islamic Jurisprudence*, Chicago, IL and London: University of Chicago Press.

Crone, M. (2006), 'The disenchantment of an Islamic state. Perspectives on secularism in Iran', *Nordic Journal of Religion and Society*, 19(2): 29–42.

Djamour, J. (1966) *The Muslim Matrimonial Court in Singapore*, London: The Athlone Press.

Dupret, B. (2012), 'What is Islamic law? A praxiological answer and an Egypt case study', in M. Diamantides and A. Gearey (eds), *Islam, Law and Identity*, Abington: Routledge.

Fleuhr-Lobban, C. (1987) *Islamic Law and Society in the Sudan*, London: Routledge.

Gerber, H. (1999) *Islamic Law and Culture. 1600–1840*, Leiden and Boston, MA, Köln: Brill.

Giunchi, E. (1994) 'The enforcement of the Zina Ordinance by the Federal Shariat Court in the period 1980–90, and its impact on women', unpublished thesis, Cambridge University.

——(2010) 'The reinvention of the shari'a under the British Raj: In search for authenticity and certainty', *Journal of Asian Studies*, 68(4): 1119–42.

——(2013) 'Islamization and judicial activism in Pakistan: What šarī'ah?', *Oriente Moderno*, 93(1): 188–204.

Gleave, R. (2005) 'Intra-madhab ikhtilaf and the late classical imami Shiite conception of the madhab', in P. Berman, R. Peters, F.E. Vogel (eds), *The Islamic School of Law. Evolution, Devolution, and Progress*, Cambridge, MA: Harvard University Press.

Hallaq, W.B. (2009a) *Sharī'a, Theory, Practice, Transformations*, Cambridge: Cambridge University Press.

——(2009b) *An Introduction to Islamic Law*, Cambridge: Cambridge University Press.

——(1997) *A History of Islamic Legal Theories. An Introduction to Sunnī uṣūl al-fiqh*, Cambridge: Cambridge University Press.

——(1993) 'Was al-Shāfi'ī the master architect of Islamic jurisprudence?', *International Journal of Middle East Studies*, 25(4): 587–605.

——(1984) 'Was the gate of ijtihad closed?', *International Journal of Middle East Studies*, 16(1): 3–41.

Hassan, S.Z.S. and Cederroth, S. (1997) *Managing Marital Disputes in Malaysia. Islamic Mediators and Conflict Resolution in the Syariah Courts*, Richmond: RoutledgeCurzon.

Hirsch, S.F. (1998) *Pronouncing and Persevering: Gender and the Discourses of Disputing in an African Islamic Court*, Chicago; IL: University of Chicago Press.

Hoexter, M. (2007) 'Qāḍī. Muftī and Ruler: Their roles in the development of Islamic law', in R. Shaham (ed.), *Law, Custom, and Statute in the Muslim World. Studies in Honor of Aharion Layish*, Leiden and Boston MA: Brill.

Hoque, R. and Khan, M.M. (2007) 'Judicial activism and Islamic family law: a socio-legal evaluation of recent trends in Bangladesh', *Islamic Law and Society*, 14(2): 204–39.

Johansen, B. (1993) 'Legal literature and the problem of change: The case of the land rent', in C. Mallat (ed.), *Islam and Public Law. Classical and Contemporary Studies*, London and Norwell, MA: Graham and Trotman.

—— (1999) *Contingency in a Sacred Law. Legal and Ethical Norms in the Muslim Fiqh*, Leiden and Boston, MA: Koln: Brill.

Kamali, M.H. (1993) 'Appellate review and judicial independence in Islamic law', in C. Mallat (ed.), *Islam and Public Law. Classical and Contemporary Studies*, London and Norwell, MA: Graham and Trotman.

Krawietz. B. (2002) 'Cut and paste in legal rules: designing Islamic norms with talfiq', *Die welt des islams*, XLII, 1: 3–40.

Lau, M. (2003), 'Article 2A: the objectives resolution and the Islamisation of Pakistani laws', in H.G. Ebers and T. Hanstein (eds), *Beiträge zum islamischen Recht*, vol. 3, Frankfurt am Main: Peter Lang.

——(2010) 'Sharia and national law in Pakistan', in J.M. Otto (ed.), *Sharia Incorporated. A Comparative overview of the Legal Systems of Twelve Muslim Countries in Past and Present*, Leiden: Leiden University Press.

Layish, A. (1971) 'Qadis and shari'a in Israel', *Asian and African Studies*, 7: 237–72.

——(1975) *Women and Islamic law in a non-Muslim State. A Study Based on Decisions of the Shari'a Courts in Israel*, Jerusalem: Israel University Press.

Lev, D.S. (1972) *Islamic Courts in Indonesia. A Study in the Political Bases of Legal Institutions*, Berkeley: University of California Press.

Lombardi, C.B. (1998) 'Islamic law as a source of constitutional law in Egypt: The constitutionalization of the sharia in a modern Arab state', *The Columbia Journal of Transnational Law*, 37: 81–112.

Masud, M.K., Peters, R. and Powers, D.S. (eds) (2005) *Dispensing Justice in Islam: qadis and their Judgments*, Leiden: Brill.

Meriwether, M.L. (1996) 'The rights of children and the responsibilities of women, women as wasis in Ottoman Aleppo, 1770–1840', in A.E. Sonbol (ed.), *Women, the Family and Divorce Laws in Islamic History*, Syracuse, NY: Syracuse University Press.

Messick, B. (1993) *The Calligraphic State: Textual Domination and History in a Muslim Society*, Berkeley: University of California Press.

Mir-Hosseini, Z. (1993), *Marriage on Trial: a Study of Islamic Family Law, Iran and Morocco Compared*, London: I.B. Tauris.

Mitchell, R. (1997) 'Family law in Algeria before and after the 1404/1984 family code', in R. Gleave and E. Kermeli (eds), *Islamic Law. Theory and Practice*, London: I.B. Tauris.

——(2005) 'Madhabs and Modernities', in P. Berman, R. Peters and F.E. Vogel (eds), *The Islamic School of Law. Evolution, Devolution, and Progress*, Cambridge, MA: Harvard University Press.

Moghadam, V.M. (ed.) (1994), *Gender and National Identity*, London: Zed Books.

Monsoor, H.T. (1999) *From Patriarchy to Gender Equality: Family Law and its Impact on Women in Bangladesh*, Dhaka: The University Press Limited.

Moussavi, A.K. (1996) *Religious Authority in Shi'ite Islam: From the Office of Mufti to the Institution of Marja'*, Kuala Lumpur: International Institute of Islamic Thought and Civilization.

Nasir, J.M. (2007) 'Shari'a implementation and female Muslims in Nigeria's shari'a states', in P. Ostien (ed.) *Shari'a Implementation in Northern Nigeria 1999–2006: A Sourcebook*, vol. III, 76–118, Ibadan: Spectrum Books.

Nurlaelawati, E. (2010) *Modernization, Tradition and Identity: the Kompilasi Hukum Islam and Legal Practice in the Indonesian Religious Courts*, Amsterdan: Amsterdan University Press.

Otto, I.M. (ed.) (2010) *Sharia Incorporated. Acomparative Overview of the Legal Systems of Twelve Muslim Countries in Past and Present*, Amsterdam: Leiden University Press.

Pearl, D. and Menski, W. (1998) *Muslim Family Law*, London: Sweet & Maxwell.

Peirce, L. (2003) *Morality Tales: Law and Gender in the Ottoman Court of Aintab*, Berkeley: University of California Press.

Peletz, M. (2002) *Islamic Modern: Religious Courts and Cultural Politics in Malaysia*, Princeton, NJ: Princeton University Press.

Peters, R. (2005) 'What does it mean to be an official madhab? Hanafism and the Ottoman empire', in P. Berman, R. Peters and F.E. Vogel (eds), *The Islamic School of Law. Evolution, Devolution, and Progress*, Cambridge, MA: Harvard University Press.

Rahman, A. (2008) 'Development of Muslim family law in Bangladesh: empowerment or streamlining of women?', *Journal of the Asiatic Society of Bangladesh*, 53(2). Available online at www.asiaticsociety.org.bd/journals/Dec_2008/contents/AnisurRahman.htm#_edn1 (accessed 13 January 2013).

Rehman, J. (2007) 'The sharia, Islamic family laws and international human rights law: examining the theory and practice of polygamy and talaq', *International Journal of Law, Policy and the Family*, 21(1): 108–27.

Reiter, Y. (1997) 'Qāḍis and the implementation of Islamic law in present day Israel', in R. Gleave and E. Kermeli (eds), *Islamic Law. Theory and Practice*, London: I.B. Tauris.

Rosen, L. (2000) *The Justice of Islam. Comparative Perspectives on Islamic Law and Society*, Oxford: Oxford University Press.

Schacht, J. (1964) *An Introduction to Islamic Law*, Oxford: Clarendon Press.

Shaham R. (1997) *Family and the Courts in Modern Egypt: a Study Based on Decisions by the Shari'a Courts, 1900–1955*, Leiden: Brill.

Stewart, D.J. (1998) *Islamic Legal Orthodoxy. Twelver Shiite Responses to the Sunni Legal System*, Salt Lake City: The University of Utah Press.

Stilt, K. (2011), *Islamic Law in Action. Authority, Discretion, and Everyday Experiences in Mamluk Egypt*, Oxford: Oxford University Press.

Tucker, J. (1999) *In the House of the Law: Gender and Islamic Law in Ottoman Syria and Palestine*, Berkeley: University of California press.

Tyan, E. (1960) *Histoire de l'organisationjudiciaire en pays d'islam*, Leiden: Brill.

Vikør, K. (2005) *Between God and the Sultan: A History of Islamic Law*, Oxford: Oxford University Press.

Vogel, E. (2000) *Islamic Law and Legal System*, Leiden: Brill.

Weiss, B.G. (2005) 'The Madhab in Islamic legal theory', in P. Berman, R. Peters and F.E. Vogel (eds), *The Islamic School of Law. Evolution, Devolution, and Progress*, Cambridge, MA: Harvard University Press, 1–9.

Welchman, L. (1990) 'Family law under occupation: Islamic law and the shari'a courts in the West Bank', in C. Mallat and J. Connors (eds), *Islamic Family Law*, London: Graham & Trotman.

——(2000) *Beyond the Code. Muslim Family Law and the Shari'a Judiciary*, The Hague, London, Boston, MA: Kluwer International.

——(ed.) (2007) *Women and Muslim Family Laws in Arab States. A Comparative Overview of Textual Development and Advocacy*, Amsterdam: Amsterdam University Press.

Wheeler, B.M. (1996) *Applying the Canon in Islam. The Authorization and Maintenance of Interpretative reasoning in Ḥanafi Scholarship*, New York: State University of New York Press.

Yefet, K.C. (2012) 'The constitution and female-initiated divorce in Pakistan: Western liberalism in Islamic garb', *Harvard Journal of Law and Gender*, 35(1). Available online at www.law.harvard.edu/students/orgs/jlg/vol342/553–616.pdf (accessed 14 January 2013).

Yilmaz, I. (2005) *Muslim Laws, Politics and Society in Modern Nation States. Dynamic Legal Pluralisms in England, Turkey and Pakistan*, Aldershot: Ashgate.

Zilfi, M.C. (ed.) (1997) *Women in the Ottoman Empire. Middle Eastern Women in the Early Modern Era*, Leiden and New York: Brill.

Zubaida, S. (2003) *Law and Power in the Islamic World*, London and New York: I.B. Tauris.

2 Shari'a Courts and Muslim Family Law in Lebanon[1]

Morgan Clarke

Introduction

Amid the burgeoning literature on shari'a courts and Muslim family law worldwide, Lebanon's courts and personal status law have received relatively little attention.[2] Lebanon is treated in a number of the standard surveys of Muslim family law (Mahmood 1972, 1987; El-Alami and Hinchliffe 1996; An-Na'im 2002; Nasir 2002), but such treatments are in certain respects incomplete, as I will discuss. This relative lack of attention may be due in part to the complexity, which is to say plurality, of Lebanon's family legal system, which has to deal with 18 official religious communities, or perhaps a perception that Lebanon, with its important Christian communities and cosmopolitan image, is not a natural place to look for shari'a courts. That would be to be misled. Lebanon is, for me at least, a very interesting context in which to think about shari'a courts and Muslim family law.

For one thing, Lebanon's religious diversity allows both the Sunni and Twelver Shi'i traditions to be studied together and compared. One could go further and consider Lebanon's three other official Muslim communities, the Druze, 'Alawis and Isma'ilis, two of whom, the Druze and the 'Alawis, have their own religious court systems, although I do not do so here.[3] For another, in large part due to the autonomy given to Lebanon's religious communities under its communitarian legal and political system and the sensitivities involved in any adjustments to it, the codification and reform of Muslim family law found across most of the Islamic world has been comparatively limited with regard to Lebanon's Sunni and Ja'fari (i.e. Twelver Shi'i) shari'a courts.[4] In contrast with some jurisdictions in the region, judges in those courts are *shaykhs*, Muslim religious specialists, trained in the religious sciences rather than the civil law. Wider controversies over the relationship between the Islamic legal tradition, the state and the gendered citizen here take on a particular form.

Given the rather slim literature on the topic, I take this opportunity first and foremost to present an introductory survey of Lebanon's shari'a courts and the law they apply. The roots of my interest lie in my previous research on Islamic medical ethics in Lebanon in 2003–4 (Clarke 2009), when I also attended a number of sessions in the Sunni appeals court and regularly sat with a Sunni initial court judge in Sidon and a Shi'i initial court judge in Beirut in order to gain a feel for Islamic law in action. I subsequently conducted a major anthropological study of the courts, based on extended fieldwork: three months research in 2007 and six months in 2008 in the initial courts of three Sunni and three Shi'i judges in Beirut. I was also an occasional visitor to the Sunni and Shi'i appeals courts. In addition to interviewing judges and other functionaries and observing the courts' wider business, I attended many tens of hearings (*jalsat*), sitting as unobtrusively as possible in the courts themselves, taking notes of the proceedings (see Clarke 2012). I should note that my account is necessarily of the courts as I found them in 2007–08. Important changes in the Sunni courts have occurred since (Ghamroun, in press).

Historical background

Modern Lebanon inherits its shari'a courts from Ottoman times. Under the Ottoman Empire, shari'a courts (*mahakim shar'iyya*) served as law courts with general competence, applying Hanafi *fiqh* (Islamic legal precepts), together with imperial edicts. But as part of a wider project of reform, these courts were superseded by new legal institutions applying codified law following the European model, and were largely left to deal with family law alone (Rubin 2009). Family law was itself the object of reform, with the 1917 Ottoman Law of Family Rights (OLFR) providing a codified and in many ways progressive text with provision for all the recognized religious communities, Muslim, Christian and Jewish (Tucker 1996).

Come the end of the Ottoman Empire, the new state of Lebanon fell under French Mandate control (1920–43). Despite some lackluster attempts to institute a fully civil state, French rule ended by consolidating Ottoman communitarian precepts and extending official recognition to 17, later 18 religious communities, which were to have exclusive jurisdiction over the family legal affairs of their members. The communitarian settlement was enshrined in the Lebanese constitution of 1926 and decree 60LR of 1936, and entrenched by the unwritten post-independence National Pact.

The Twelver Shi'a, who had not been so recognized under Sunni Ottoman rule, were deemed, under decree 3503 of 1926, an 'independent [Ja'fari] *madhhab*' (i.e. legal school), and set up their own separate personal status courts. A 1942 law of procedure (superseded by a later law of 1962) regulated shari'a courts, now subdivided into Sunni and Ja'fari personal status tribunals. The Christian communities had their own spiritual courts (*mahakim ruhiyya*) to deal with their family legal matters; the Druze gained separate *madhhab* courts (*mahakim madhhabiyya*), under the general ambit of, but independent from, the shari'a court system. Unlike the Christian courts, which are generally considered independent of the state, the shari'a courts remain part of it, continuous with their Ottoman roots. That means, among other things, that their functionaries, including the judges, are state employees (Rabbath 1986: 93–156; Thompson 2000: 113–70; Saadeh 2002: 451; Weiss 2010: 92–126).

This legal apparatus remains in effect now. Religious courts have exclusive jurisdiction over cases concerning marriages contracted in Lebanon by Lebanese citizens, whether they are religiously committed or not.[5] In the case of a mixed marriage between a couple from different religious communities, the courts of the husband's community have jurisdiction. However, if a couple contract a civil marriage abroad, such as in neighbouring Cyprus, then disputes arising can be taken to a civil court, where they are arbitrated according to the law of the country where the marriage was contracted (Qazzi 2007: *passim*).[6] This is one recourse for couples either wishing to live under a civil rather than religious regime of marriage or to contract a marriage that would be ruled out under religious precepts, as in the marriage of a Christian man to a Muslim woman, prohibited under Islamic law, Sunni and Shi'i (Weber 2008). The only alternative is for one or other party to convert to a different religious affiliation. Such conversions of convenience are a well-attested means of forum shopping more generally, famously employed by some high-profile political personalities. Legislation has been enacted to limit these possibilities (Bilani *et al.* 1985: 272).

The religious courts have been the target of fierce criticism from civil society activists who see them as crucial to the sectarian divisions that have disfigured the country's modern history, as well as from women's rights activists dissatisfied with the patriarchal precepts employed (Zalzal 1997; Shehadeh 1998; Zuhur 2002). There have been several post-independence attempts to introduce a unitary civil family law for all Lebanese citizens, but all have failed (El-Cheikh 2000). Nevertheless, some civil court judges are, controversially, not averse to pushing the boundaries of their jurisdiction (see Qazzi 2007 for examples pertinent to the Christian courts). Given the high number of Lebanese living, marrying and divorcing abroad while maintaining close ties to the homeland, international conflicts of laws are also common. Where there is a dispute over which court system should have jurisdiction, then the civil Court of Cassation (*mahkamat al-tamyiz*), the highest court in the land, has the ultimate say. We should thus remember that, despite the religious courts' prerogatives, they still ultimately reside under a civil state and judiciary.

The relevant legislation

The 1962 Law of the Shari'a Courts (*qanun al-mahakim al-shar'iyya*), the code of procedure that governs the courts, restated one crucial section from the 1942 law it superseded. Until 2011, when a significant modification was made regarding the law applied to Sunnis, Section 242 read:

> The Sunni judge issues his ruling according to the preponderant statements of the school of Abu Hanifa, except in those cases where the [Ottoman] Law of Family Rights of 8 Muharram 1336/25 October 1917 speaks, whereupon the Sunni judge applies the rulings of that law; and the Ja'fari judge issues his ruling according to the Ja'fari *madhhab* and, where it is in harmony with this school, from among the rulings of the Law of the Family.[7]

Law 177 of 29 August 2011 now instructs the Sunni judge in the first instance to follow the rulings of the community's Supreme Islamic Shari'a Council, and then the OLFR and the Hanafi school (Ghamroun, in press). Lebanon is thus now the only country where the Ottoman Law of Family Rights of 1917 applies (to Muslims), albeit in qualified fashion.[8] Indeed, one might take the impression from some of the standard international surveys of Muslim family law that the text of the OLFR was largely sufficient for understanding the law applied in Lebanon (e.g. Mahmood 1972: 35–47,

1987: 93–106; El-Alami and Hinchcliffe 1996: 147–80). Beyond the far from comprehensive stipulations of the OLFR, however, which does not, for instance, discuss child custody (*hadana*) or indeed inheritance, section 242 points Sunnis to the Hanafi school, a very much larger field.[9]

'Arif al-Zayn's (2003) comprehensive compilation of the legislation applicable in the Muslim courts includes the sections on bequests and inheritance from the late-nineteenth-century Egyptian Hanafi codification by Muhammad Qadri Pasha (*Kitab al-Ahkam al-Shar'iyya li-l-Ahwal al-Shakhsiyya 'ala Madhhab al-Imam Abi Hanifa al-Nu'man*), because of, he claims, the Sunni courts' 'reliance upon it' (2003: 5). I have certainly heard it mentioned as a source of reference, but it is in no sense a stipulated authority. Initial court rulings do on occasion refer to Qadri Pasha. But those rulings in the Sunni courts that make reference to wider Hanafi debates, especially at the appeals court level where most 'difficult' cases end up, more often cite more prestigious and classical Hanafi commentaries and compilations, pre-eminently Ibn 'Abidin's nineteenth-century *Radd al-Muhtar* (Homsi 2003: *passim*).

Ja'fari *fiqh*, however, in fact disagrees with the OLFR on almost every point. So, under the terms of section 242, the Ja'fari courts are, by contrast, largely free to follow their own path, nominally applying the majority position of the school (*al-mashhur*). This makes it rather harder to identify what the 'Ja'fari law' applied in the courts is than the sanguine passing statements in the standard academic surveys might suggest. Zayn (2003: 6) cites two sources, one being the handbook published by a previous president of the Lebanese Ja'fari courts, Shaykh 'Abdallah Ni'ma (1996), *Dalil al-Qada' al-Ja'fari*, which again I have heard referred to as a useful resource, for lawyers, say (and for me here), and the other a manual by the late Ayatollah Abu-l-Qasim al-Khu'i (d. 1992), who was one of the foremost *maraji'* (sing. *marja'*) *al-taqlid* (sources of emulation), or religious authorities, of his day and the leading figure in the prestigious seminary city of Najaf, Iraq. I have seen Khu'i's works on judges' desks, along with those of his pupil and successor Ayatollah 'Ali al-Sistani, perhaps the most widely followed *marja'* in the Shi'i world today. But again, these works are not stipulated authorities binding on the courts. And while I have seen an initial court ruling that refers to them (Barakat 2005: 166–68), most appeals court rulings rather surprisingly (to me) would seem to eschew references to any *fiqh* sources at all, at least according to my survey of one lawyer's collection (Barakat 2005).

This brings us to what I perceive as a problematic issue. In (Usuli Twelver) Shi'i Islam, if one has not mastered the shari'a oneself, one is bound to follow the opinion of one who has: that is, a living *mujtahid*, capable of deriving legal rulings from scripture through *ijtihad*, who has consented to serve as a *marja' al-taqlid*, or source of emulation. This emphasis on living *ijtihad* is commonly cited as giving the school a greater flexibility in changing times. The majority opinion holds that only a *mujtahid* can serve as a judge, although there are opinions that allow otherwise (Gleave 2008: 237–39). To be a *mujtahid* is to stand at the top of the clerical hierarchy, and a claim to such status is a very considerable one in Lebanon, a country that is marginal to the great centres of Shi'i learning in Iran and Iraq. There are those who would say there are no *mujtahids* to be found locally at all, at least not 'absolute' (*mutlaq*) ones; and very few, if any of the judges serving in the courts, and certainly not those working at the initial court level, would make or could defend such a claim. While I may be reading the issue overly formally, arguably judge who cannot claim to be *mujtahids* should then be bound to follow the opinion of a current *marja'*, such as Sistani. But this issue does not arise in practice: judges feel comfortable issuing rulings within the known parameters of the mainline thought of the school and, broadly speaking, the line taken by the Supreme Court.[10]

As regards other relevant legislation, the 1962 law is the most crucial. Although in essence a procedural law and not a codification of Muslim family law, as some academic commentary implies (El-Alami and Hinchcliffe 1996: 147; Shehadeh 1998: 502), it nevertheless contains some significant clauses in pertaining to family issues, as we will see.

With regard to the substantive family law applied, we are thus faced with a rather different situation from that in much of the rest of the region, where more comprehensive and progressive modern codifications of the shari'a are in place, in many cases now into their third phase of reform according to leading scholar Lynn Welchman (2007: 42–43 and *passim*), who observes that academic commentary 'can scarcely keep pace with events' (ibid.: 40). She lists a series of recent legislative initiatives around the region, none associated with Lebanon. In Lebanon's shari'a courts, one is thus, with regard to legal reform, several steps closer to earlier shari'a models.[11]

Of course this is not to suggest that Lebanon's is in any way a 'pure', 'traditional' or 'unreformed' shari'a system, should such a thing ever have existed. The shari'a courts have strictly limited competence, within an encompassing civil legal and modern bureaucratic system; and the initial courts across the country are under the authority of supreme, appeals courts, Sunni and Ja'fari, in Beirut, which are subject to the advice and scrutiny of a civil judge (*al-na'ib al-'amm*, or prosecutor general) who sits on their panels. Nevertheless, the comparatively unreformed situation with regard to the legislation applied is certainly the subject of critique, from activists, lawyers and a good number of religious specialists, including many judges. There have been a series of important attempts to reform family law in Lebanon. But, as already noted, these have taken the form of proposals for a unitary civil law for all the communities, and have thus been closely bound up with highly political debates over the secularization of Lebanon's entire confessional political and legal system, rather than family law reform alone (El-Cheikh 2000; Zuhur 2002).

Marriage

The OLFR raised the minimum age of marriage to 18 for males and 17 for females, below which special permission would be required from the court, and ruled out forced marriage (sections 4–7, 57).[12] Considerable authority (more than the Hanafi norm) was, however, given to the guardian (*wali*) of the bride, even when she was of age and even when not a virgin, a distinction commonly drawn in the *fiqh* discussions and still pertinent to Lebanese shari'a court practice. The OLFR requires the judge to consult the *wali* before allowing the marriage, while stating that should a woman marry without her guardian's consent, the marriage will stand so long as the groom satisfies the condition of equality of status (*kafa'a*) with her. If he does not, the wali may apply to have the marriage annulled (sections 8, 47, 50).

While these stipulations are arguably somewhat ambivalent, the requirement of the *wali*'s consent is read as mandatory for all marriages in the contemporary Sunni and Ja'fari courts, as I observed them at least.[13] This requirement is far from unusual across the wider region, but is commonly seen – including in Lebanon – as highly objectionable by women's rights campaigners (Welchman 2007: 69–75). Polygamy, another important women's rights issue and subject of reformist activism (Welchman 2007: 77–87; Tucker 2008: 75, 77–80), was preserved by the OLFR and still pertains in Lebanon. I witnessed instances of polygynous marriages in the courts, but limited in number, it should be said. The OLFR (section 38) recognized the validity of conditions added to the marriage contract limiting this male prerogative, or otherwise increasing the wife's rights, by delegating a husband's right of divorce to her (*talaq al-tafwid*) for instance. Mechanisms such as this are commonly emphasized by progressive and reformist voices in Lebanon as elsewhere (Welchman 2007: 99–102; Tucker 2008: 49–50, 61–63), and are variably admissible in both court systems. In practice, however, in my experience at least, they are rather uncommon and not well regarded in many circles as they are seen as indicating a lack of trust between the parties.

Marriages are to be registered with the authorities, following the OLFR (sections 34, 37), a 1951 law on the registration of personal status documents (sections 2, 22–29; Zayn 2003: 30–33) and the 1962 law of the shari'a courts, which requires that the marriage contract be supervised by the shari'a court judge or relevant official and state the name and domicile of the couple, their religious community, date of birth, the names of their guardians and whether or not the bride is a virgin, as well as the names of two witnesses and the amount of the bride's dower (*mahr*) (sections 348–56). A law of 1983, modified in 1994, required couples of all communities to provide before marriage a medical certificate with the results of examinations for various sexually and genetically transmitted diseases and conditions, as is now common elsewhere (Zayn 2003: 37–38; Welchman 2007: 55–56).

The requirement that the marriage be supervised by an officially mandated religious specialist is no mere formality: debates over marriages outside of the purview of the state are very much current, like those regarding 'customary marriage' (*zawaj 'urfi*) elsewhere. In Lebanon, the commonly remarked upon weakness of the Lebanese state entails worries as to the resulting strength of a multiplicity of non-state religious actors, paradigmatically, the Lebanese Hizballah. The Sunni courts strictly require the writing of marriage contracts to be supervised by an official authorized by the court, and are supposedly only willing to register unofficial marriages in the case of pregnancy; but I know of at least one powerful Sunni *shaykh* outside the court system who was willing to contract marriages on his own authority and without requiring the permission of the (adult) bride's guardian, in accordance with much Hanafi opinion. This points up a theme of more general importance: the vast field of shari'a discourse provides ample opportunities for dissenting opinions from those employed by the state-sponsored courts and from rivals to their authority.

The Ja'fari courts are not bound to apply the OLFR and could in theory allow lower ages of marriage and indeed marriages of minors without their consent at the request of their guardians, in accordance with the opinions of the school. This is the position relayed in the academic surveys that touch on the topic (Bilani *et al.* 1985: 274, 279–81;

Nasir 2002: 50, 54–55), although I never saw or heard of any such instance.[14] More significantly, the Ja'fari courts are more willing to 'establish' (*ithbat*) and register marriages
conducted by *shaykhs* outside of the courts, which would seem to contravene the 1962
Law of Shari'a Courts.[15] 'Temporary marriage' (*zawaj mu'aqqat*; also 'limited' marriage
(*zawaj munqati'*) and, more pejoratively, 'pleasure marriage' (*zawaj al-mut'a*)) was ruled
out by the OLFR (section 55), but is, notoriously, a possibility for Twelver Shi'a, and
would be recognized by the courts. In practice, however, in Lebanon at least, it is rarely
admitted to, being rather shameful (Mervin 2008), and I did not myself see such cases.

With regard to the dower (*mahr*), often referred to as the wife's 'right' (*haqq*) – the
most prominent of her religious-legal rights (*huquq shar'iyya*) – the OLFR validated the
practice, recognized within Hanafi *fiqh* and common historically and currently in this
part of the region, of dividing the *mahr* into two portions: prompt (*mu'ajjal*), payable
on marriage, and deferred (*mu'ajjal, mu'akhkhar*), to be paid on the husband's death or
divorce (sections 81–82; Tucker 2008: 47). This holds in both the contemporary Sunni
and Ja'fari courts. The deferred dower is thus the wife's most important hedge against
divorce and the husband's most powerful disincentive to divorce. While it is perhaps
somewhat misleading to talk of averages, in the interests of giving some impression of
the sums involved from my own observations, one is speaking in the order of thousands
of US dollars (the standard most commonly employed): as a very crude rule-of-thumb,
a common sum for lower- to lower-middle-class marriages might be around $10,000
deferred; a more middle-class marriage might involve $20,000 and up. Prompt dowers
vary, sometimes covering the furnishing of the marital home, sometimes cash, but often
only a token stipulation, such as a copy of the Qur'an.

The savage inflation of the civil war period (1975–90) rendered many women's *mahr*
portions worthless, unbalancing this structure; and progressive elements in the courts
argue for the possibility of 'changing the *mahr*' (*ta'dil al-muhur*) to be in proportion
with its previous buying power (as now in Iran; see Mir-Hosseini 2000: 275). Those
arguments have not gained much traction in the Sunni courts, but are viable in the
Ja'fari system, testament, some would claim, to their greater scope for change, given
the lack of codification and nominally greater scope for *ijtihad* (but see above).[16]

Marital disputes in the courts

Marriages are put under stress for all manner of reasons, not least, at the time of my
fieldwork, the dire economic situation. Prolonged political uncertainty, a string of car-
bomb assassinations and, especially in the Shi'i southern suburbs of Beirut, the aftermath
of the 2006 war with Israel, had driven away investment and the vital tourist industry.
Unemployment and inflation were running very high. Such economic problems have
been common in Lebanon's modern history, and Lebanese men have long pursued
employment overseas, leaving, and sometimes abandoning, wives and families at home.

If the relationship breaks down, a woman's first move will very often be to leave the
marital home, should there be one. If she has recourse to the courts, she will most
often begin by suing for maintenance (*nafaqa*), her other crucial right. A husband's
response – if not just to settle up or separate – will very often be to sue in his turn for
'obedience' (*ita'a*). This does not imply literal coercion to obey his will. Rather, he must

first prove that he has provided a legally satisfactory marital home (*maskan shar'i*), another common legal demand on the part of women: a wife is entitled to an adequately equipped home to herself, not one shared with her husband's relatives. If he can prove that he has provided such a home (and the court will have it inspected) and his wife is then not willing to live in it with him, she has shown 'recalcitrance' (*nushuz*) and is not entitled to maintenance. This follows the OLFR (sections 70–73, 92–101), and is a familiar dynamic, turning on a largely unchallenged 'gender contract' throughout the region: women have a right to maintenance and a home; 'disobedience' means they lose it (Welchman 2007: 93–99; Tucker 2008: 50–56, 63–64, 67–68, 73–75).

Bringing a case before the courts, let alone getting the verdict you want, is a laborious and trying undertaking. The bureaucratic procedures required are complex and time-consuming. One must submit an appropriately constructed case and pay the requisite fees, then obtain a date for a hearing (*jalsa*), often months away. The respondent will need to be informed, an unavoidable but problematic bureaucratic hurdle, especially if the respondent lives abroad. One hearing will in any case very rarely be sufficient, and further hearings, at necessarily distant intervals, will have to be arranged. Given the volume of the courts' business, cases can thus take months if not years to work through the system, and plaintiffs frequently become highly exasperated, sometimes abandoning proceedings.

The judges, it should be said, share their frustration. As 'men of religion' (*rijal al-din*), their vocation, many feel, is one of sincere engagement with people's problems rather than pedantic adherence to bureaucratic strictures, although the latter is inevitable if one wants to enact rulings that cannot be overturned by lawyerly arguing before the appeal court (Clarke 2012). People are allowed to employ legal representation (indeed, they have to at the appeals court level), and lawyers are a common presence. Lawyers, in contrast to the judges, are not shari'a specialists and have been trained in the civil law. Indeed, while many are ostensibly and rhetorically pious, they nevertheless often bemoan the *shaykhs'* lack of civil legal expertise and procedural precision. Although debates over the shari'a are of course fundamentally important, it is thus, in fact, procedural law that is the most obvious feature of court practice and hindrance to plaintiffs' pursuit of redress. Judges' rulings are written 'In the name of God' (*Bismillah*), to be sure. But they are generally dominated by reference to laws of procedure rather than Islamic legal texts. I was frequently told that, say, 90 per cent of what goes on in the courts is civil procedural law (*qanun*), not shari'a. This was consonant with a broader downplaying of the religious nature of the courts by the religious specialists I worked with. While it is of course important to many that shari'a courts do handle family law for Muslims – and their removal would be a red line for many – I was warned not to look within them if I wanted to understand the shari'a proper. This tension between the courts' religious and civil elements, or between the idealized shari'a and mundane law (*qanun*), is thus a trope with wider resonance: dissatisfied plaintiffs may themselves express disbelief that the Lebanese shari'a courts as they experience them represent a manifestation of divine intention.

Sooner or later, the couple, or their representatives, will find themselves before the judge. In contrast with the highest, and thus grandest, appeal courts, the initial courts are very often just offices, with a desk for the judge and his recorder (*katib*). Again, the judges in both the Sunni and Ja'fari courts are *shaykhs*, religious rather than legal professionals, and are dressed in their turbans and robes, which differ slightly between the two traditions and are the most superficially obvious marker of the nominally religious character of the courts. Women appearing before the judges are generally supposed to wear modest dress (*hijab*), covering their hair and not taking too obvious liberties in any case. For those who do not habitually wear a headscarf, who number a good proportion of Lebanon's Muslim women, this can grate.

The judge is enjoined in the first instance to seek reconciliation (*sulh*) between the couple (as elsewhere, Welchman 2007: 50–52). That generally means sending them away for a month to talk things over, most often to the wife's disappointment – they will often already have sat through many a family meeting – or horror in the case of an abusive husband. The judge may attempt some sermonizing in their guidance of the parties before them, invoking religious morals and principles. Here then we have a practice that resonates with popular understanding, as well as the judges' own understanding, of the proper role of a *shaykh*, or Muslim man of religion, which would include moral exhortation, mediation and reconciliation. Such work may extend over weeks and months and involve conversations with parties beyond the couple, especially their families. This is the hard graft of the shaykhly vocation, often stressed to me as such by the judges I sat with.

Ideally, the couple will come to an understanding, facilitated by the judge's efforts: either positive (*sulh ijabi*), that is, to return to marital life according to agreed conditions, or negative (*sulh salbi*), that is, to separate on agreed terms. Such an agreement is, for the judges, in several respects the preferred way to resolve disputes. Beyond the valorization of the work of mediation itself, this is because an agreement registered with the courts (referred to as *sulh*) constitutes a binding solution, and one that cannot be appealed. Such agreements are ideally as detailed as possible, ensuring that property and financial issues between the spouses and arrangements concerning the custody, visitation, maintenance, education and health care of children are all specified and agreed. So long as their terms are not in blatant contradiction of the shari'a, such agreements allow much flexibility – and hence, ideally, equity – in outcome, more so than may be possible if the judge were just to rule on one case within the wider complex of issues a dispute will involve and within the legal constraints that bind him.

Such work looms very large in the actual practice of the courts. Should agreement prove impossible, then the judge will of course need to issue a ruling (*hukm*), but these are a less prominent feature of court activity than one might expect, certainly from the academic literature on historical shari'a courts, which is by necessity bound to focus on the rulings preserved in archives rather than the ephemera of attempts at mediation (Othman 2007). And in any case, while academic interest might concentrate on cases that involve especially interesting points of law, again, in practice, these rulings are rarely, if ever, such exercises in shari'a erudition and argumentation.[17]

Divorce

This is not, of course, to say that the portions of the shari'a applied are unimportant: they fundamentally dictate the terms of engagement between couples and the state.

This is crucially so with regard to divorce, the ultimate point of many of these disputes. Where the Ja'fari courts take a more relaxed line with regard to the official supervision of marriages, the pattern of relative supervision and restriction between the two court systems plays out in the opposite way here, leading to the common observation that for Sunnis (in Lebanon), marriage is hard and divorce is easy, while for Shi'a, conversely, marriage is easy and divorce is hard. Here it is difficulty that is seen as commendable, for many of the lawyers I worked with at least, who feel that state control and over-sight is all to the good in these matters. But while restraining the Muslim husband's powers of unilateral repudiation (*talaq*) is to women's benefit, the relatively greater difficulty for a woman to initiate a divorce in the Ja'fari courts has a profound effect on the dynamics of marital disputes, as we will see.

For Sunnis, as in the OLFR, a husband's powers of *talaq* are largely untempered, although he is in theory obliged by both the OLFR (section 11) and the 1951 law of the registration of personal status documents at least to register the divorce officially.[18] In the Ja'fari courts, by contrast, the conditions for the validity of a husband's unilateral repudiation are more rigorous, in accordance with the Ja'fari school: the wife must not have been menstruating when the divorce was pronounced; the couple must not have had sexual relations during the current menstrual cycle; the husband must use the correct formula (*anti taliq*, 'you are divorced'); and there must be two trustworthy witnesses to his so doing (Ni'ma 1996: 125–38). This makes the casual pronouncement of divorce much more difficult and the scrutiny required for the registration of divorces enacted outside of court more exacting. Divorce is thus generally more closely supervised.

Should unilateral divorce by the husband take place, the deferred portion of the *mahr* promised at marriage will become due. Husbands may thus be reluctant to divorce when a marriage breaks down and a miserable wife may be trapped within the mar-riage, while her husband can seek another. A wife can, however, offer her husband a financial incentive to divorce, as in *khul'*, divorce for a consideration.[19] That most often takes the form of her renouncing her rights (*huquq*), that is, her *mahr* owed and most often the maintenance she is due during the post-divorce waiting period (*'idda*). She may even have to pay him a sum over and above that, as very frequently happens in the Ja'fari courts (but not the Sunni ones), for reasons we will come to below.

Should the husband not consent to divorce then the wife will need to apply to the courts for a judicial divorce. Here the two court systems differ significantly. Judicial divorce (*tafriq*) was legislated for in the OLFR. This was important because Hanafi precepts were notoriously restrictive in this regard, and the OLFR expanded the possible causes for such a divorce by drawing on the other Sunni schools (Tucker 2008: 107–09, 119; Welchman 2007: 109). What is envisaged here is more a matter of annulment (also, and perhaps more usually in court discourse, termed *faskh*) for reasons such as impotence or apostasy. That is certainly still possible in the contemporary Lebanese courts, but hard to prove.

The OLFR also paved the way for the mechanism that has become by far the most common means for a woman to divorce her unwilling husband in the Sunni courts, judicial separation for reasons of marital discord and strife (*tafriq li-l-shiqaq wa-l-niza'*). Section 130 laid down the requisite procedure: should such discord arise and one of the spouses applies to the judge, the judge will appoint a family council made up of two arbitrators, either from each of their families or, if no one suitable is available, then from outside them. If reconciliation is not possible, then if the fault is deemed to be the husband's the judge will divorce them (*tafriq*); if the wife's, then *khul'* will be enacted in return for all or part of the *mahr*.

The 1962 LSC also legislates on this point (sections 337–43), in a genuine, if modest, substantive reform amplifying the provisions of the OLFR, specifying that either spouse can request divorce (*tafriq*) on the grounds of harm (*darar*) arising from discord (*shiqaq*) or ill-treatment within the marriage, such as physical and verbal abuse (*al-darbwa-l-sabb*), coercion to engage in something prohibited (*muharram*) or the performance of prohibited acts. The judge must establish that such harm does indeed exist and must enjoin an attempt at reconciliation (*islah*) between the couple for not less than one month. He will then designate two arbitrators as above, but who are now envisaged as professional experts (usually *shaykhs* working within the system, who must be paid for their time), who will attempt to reconcile the couple in council and, if they fail in that, will provide the judge with a detailed report assigning relative responsibility between the couple. The judge will then divorce them as above.

This has become a relatively easy case for wives to win, albeit a time-consuming and comparatively expensive one (although costs may be later recovered in proportion with the allocation of responsibility), and thus very common in the Sunni courts. A potential stumbling block, as with similar provisions elsewhere (Welchman 2007: 111), is establishing ill-treatment within the intimate sphere of the marital home. While some instances of physical abuse are so bad as to occasion medical treatment, more usually witnesses will be required; when they can be found, marshalling them to come to the court during the working day, where they will inevitably have to wait around for some time before the case comes up, can be problematic.

Judges have some leeway in establishing ill-treatment, and this is one of the domains where they can show how open-minded they are. Some argue that the wife's bringing such a case, still more so if it comes, as it usually does, on top of a series of other cases, in itself serves to demonstrate marital strife. And, very commonly, during a hearing or in a written response, a husband will make the mistake of disagreeing forcefully with his wife's claims, and perhaps making his own claims of bad conduct on her part. That can certainly be argued to demonstrate discord.

Lawyers can use tactics here, encouraging a woman to provoke her husband, through an accusation of impotence for example. Any violent reaction on his part will serve to show the discord between them. Similarly, in the family council, the arbitrators are required to allocate responsibility in percentage terms between the couple, and it is thus in the husband's interests to appear as agreeable as possible. That would leave the wife in an awkward position: as the instigator of the process, responsibility for the discord will appear largely hers. In practice, however, at least as regards the arbitration sessions I attended, a more realistic picture of the relations between the couple will generally emerge. A ruling of 100 per cent responsibility on either party's side is rare.

In the Ja'fari courts, by contrast, a judicial separation for reasons of marital strife is not possible, as it is contrary to the precepts of the school, and the 1962 LSC (section 346) exempts Ja'fari courts from the relevant stipulations. It is possible, but, again, rare and difficult, to sue for an annulment on grounds such as physical incapacity. The approx-imate equivalent to *tafriq li-l-shiqaq wa-l-niza'* in the discourse of the courts is *talaq al-hakim* (divorce by the judge) on ground of neglect or abandonment (Ni'ma 1996: 168). Here 'the judge' (*al-hakim*) is interpreted as being, perforce, a religious scholar of the very highest rank, a mujtahid, or indeed a Grand Ayatollah, *a marja' al-taqlid*. This is consonant with the gravity assigned to a judicial divorce without the husband's consent, an egregious usurpation of his rights in the terms of the *fiqh* discourse, and also with the perceived danger of assigning such a power to an 'ordinary' judge, who might be tempted to divorce a woman in his own interests, rather than to a figure of unimpeachable moral standing. The conditions for establishing a case of *talaq al-hakim* are correspondingly exacting, and winning one is thus extremely difficult and almost, but not entirely, unheard of in practice. Should one be won, I was told, the courts now rely on the imprimatur of Ayatollah Sistani, who has given the official head of the Lebanese Shi'i community, Shaykh 'Abd al-Amir Qabalan, the authority to act as his agent (*wakil*) in such cases.[20]

This has the consequence of changing the dynamics of the way disputes play out in the Ja'fari courts. In effect, the husband has a much better hand, as his consent is in practice required for a divorce. Women very often have not only to give up their rights to the deferred dower and post-divorce maintenance, but also have to pay even more, sometimes thousands of dollars, over and above that to obtain that consent. That then requires greater efforts on the part of the judges in order to bring the couple to an agreement, even if the negative one of divorce. The Ja'fari judges themselves note this additional effort, sometimes comparing their practice favourably to that of the Sunni courts and explaining it by the historically greater independence of their tradition from state law and bureaucratic procedure (Clarke 2012: 112–13). I prefer to explain it by the fundamental structural difference in the law applied in the two court systems.

Finally, as regards subsequent custody (*hadana*) of children, the OLFR is silent. Until recently the Sunni courts have thus followed Hanafi precepts, giving custody to the father at seven years for a boy and nine years for a girl. The Ja'fari courts are known to be still more patriarchal, commonly supposed to award a son to their father at two years (i.e., after the end of breast-feeding) and a daughter at seven, the majority position (Bilani *et al.* 1985: 325; Ni'ma 1996: 119). This is another area where the courts are widely seen to be behind the times, and, under pressure from women's rights organizations, the Sunni authorities have recently issued guidance to change the presumption to 12 years for children of both sexes (Ghamroun, in press). But judges who are so minded are within their rights to look to the interests of the child first and foremost, which they very often deem to lie with custody by the mother even if at ages later than those stipulated (as elsewhere, Welchman 2007: 133–42, 219–20 note 4). One reform-minded judge in the Sunni courts bolsters such rulings with psychiatrists' reports. And once the child is of age, as construed in religious law – considerably earlier than in civil law – they are in any case free to choose themselves.

Conclusion

The Lebanese shari'a courts are situated within a pluralistic, religious, family legal system that is both emblematic of and crucial to Lebanon's distinctive communitarian political and legal settlement. The law applicable is comparatively unreformed, the Sunni courts still largely applying the 1917 OLFR, and the Ja'fari courts largely free to apply the *fiqh* of their school. In the latter case, the lack of a codified law could be seen as a boon, allowing room for a scholar-judge to exercise *ijtihad*, deriving rulings from the fundamental texts in keeping with the times. However, few of the scholars working in the courts could, or would, claim such status for themselves and changes have been modest.

The shari'a courts are thus widely, rightly and perhaps surprisingly, given Lebanon's liberal image, seen as relatively conservative in the context of the region. One should keep in mind the importance of the religious courts for the Lebanese communitarian state: proposals for reform, which have taken the form of unified civil codes of family law for all Lebanese citizens, are politically fraught. But for those having recourse to and working in them, the genuinely religious nature of the courts is nevertheless contestable: procedural concerns are crucial to court practice. Judges thus very often see their distinctive work, as religious professionals, as that of mediation rather than the exercise of religio-legal judgement. For many of them, family disputes require the facilitation of reconciliation (*sulh*) more than intellectual virtuosity in ruling (*hukm*). But for others, a minority perhaps, the introduction of more progressive readings of the shari'a would constitute the best means to secure the authentically Islamic nature of court practice.

Notes

1 I must thank all those who helped in my researches in Lebanon, most especially my much-missed friend and mentor, the late Dr Talal Khodari, as well as Samer Ghamroun for sharing his recent work with me. The situation in the immediate region is obviously terribly disturbed as I write, in ways that look very ominous for Lebanon but with which I cannot engage here.
2 Lebanon finds no mention in two recent review articles of the field (Hirsch 2006; Agmon and Shahar 2008), and only passing mention in Welchman (2007) and Tucker's (2008) recent overviews, for instance. For sociological and historical treatments of the shari'a courts, besides my own ethnographic piece (Clarke 2012), one could, however, cite Max Weiss's (2010) work on the Ja'fari courts in the French Mandate period and Zouhair Ghazzal's (2007) treatment of the late Ottoman court of Beirut.
3 I should say that I have no first-hand knowledge of the 'Alawi courts, which were instituted by relatively recent (1995) legislation (Zayn 2003: 315) and remain obscure to me.
4 This is not so true of the Druze courts, which apply the thoroughly reformed law of 1948, described by Layish (1982: 10) as 'the most impressive family law so far enacted in any Middle Eastern Arab state' for its 'far-reaching reforms'. The comparative lack of reform and indeed accessible legal codes for the Sunni and Ja'fari courts may partly explain why the literature on Muslim family law in Lebanon is relatively exiguous.
5 That means that it is impossible for members of unrecognized faiths to marry, as is the case for Baha'is, for instance (Zalzal 1997: 38).
6 The shari'a courts, however, also claim jurisdiction over marriages contracted by Muslims abroad where the country where the marriage is contracted follows Islamic marriage law, where two Lebanese Muslims or a Lebanese Muslim and a foreign Muslim marry in a country applying civil marriage law, and, more debatably, the marriage between a Lebanese Muslim and a non-Muslim foreigner in a country applying civil marriage law (Bilani et al. 1985: 269–71).
7 Zayn 2003: 75; see also Nasir 2002: 36. For the text of the 1962 LSC, I use Zayn (2003: 49–105) throughout.

8 The OLFR has also historically been applicable in Palestine, but the current situation is more complex (Welchman 2000).

9 As also in Egypt, Syria and Jordan, which nevertheless have more substantial and recently codified laws in place (Welchman 2007: 45).

10 The strictness of the formal hierarchy might, however, possibly explain the lack of explicit *fiqh* argumentation in the rulings I have so far surveyed.

11 An-Na'im (2002: 128) refers to areas governed by 'classical law'.

12 I refer to the Arabic text reproduced in Zayn 2003: 131–43. See also the translations in Mahmood 1972: 40–47, 1987: 97–106 and El-Alami and Hinchcliffe 1996: 147–71. On the OLFR's reforms and the wider debates here and below, see Welchman 2007: 53–59, 63, 72–73; Tucker 2008: 35, 59–61, 66–67, 70–73.

13 The necessity of the *wali*'s consent is, in fact, debatable in Ja'fari *fiqh*. Ni'ma (1996: 70) finds it not required, while noting the complexities; others, Ayatollah Khu'i for instance, think it best practice in the case of a virgin bride (Zayn 2003: 248). If the *wali* is deemed unreasonable in his opposition then the judge can overrule him, as Sunni and Ja'fari judges told me they had done on occasion. Cases to annul a marriage on the basis of *kafa'a* are by all accounts extremely rare in the Sunni courts. *Kafa'a* does not have the same prominence in Ja'fari *fiqh*.

14 While these were important topics in the first wave of reform, public concern in Lebanon would seem now to turn more on the relatively late average age of marriage (Drieskens 2008: 98).

15 They are also not bound, in terms of the rulings of the school, to insist on two witnesses, witnessing of the marriage being only recommended (*mustahabb*) rather than obligatory under Ja'fari precepts (Ni'ma 1996: 11).

16 On reformist issues around *mahr* more widely, see Welchman 2007: 90–93.

17 That is, beyond the sums to be awarded. The shari'a courts are often accused of being far too mean in this regard.

18 The 'triple divorce', three divorces in one utterance eliminating the possibility of reconciliation and return to marriage, is recognized and enforced in the Sunni courts.

19 The OLFR does not mention *khul'* in these terms, although it does, confusingly, in a section regarding judicial divorce (see below and Tucker 2008: 121), but it is common in both sets of courts. In current practice, this is *khul'* as classically understood, and not to be confused with the controversial version of *khul'* introduced in Egypt and Jordan, which does not require the husband's consent (Tucker 2008: 128–29; Welchman 2007: 112–19).

20 Previously, Qabalan's predecessor, the distinguished scholar Shaykh Muhammad Mahdi Shams al-Din, had apparently undertaken such divorces himself (Barakat 2005: 157). See also, Clarke 2010: 366–67.

Bibliography

Agmon, I. and Shahar, I. (2008) 'Introduction', in I. Agmon and I. Shahr (eds) *Shifting Perspectives in the Study of Shari'a Courts: Methodologies And Paradigms, Islamic Law and Society* (theme issue): 1–19.

An-Na'im, A. (2002) *Islamic Family Law in a Changing World: a Global Resource Book*, London: Zed Books.

Barakat, S. (2005) *Al-Qada' al-shar'i al-ja'fari: ijtihadat, nusus*, Beirut: ManshuratZayn al-Huquqiyya.

Bilani, B., Najjar, I. and El-Gemayel, A. (1985) 'Personal status', in A. El-Gemayel (ed.) *The Lebanese Legal System*, vol. 1, Washington, DC: International Law Institute.

Clarke, M. (2009) *Islam and New Kinship: Reproductive Technology and the Shari'ah in Lebanon*, New York: Berghahn Books.

——(2010) 'Neo-calligraphy: religious authority and media technology in contemporary Shiite Islam', *Comparative Studies in Society and History*, 52(2): 351–83.

——(2012) 'The judge as tragic hero: judicial ethics in Lebanon's shari'a courts', *American Ethnologist*, 39(1): 106–21.

Drieskens, B. (2008) 'Changing perceptions of marriage in contemporary Beirut', in B. Drieskens (ed.) *Les metamorphoses du marriage au moyen-orient*, Beirut: Presses de l'IFPO.

El-Alami, D. and Hinchcliffe, D. (1996) *Islamic Marriage and Divorce Laws of the Arab World*, London: Kluwer Law International.

El-Cheikh, N. (2000) 'The 1998 proposed civil marriage law in Lebanon: the reaction of the Muslim communities', in E. Cotran (ed.) *Yearbook of Islamic and Middle Eastern Law, vol. 5 (1998–99)*, London: Kluwer Law International.

Ghamroun, S. (in press) 'La communauté Sunnite libanaise saisie par les femmes', in F. Rochefort and M. Sanna (eds) *Normes religieuses et genre*, Paris: Armand Colin.

Ghazzal, Z. (2007) *The Grammars of Adjudication: the Economics of Judicial Decision Making in fin-de-siècle Ottoman Beirut and Damascus*, Beirut: Institut Français de Proche-Orient.

Gleave, R. (2008) 'The qadi and the mufti in Akhbari Shi'i jurisprudence', in P. Bearman, W. Heinrichs and B. Weiss (eds) *The Law Applied: Contextualizing the Islamic Shari'a*, London: I.B. Tauris.

Hirsch, S. (2006) 'Islamic law and society post-9/11', *Annual Review of Law and Social Science*, 2: 165–86.

Homsi, N. al- (2003) *Majmu'at al-mabadi' wa-l-qawa'id al-shar'iyyawa-l-qanuniyya allati tabbaqat-ha al-mahakim al-shar'iyya al-sunniyya*, Beirut: Manshurat al-Halabi al-Huquqiyya.

Layish, A. (1982) *Marriage, Divorce and Succession in the Druze Family: a Study Based on Decisions of Druze Arbitrators and Religious Courts in Israel and the Golan Heights*, Leiden: Brill.

Mahmood, T. (1972) *Family Law Reform in the Muslim world*, Bombay: Indian Law Institute.

——(1987) *Personal Law in Islamic Countries: History, Text and Comparative Analysis*, New Delhi: Academy of Law and Religion.

Mervin, S. (2008) 'Normes religieuses et loi du silence: le marriage temporaire chez les chiites du Liban', in B. Drieskens (ed.) *Les metamorphoses du marriage au moyen-orient*, Beirut: Presses de l'IFPO.

Mir-Hosseini, Z. (2000) *Islam and Gender: the Religious Debate in Contemporary Iran*, London: I.B. Tauris.

Nasir, J. (2002[1986]) *The Islamic Law of Personal Status*, London: Kluwer Law International.

Ni'ma, A. (1996) *Dalil al-qada' al-ja'fari*, Beirut: Dar al-Balagha.

Othman, A. (2007) '"And amicable settlement is best": *sulh* and dispute resolution in Islamic law', *Arab Law Quarterly*, 21: 64–90.

Qazzi, J. al- (2007) *Al-Zawaj al-madani: al-qadi al-lubnani fi muwajahat qawanin al-'alam*, Beirut (privately published).

Rabbath, E. (1986) *La formation historique du Liban politique et constitutionnel: essai de synthèse*, Beirut: Librairie Orientale.

Rubin, A. (2009) 'Ottoman judicial change in the age of modernity: a reappraisal', *History Compass*, 7(1): 119–40.

Saadeh, S. (2002) 'Basic issues concerning the personal status laws in Lebanon', in T. Scheffler (ed.), *Religion Between Violence and Reconciliation*, Würzburg: Ergon Verlag in Kommission.

Shehadeh, L. (1998) 'The legal status of married women in Lebanon', *International Journal of Middle East Studies*, 30(4): 501–19.

Thompson, E. (2000) *Colonial Citizens: Republican Rights, Paternal Privilege, and Gender in French Syria and Lebanon*, New York: Columbia University Press.

Tucker, J. (1996) 'Revisiting reform: women and the Ottoman law of family rights, 1917', *Arab Studies Journal*, 4(2): 4–17.

——(2008) *Women, Family, and Gender in Islamic Law*, Cambridge: Cambridge University Press.

Weber, A. (2008) 'Briseret suivre les norms: les couples islamo-chrétiens au Liban', in B. Drieskens (ed.) *Les metamorphoses du marriage au moyen-orient*, Beirut: Presses de l'IFPO.

Weiss, M. (2010) *In the Shadow of Sectarianism: Law, Shi'ism, and the Making of Modern Lebanon*, Cambridge, MA: Harvard University Press.

Welchman, L. (2000) *Beyond the Code: Muslim family Law and the Shar'i Judiciary in the Palestinian West Bank*, The Hague: Kluwer Law International.

——(2007) *Women and Muslim Family Laws in Arab States: a Comparative Overview of Textual Development and Advocacy*, Amsterdam: Amsterdam University Press.

Zalzal, M.R. (1997) 'Secularism and personal status codes in Lebanon', *Middle East Report*, 203: 37–39.

Zayn, 'A. al- (2003) *Qawanin wa-nusus wa-ahkam al-ahwal al-shakhsiyyawa-tanzim al-ta wa'if al-islamiyya fi lubnan*, Beirut: Manshurat al-Halabi al-Huquqiyya.

Zuhur, S. (2002) 'Empowering women or dislodging sectarianism? Civil marriage in Lebanon', *Yale Journal of Law and Feminism*, 14(1): 177–208.

3   The Application of Muslim Personal Law in India

A system of legal pluralism in action

Sylvia Vatuk

Introduction

In this chapter I describe the way in which Islamic family law is applied to Muslim citizens of India today, both in the state courts and in a variety of non-state religious and community-based dispute-settlement venues. I draw upon the extensive secondary literature, as well as some of the relevant case law, supplemented by ethnographic and archival data from research that I have been carrying out over the past 13 years on various aspects of Muslim personal law in India and its impact upon women's welfare. In the course of this research I spent nine months in 1998–99 in Chennai carrying out ethnographic fieldwork, interviewing Muslim women litigants and examining case files in the Chennai Family Court and in one of the city's All-Woman Police Stations. In the fall of 2001 I did a similar, though less extensive, study of Muslim personal law cases in the Hyderabad Family Court, while also examining a large body of marriage records that, by law, are required to be deposited in the Andhra Pradesh State Archives by the government *qazis* who preside over most weddings that take place in that city. I also interviewed several of those *qazis* in their respective offices and was given permission by one of them to copy a substantial sample of his recent divorce records. In the fall and winter of 2005–06 I spent one month in Delhi and three months in Hyderabad observing the proceedings and examining the files of divorced Muslim women's maintenance cases in the magistrates' courts of the two cities.[1]

Legal pluralism in India

The Indian system of family law (or personal law, as it is usually called in that country) is characterized by legal pluralism, a concept defined and used in a variety of different ways but generally employed to refer to situations in which more than one legal regime or order is operative within a society at a particular point in time (see, for example, Galanter 1981; Griffiths 1986; Merry 1988; Tamanaha 1993; Fuller 1994).[2] India's legal system is plural in two senses. The first is in what Griffiths has called its 'weak' or 'juristic' sense, which refers to situations wherein the state commands different bodies of law for different categories of persons in the population (1986: 5). Thus in India, insofar as matters of marriage and the family are concerned, distinct legal codes govern the adherents of each of the religions represented in the population: one for Hindus, another for Muslims, a third for Christians. Parsis and Jews also have their own codes of personal law.[3] When someone approaches the court to resolve a personal law issue, the judge determines the litigant's religious affiliation and applies the appropriate code.[4]

Personal law cases are heard in the regular state-run civil courts – or, in large cities, in specialized family courts – by government-appointed judges. Neither are there any government-run religious courts, nor does the state retain a cadre of religiously trained Muslim judges to hear cases filed under Muslim personal law. The religious identity of a judge is not taken into account when he or she is appointed, and it is not considered in the assignment of cases to a particular court.

Since the vast majority of Indian judges are Hindu and some of the rest are Christian or Parsi, it is only rarely and entirely a matter of chance that a Muslim personal law (MPL) case will be heard by a Muslim judge.[5] And even a judge who is Muslim by faith is unlikely to have any particular expertise in Islamic jurisprudence. Like their non-Muslim colleagues, they have been trained almost exclusively in western law and have received only minimal exposure to the rudiments of MPL. Judges in the lower courts, when confronted with an MPL case, typically refer for guidance to a recent edition of one of the better-known standard Indian textbooks or manuals on MPL compiled during or shortly after the end of the colonial period. Judges at the higher levels of the judiciary are similarly unlikely to have received any formal training in the fine points of Islamic law and few, if any, can read the original Arabic sources. However, some have made it a point to acquire considerable erudition on the subject of Islamic law and in their judgments cite relevant passages from authoritative English translations of the Qur'an, quote from some of the older pre-colonial Indian legal texts and compilations (for example, the Mughal-era *Fatawa-i Alamgiri*) and reproduce, on occasion, passages from works on the law by prominent contemporary Islamic scholars.

MPL in non-state dispute-settlement venues

The second, strong, sense in which the Indian system of personal law is pluralistic is that, insofar as the settlement of personal law disputes are concerned, there is a plurality of normative codes and a variety of venues for dispute resolution that are regarded by the public as valid and even preferred alternatives to the state-sponsored courts. Hindus and Muslims alike turn to the traditional village, caste (*jati*) or neighborhood council (*panchayat*) to resolve family conflicts. Specifically Muslim venues include mosque committees (*jama'at*) and *qazi* or *shari'a* courts (*dar-ul quzat*), some sponsored by religious institutions – such as the *madrasa* at Deoband or the Bihar-based Imarat-Shari'ah – or by multi-sectarian organizations of religious scholars such as the All India Muslim Personal Law Board (AIMPLB).[6]

These bodies are invariably presided over exclusively by men and some do not even allow women complainants to present their cases in person but insist that they be represented by a male relative. Feminist activists, believing that all-female mediation bodies can better meet women's needs, have recently promoted the formation of so-called women's courts (*mahila* or *nari adalat*). They can now be found in many rural and in most urban areas of India. Poor women, in particular, find it easier to narrate their marital problems before a sympathetic and understanding audience of their own sex and background. These bodies strive to reach resolutions that are more attentive to the social and cultural context of women's lives than those that either the state courts or the traditional community councils provide.[7]

None of these non-state bodies have any legal authority to enforce their edicts; they can only use social pressure and the force of public opinion to help ensure that the parties adhere to the agreements they have forged. But it is to such venues that the vast majority of Muslims prefer to take their marital and other family disputes, at least in the first instance, turning to the state courts only as a last resort. Consequently, only a very small minority of the marital and other family disputes that could theoretically be handled by the judicial system ever come to its attention.

The reasons for this are many. To go to court is expensive – fees are imposed at every stage of the process and under-the-table payments to court staff are typically required to ensure that one's case is proceeding in a timely manner. And a favorable outcome can hardly be hoped for unless one engages an advocate and compensates him (or her) generously for constructing a credible case and making the necessary court appearances.[8]

Furthermore, court cases are known to drag out interminably, particularly if they are contested: prolonging a case to the point where one's adversary gives up in disgust is a favorite strategy of skilled advocates. Finally, it is considered shameful – especially for a woman – to take one's private family conflicts to a court of law, rather than resolving them within one's own kin group or having them mediated by community-based bodies.

Resistance to the state's official system of justice

In her 1988 review of the state of research on legal pluralism at that time, Merry called particular attention to the need for further research on questions about 'the dynamics of the imposition of law and of resistance to [state] law ... from other normative orders' within the society (Merry 1988: 890). Such issues are of particular importance at the present time in relation to MPL in India. On the one hand, the government has for some time been establishing – and encouraging others to form – alternative dispute resolution (ADR) bodies. It has also been promoting arbitration over judicial decision-making, at least for certain types of cases (see Galanter and Krishnan, 2003). At the same time, both the government and the public at large are becoming increasingly suspicious and critical of the activities of such existing non-state ADR bodies as caste *pancayats* and shari'a courts, mainly because the decisions they issue are often biased against women. Erin Moore, for example, related the travails of a rural Muslim woman who for years fought her community council for the right to live apart from her abusive husband (Moore 1998). A similar Muslim village council attracted considerable media publicity a few years ago after a young Muslim woman alleged that her father-in-law had raped her. She was told to cease conjugal relations with her husband because, since she had engaged in sexual relations with her husband's father, the couple would have to treat one another as 'mother' and 'son' (Reddy 2005; Metcalf 2006).[9]

The state claims sole legitimate authority to change the law and many policymakers, concerned about certain provisions of MPL that create special hardship for Muslim women, feel a positive responsibility to see that the MPL is made to conform to the principles of gender equity enshrined in the Indian Constitution. For decades there has been an active and ongoing campaign, led initially by feminist activists and later taken up – though for other reasons – by right-wing Hindu chauvinist politicians,[10] to abolish the entire existing personal law system and replace it with a uniform civil code (UCC) that would apply to all citizens. But, largely for political reasons related to the position of Muslims as a minority group within a largely Hindu citizenry, the legislature has not ventured to take any concrete action in this direction.

From the side of the Muslim religious establishment there is a counter-movement of increasingly organized resistance to the state's attempts – through both legislation and judicial activism – to expand the scope of its legal hegemony over matters that the clerics would like to protect from outside interference and reserve, as far as possible, for resolution by their own quasi-judicial religious institutions. These issues have been highly contested for a very long time, but particularly so since India achieved independence in 1947. And there is considerable evidence of hardening attitudes on both fronts in recent decades.

Some religious leaders are indeed strongly resistant to the very notion that any MPL disputes should be dealt with by non-Muslim judges in the regular civil courts. Thus there is a growing move to press for the establishment of a greater number of Islamic dispute resolution fora and to encourage Muslims to use them in preference to the state-run legal institutions. The AIMPLB, in particular, has been trying for some time to persuade Muslims experiencing marital difficulties to approach *shariat* courts (*dar-ul quzat*) rather than resort to the state-sponsored judiciary. This was, for example, one of the explicit recommendations of a model marriage contract that they drafted and disseminated in 2005 (All India Muslim Personal Law Board 2005).

But during the past decade there has been increasing concern expressed in the society at large about whether the activities of informal religious dispute-settlement bodies, such as shari'a courts, are harmful to Muslim women or even pose a threat to the state-run judicial system. An active public interest movement to ban their operation altogether is underway. A writ petition was submitted to the Supreme Court in 2005 by a politically active Hindu lawyer, demanding that 'a courts be banned from continuing to operate in India as what he characterizes as 'a parallel legal system' that, in his view, poses a serious 'challenge to the judicial system' of India.[11] The Supreme Court solicited and received responses to this petition from the AIMPLB and other Islamic institutions but to date no judgment has been issued. The continuing controversy is symptomatic of a heightened level of confrontation over the issue of how much autonomy the Muslim community ought to be allowed to exercise in the administration of MPL.

The Muslim clerical leadership has tried to defuse public criticism of these courts by characterizing them as engaged purely in mediation or conciliation and counseling activities. But at the same time – and possibly in part as a reaction to criticism from outside the community – they have been making efforts both to expand the geographic coverage of the shari'a court network and to strongly encourage the faithful to use such venues in preference to taking their family and marital disputes to the state's civil or criminal courts. It is, of course, impossible to predict the outcome of these counter-vailing forces of imposition and resistance, emanating respectively from the state and the Muslim clerical leadership. But the fascinating dynamics of this contestation between the two normative orders of this legally pluralistic society warrant continued scrutiny and further in-depth investigation and analysis, as it continues to develop in the years to come.

Muslim women's groups generally feel that encouraging Muslims to rely upon shari'a courts to settle marital disputes would be detrimental to women's interests. In the mid-1980s Muslim women in cities throughout the country began organizing around attempts to reform Muslim personal law in such a way as to enhance gender equity (Vatuk 2008b, 2013a; Kirmani 2009, 2011; Schneider 2009). Like the male religious leaders of their community, many Muslim women's groups believe in working within the Muslim community itself to bring about reform of those provisions of MPL that discriminate against women, rather than encouraging or relying upon the state to do so. For the most part, they use religious, rather than secular, human rights arguments for overcoming the gender bias that characterizes MPL, as it is interpreted and administered in India today. Based on their own readings of the Qur'an and *hadith*, they claim that patriarchal interpretations of those holy texts have been foisted upon the ignorant lay Muslim population for centuries by self-interested male *'ulama'*. They demand of the clerical establishment that they give Indian women the rights that God vouchsafed to them in His revelations to the Prophet Muhammad. They specifically point to certain provisions of MPL that have an especially negative impact on women, such as the man's right to dissolve his marriage by pronouncing an extrajudicial, unilateral divorce (*talaq*) and his right to marry multiple wives. They also excoriate the religious authorities' failure to effectively enforce various male religious obligations, such as the payment of *mahr* upon divorce.[12]

Muslim leaders react strongly to any sign that the state intends to introduce changes in MPL, whether through legislation or by judicial decree. They take the position that Muslim personal law is divinely inspired and therefore cannot be altered – even though in the past some of their number have sponsored the passage of statutes that have done just that. Some *'ulama'* do acknowledge the possibility that minor modifications of existing laws might be possible but insist that only their own religio-legal experts are qualified to undertake them.

Muslim clerics and clerical organizations have also resisted the enactment of laws applicable to all citizens that could potentially impinge, directly or indirectly, on matters that, in their view, properly fall within the scope of personal law. The AIMPLB and others have voiced objections, for example, to government moves to introduce a system of compulsory registration of marriages (Venkatesan 2007).[13] Their stated rationale is that records of Muslim marriages are already kept by the clerics who write up the marriage contract (*nikahnama*) when they preside over a wedding (Anwar 2007). There have also been demands to exempt Muslims from the Prohibition of Child Marriage Act 2006 that makes it an offense to solemnize the marriage of a girl under the age of 18 (or a boy under 21).[14] Its opponents contend that, inasmuch as shari'a law considers a girl eligible for marriage once she has attained puberty, to impose a higher minimum marriage age on all females, regardless of religion, constitutes undue interference with MPL. These two issues are, of course, not unrelated: if all marriages are required to be registered with the state, it will be more difficult to evade the law against marrying underage girls.

Laws that address gender violence, particularly section 498a of the Indian Penal Code (IPC), have also come under criticism by some Muslim leaders who, like many other Indians, believe that they are widely misused by malicious wives and daughters-in-laws, in retaliation for attempts to discipline them for neglecting their household duties or diverging from other accepted standards of feminine comportment.

Muslim personal law: the statutes

MPL is broadly based upon shari'a law, as interpreted and modified – from the late-eighteenth century onward – by successive British colonial and later post-independence Indian courts. It is largely uncodified but includes a small number of legislative acts, all but one of which was enacted before India gained independence from Great Britain in 1947. The statute with the widest scope, the Muslim Personal Law (Shariat) Application Act 1937 (SAA), provides the overall framework within which Indian Muslims are governed today in terms of personal law.[15] It was originally conceived by Muslim community leaders who were disturbed by the fact that many Indian Muslims, instead of being governed by Islamic law, were in practice being subjected to whatever form of customary law prevailed in their respective local regions, which often ran directly counter to the dictates of Islam, especially insofar as rules of inheritance were concerned. Islam gives daughters and widows defined shares in a father's or husband's estate, but in most parts of India real property was (and in many cases still is) divided exclusively among the deceased's male heirs. The SAA states that in all matters of inheritance, marriage, divorce, maintenance, dower, guardianship, endowments, etc., shari'a is to prevail over local custom.[16]

Each of three other legislative acts that form part of MPL address very specific points of Islamic law. The Mussalman Wakf Validating Act (MWVA) was enacted in 1913 in response to controversies raging at the time over the legality – under shari'a – of setting up a religious endowment or trust (*waqf*, pl. *auqaf*) for the sole benefit of one's own family and descendants.[17] Numerous court cases were fought over the question until the Privy Council, in a precedent-setting appellate decision in 1894, declared such *auqaf* to be invalid because they have no religious, pious or charitable purpose as is required by shari'a. This judgment ignited furious condemnation from the Muslim community and led to an eventually successful campaign for legislation to confirm the legal validity of family *auqaf* (Kozlowski 1985; Powers 1989: 554–63).

The Dissolution of Muslim Marriages Act 1939 (DMMA) made it possible for a Muslim woman to obtain a divorce from an unwilling or untraceable husband. In Hanafi law (followed by the vast majority of Indian Muslims) a woman cannot divorce without her husband's consent. But the Indian courts had long upheld the principle that she could have her marriage automatically voided if she renounced her faith. Some leading '*ulama*', concerned that increasing numbers of women were converting to Christianity for this purpose, drafted a bill setting forth a number of approved grounds under which a woman could get a divorce from a court of law. These included desertion, insanity, obstructing the wife's right to practice her religion, disposing of her property without her consent, charging her falsely with adultery or subjecting her to mental or physical cruelty. At the same time, the act rescinded the option of voiding one's marriage through apostasy.[18]

The Muslim Women (Protection of Rights on Divorce) Act 1986 (MWA) was the most recent legislation to be enacted and the only one since independence. It also came about at the initiative of Muslim leaders and was meant to ensure that a Muslim man would not be held responsible for the support of a wife whom he had divorced, beyond an approximately three-month post-divorce waiting period (*'iddat*). Should she have no other means of maintaining herself thereafter, the law provides that she can ask a magistrate to order her adult children (if any) or one or more of her natal relatives to maintain her.[19] Otherwise, the *waqf* board[20] of the state in which she resides may be ordered to pay her a monthly living allowance.

The precipitating event for this legislation was a 1985 Supreme Court decision (*Mohd. Ahmed Khan vs Shah Bano Begum*) rejecting a well-to-do husband's appeal against a maintenance order awarded by a lower court to his divorced wife under section 125 of the Criminal Procedure Code (CrPC).[21] This judgment was widely publicized and, both because of its substance and because the (Hindu) justice had ventured to interpret the Qur'an and had interjected his views on the need for a UCC, created a furor among the Muslim religious establishment. There were mass demonstrations, petitions and public speeches protesting this unwarranted interference with MPL. The issue was extensively debated in the media and Parliament bowed to political pressure and soon passed the act.

MPL in the higher courts

Those aspects of MPL that have been most controversial in recent decades are maintenance for divorced women, unilateral divorce (particularly by the so-called triple *talaq*) and polygamy. Case law on these issues – particularly the first two – goes back to the early British colonial period. However, since independence those aspects have been brought to the attention of India's courts much more frequently and some recent judicial pronouncements have produced new directives for their interpretation in the context of MPL.

Maintenance for divorced women

The passage of the MWA was, from the outset, deplored by feminist and human rights activists. It was characterized as highly discriminatory, singling out Muslim women for deprivation of a fundamental right that all other women possessed and in the process contravening India's constitutional guarantee of equality for all under the law. It was widely assumed that the MWA would have serious consequences for all divorced Muslim women. In the Indian cultural context, it was believed unreasonable to expect a woman to file a maintenance suit against an adult child, parent or sibling, no matter how needy she might be.[22] Consequently, untold numbers of Muslim divorcees would be left penniless, with no avenue of recourse.

The MWA does indeed provide a convenient escape for men threatened by maintenance suits. Advocates routinely advise clients that they can avoid a maintenance order by simply pronouncing *talaq*. Civil and family court judges often have a similar understanding of the act's intent: upon learning that a Muslim petitioner under section

125 has been divorced by her husband, they frequently dismiss her case immediately. The legal efficacy of this tactic has been seriously undermined by recent High Court and Supreme Court decisions, but unfortunately the lower courts are not always cognizant of the applicable case law and continue to reject women's maintenance applications on this basis.

Soon after the act's passage, decisions from various high courts began to accumulate that indicated the willingness of some judges to interpret the law quite differently from the way its authors had intended.[23] A number of men whose wives had been granted maintenance awards by lower courts appealed to a higher jurisdiction, claimed that they had divorced their wives and cited the MWA to the effect that after their wives completed their *'iddat*, their financial obligations were at an end. But several appeals of this kind were rejected by the high courts and the men were instead ordered to make longer-term financial provisions for their ex-wives in the form of lump-sum payments.[24]

The key concept here was the 'reasonable and fair provision', which the MWA directs the husband to make for his ex-wife during the *'iddat* period. Those who drafted the original legislation had meant to ensure that a Muslim man would have no further financial responsibility for his ex-wife after *'iddat*. But in at least 15 of the reported cases decided under the act between 1987 and 2000, the woman's right to a 'reasonable and fair' amount *in addition to* her *'iddat* expenses was upheld by an appeals court (Agnes 2001: 32–41).[25] In 2001 a Supreme Court settled the issue with its decree that during the *'iddat* period a Muslim man is liable to make a payment to his ex-wife sufficient to sustain her in the future (*Danial Latifi & Anr. v Union of India*). Since then, courts have begun in increasing numbers to order husbands to transfer substantial lump-sum cash amounts or material assets, such as land, a house, gold jewelry or stocks, to their ex-wives.

This has led some feminist legal scholars to take a revisionist view of the 1986 law, suggesting that it has had an unintended *positive* effect on the ability of divorced Muslim women to obtain financial assistance from their ex-husbands. They claim that, rather than being disadvantaged by their inability to resort to section 125, Muslim women are finding the 1986 act 'a blessing in disguise, bringing ... newer alternatives for a more viable economic settlement' and 'scope for more innovative safeguards' for women's financial well-being after divorce (Agnes 2001: 72). While there is much to be said for this assessment of the impact of the act, it has to be emphasized that its benefits accrue mainly to women of the middle and upper classes who were married to men who can afford to pay substantial amounts as alimony. Women in poverty who, in the past, could have received maintenance awards under section 125 CrPC, are less likely, even if awarded a judgment under MWA, to be able to collect any substantial amounts from ex-husbands whose incomes are low and often unpredictable and who lack any appreciable assets.

Unilateral divorce by triple *talaq*

The issue of extrajudicial, unilateral divorce has also generated a good deal of case law in recent years. In Agnes's words, '[t]he entire discourse on Muslim women's rights revolves around this issue' (2011: 60). The question for the Indian courts has not been whether a Muslim man can dissolve his marriage by pronouncing *talaq* (divorce) three times – since shari'a clearly allows this, it has not been seriously questioned, either by the judiciary or by legislators. The issue has been whether he can utter the word three times *in rapid succession*, or 'at one sitting'. This procedure, popularly known as triple *talaq*, is the one most frequently used in India to effect a Muslim divorce. The Arabic term is *talaq-ul bida'at* (innovative divorce), so called because it was unknown in the early days of Islam and introduced only at a later date. In the eyes of some Islamic scholars, it is of questionable validity. Some contend that when pronounced in this way it should be counted as a single *talaq* and is therefore revocable, just as if the man had pronounced the word only once. Most Indian Sunni clerics, however, while they may acknowledge that it is an undesirable and even sinful practice, consider the triple *talaq* to be a legally permissible way of effecting an irrevocable divorce. Until recently, the British and post-independence Indian courts followed this interpretation, typically citing the 1905 decision in *Sarabai vs Rabiabai*. The judge in that case, while admitting that in shari'a the *approved* method is to leave one month between the first and second and the second and third *talaqs* in order to allow for the possibility of reconciliation, declared an irrevocable divorce by triple *talaq* to be 'good in law, though bad in theology'.

In the 1980s the appellate courts began to turn away from this approach to the question. The issue of triple *talaq* has not often arisen directly, but rather in connection with maintenance cases. Typically, a lower court has ordered a man to pay his wife a monthly stipend under section 125 CrPC. He appeals the decision, claiming that he has pronounced *talaq* and made all the religiously required *mahr* and *'iddat* payments and returned her wedding gifts. Therefore, he contends, he has no legal obligation to maintain her further. The wife, in response, claims that the divorce never took place or was improperly executed. In 1981, Justice Baharul Islam of the Gauhati High Court (later of the Supreme Court) – one of the few Muslims in the higher ranks of the judiciary – took the opportunity presented by one such case to declare instantaneous divorce by triple *talaq* invalid. The judge's argument was *talaq* could only be for a reasonable cause and that a relation of each the husband and wife must make attempts to effect a reconciliation between the parties. In his view, it was the Qur'an that stated the correct law of *talaq*. Further, the judge stated that Qur'anic law did not provide a husband with an unfettered right to end the marriage; the husband could not act on a whim as long as the wife maintained her faithfulness and obedience to the husband (*Jiauddin vs Anwara Begum*).

Justice Baharul Islam made a similar decision in a subsequent case (*Rukia Khatun vs Abdul Khalique Laskar*) and some other high courts followed his lead. A 2002 Supreme Court ruling in *Shamim Ara vs State of U.P.* effectively settled the issue. The appellant was the wife. A lower court had refused to consider her maintenance plea, on the basis that, as a divorced Muslim woman, the MWA made her ineligible for relief under section 125 CrPC. As evidence of the divorce the lower court had accepted the husband's affidavit, which had been prepared in connection with an entirely different case but happened to mention his having divorced his wife some time previously. The apex court was asked to decide whether such a declaration proved that a divorce had actually taken place. The justice ruled that it did not and therefore the lower court should not have relied upon it when rejecting the wife's maintenance application. The marriage still subsisted and the husband remained liable to pay maintenance until it was legally dissolved.

In reaching his decision, Justice Lahoti cited two respected authorities on MPL – a standard 1906 law manual (*Mulla's Principles of Maomedan Law*: Hidayatullah and Hidayatullah 1990) and a textbook by a respected contemporary legal scholar (Mahmood 1980) – and strongly rejected the position held by both, that 'a mere plea of previous talaq … , though unsubstantiated', is sufficient to prove a divorce. He pointed to earlier High Court decisions establishing that a *talaq* is not effective without the husband providing adequate justification and making serious attempts at reconciliation. The present case met neither of these conditions.

Polygamy

The fact that MPL allows a man to have as many as four wives at a time, while men of other religions are limited to one, is repeatedly criticized in the Indian media and by the non-Muslim public more generally.[26] Yet the issue has generated relatively little case law. To the extent that the judiciary has been inspired to express its views on the matter, its usual position is that although polygamy is an undesirable practice, causing untold suffering to Muslim wives, it is clearly permitted by the Qur'an and therefore, inasmuch as the SAA requires Muslims to be governed in all family matters by shari'a, it can be neither banned nor restricted by the Indian state. In the words of Justice R. Basant of the Kerala High Court:

> Polygamy is permitted, tolerated and accepted and enforced by the Indian courts only because the Muslim Personal Law (Shariat) Application Act, 1937 mandates that the Muslim Personal Law (Shariat) … has to be followed by the Indian courts. The stipulation regarding polygamy is therefore accepted and enforced … . In that view of the matter, the law permitting polygamy will also have to pass the test of constitutionality under Art. 13 (*Abdurahiman vs Khairunnessa*).

The Supreme Court has been asked on more than one occasion to declare this provision of MPL unconstitutional, but each time has refused to do so.[27] Thus, in 1996, a writ petition, asking that the laws under which Muslims are allowed to practice polygamy, extrajudicial unilateral divorce and discrimination against females in inheritance be declared void (*Ahmedabad Women Action Group (AWAG) vs Union of India*).[28] The court dismissed it, saying that 'these are all matters for legislature', not the courts, to decide. In 2006 a public interest litigation (PIL) suit challenging those same practices on constitutional grounds was likewise dismissed. That two-justice bench declared that only Parliament has jurisdiction over such matters: 'If the law provides that Muslims can have four wives, we cannot change it' (TNN 2006). The Supreme Court also rejected a 2001 plea – by a woman whose husband had taken a second wife and then divorced her – to declare polygamy unconstitutional, on the grounds that it constitutes 'a denial of equality, personal liberty and human rights' (*Julekhabi vs Union of India*). She was instructed to approach Parliament for a remedy (TNN 2001).

Some judges have referred to an argument put forward by Muslim women activists and others that, inasmuch as the Qur'an requires a polygamous husband to treat all wives equitably but acknowledges that this condition is close to impossible to fulfill in practice, the proper meaning of the injunction is that a man should have only one wife. However, these observations have been merely *obiter dicta*: they have not de-legitimized the practice, as such.

The main contexts within which polygamy appears in case law is in connection with suits for divorce, maintenance or restitution of conjugal rights (RCR).[29] Under the DMMA, the simple fact that one's husband has taken another wife is not a ground for divorce. However, a woman may sue for dissolution on grounds of cruelty, if her husband 'does not treat her equitably in accordance with the injunctions of the Qur'an' (DMMA s. 2 (viii)(f)). This was the issue in *Abdurahiman vs Khairunnessa* (cited above). In dismissing the husband's appeal against a lower court's award of a divorce decree to his wife, the presiding justice cited three relevant *ayats* (verses) from the Qur'an and the commentary of its translator (Yusuf Ali 1983)[30] and on that basis concluded that Islamic law clearly gives a woman the right to exit a polygamous marriage if she has been unfairly treated by comparison with other wives. She needs not even provide any evidence: 'it is the assertion of the woman that matters. She is the best Judge to decide whether she has been treated equitably or not' (p. 33). Various high courts have used similar reasoning when rejecting a husband's plea for restitution of conjugal rights,[31] and it has been successfully employed by married Muslim women, when filing for maintenance under section 125 CrPC, to justify their residing separately from their husbands.

In 1995 the Supreme Court addressed the issue of Muslim polygamy in *Sarla Mudgal vs Union of India,* when hearing together the cases of four different couples. All of the parties were born Hindu and the men's first wives were Hindu as well. Each of the men, unable to divorce their wives but desiring to marry other women, converted to Islam and married according to Islamic rites, hoping in this way to circumvent the monogamy clause in the Hindu Marriage Act. The author of this decision cites a number of analogous cases involving conversion and remarriage that go back to the late-nineteenth century and concludes that a second marriage contracted by an already-married Hindu convert to Islam is void and the man guilty of the offense of bigamy (under section 494 IPC). This judgment has, of course, no bearing on the validity of multiple marriages contracted by men born to Muslim parents.

Recurring themes in appeal court decisions on issues of MPL

In formulating their decisions on cases of MPL, all justices refer at least briefly to the text of the Qur'an, many of them discoursing at length upon those passages of the Holy Book that pertain most directly to the issue at hand, referring to English translations, usually those produced by Indian Muslim Islamic scholars of an earlier age. They also quote liberally from standard Indian textbooks of Islamic law, as well as citing relevant case law, sometimes excerpting lengthy passages from earlier, precedent-setting High and Supreme Court judgments. Occasionally, a justice will also refer to legislation passed by other – usually Muslim-majority – countries, which they believe could serve as models for a particular interpretation of shari'a or as an indication of the kind of reforms that could be introduced into MPL in India – in terms of, for example, imposing limits on or regulating the ability of men to discard their wives unilaterally or marry more than one wife.

Another recurrent theme in the recent case law is the need for a uniform code of family law to replace the existing pluralistic legal system. Justices dealing with issues of MPL repeatedly deplore the fact that, although Article 44 of the Indian Constitution enjoins the state to 'endeavour to secure' a UCC for all its citizens, it has, in the words of Justice Chandrachud in *Mohd. Ahmed Khan vs Shah Bano Begum & Ors*:

> remained a dead letter. There is no evidence of any official activity for framing a common civil code ... . Inevitably, the role of the reformer has to be assumed by the courts because it is beyond the endurance of sensitive minds to allow injustice to be suffered when it is so palpable. But piecemeal attempts of courts to bridge the gap between personal laws cannot take the place of a common civil code.

The necessity, when interpreting particular provisions of MPL, of taking into account the gender imbalance in Indian social structure is also mentioned very frequently in these judgments. Thus, for example, Supreme Court Justice S. Babu writes in *Danial Latifi & Anr. vs Union of India*:

> where matrimonial relationship is involved, one has to consider the social conditions prevalent in the Indian society ... [in which] there exists a great disparity in the matter of economic resourcefulness between a man and a woman. Indian society is male dominated both economically and socially and women are assigned, invariably, a dependent role.

Expressions of sympathy for the sufferings of Muslim women under particular provisions of MPL appear frequently in these judgments. For example, in a 1968 Kerala High Court decision the justice laments:

> Should Muslim wives suffer ... [their husbands'] tyranny for all times? Should their personal law remain so cruel towards these unfortunate wives? ... My judicial conscience is disturbed at this monstrosity. The question is whether the conscience of the leaders of public opinion of the community will also be disturbed (*Pathayi vs Moideen*).

Justices often express the idea that the very concept of marriage has changed from what it was in earlier times. Justice R. Basant of the Kerala High Court points out in *Abdurahiman vs. Khairunnessa* (2010) that '[m]arriage as an institution has totally different purposes and incidents in the modern world'. He then goes on to cite an earlier decision, by the same court, to the effect that marriage is no longer:

> an arrangement between the master and a slave or domestic maid hired for life for performing the domestic chores ... [but for] the pursuit of the mission of life by

equal adult partners seeking perfection, ... happiness and contentment in life (*Aboobacker vs Rahiyanath*).

Likewise, in a much earlier (1960) case the issue was whether a woman whose husband had taken a second wife was legally justified in choosing to live apart from him. S. S. Dhavan of the Allahabad High Court rejected the husband's contention that she was not and remarked that:

> in any particular case, the Court cannot ignore the prevailing social conditions, the circumstances of actual life and the change in the people's habits and modes of living. Today Muslim women move in society, and it is impossible for any Indian husband with several wives to cart all of them around. He must select one among them to share his social life, thus making impartial treatment in polygamy virtually impossible. (*Itwari vs Smt. Asghari*)

The fact that views of the kind outlined here are so widely shared among justices at the higher levels of judiciary, and are reflected in their decisions on important cases involving unilateral divorce, polygamy and maintenance, has meant that significant changes have occurred in MPL over the past 20 years, all in the direction of greater gender equity. These have occurred in spite of the fact that the judiciary consistently declines to declare any specific provisions of the law unconstitutional and the legislature refrains from taking any action that the Muslim community might regard as threatening its legal autonomy.

MPL in the lower courts

Lower court cases are very rarely officially reported and therefore data on how issues of MPL are dealt with at that level of the system are not easily available. To obtain them it is necessary to personally examine case files in court record rooms. Furthermore, under family court rules (as laid out in the Family Courts Act 1984), all hearings are held in camera and in neither of the family courts whose files I examined had the judges issued any written decisions beyond brief notes in the file indicating the mode of disposal of the case. My research (see Vatuk 2001, 2003, 2005) shows that the vast majority of MPL cases are brought by women. Thus, 70 percent of the petitioners in the 540 Muslim suits filed in the Chennai Family Court between 1988 and 1997 were female. More than two-thirds of the women were applying either for maintenance (232 cases) or divorce (63 cases).[32] This predominance of women petitioners is not surprising. Muslim men can divorce extrajudicially and cannot obtain maintenance orders against their wives. The only matrimonial relief available to them in the state courts is for RCR; in most cases they file such suits not to get their wives back but rather to defeat their wives' petitions for divorce or maintenance.[33]

Divorce

Typically a Muslim women files for divorce under DMMA only after trying other remedies, either negotiating with her husband for an extrajudicial *khul'* divorce or persuading a religious official to dissolve her marriage, without her husband's agreement, by *faskh*. Either alternative is much cheaper, more expeditious and less complicated than filing suit in a court of law. My data from the two family courts thus indicate that the DMMA is relatively infrequently resorted to. The Chennai Family Court began operation in 1988. Over the next ten years, in a city with a Muslim population of 333,672, only 6.3 suits (on average) were filed under the act per year. In Hyderabad, with a Muslim population somewhat over four times as large, the corresponding figure was 32.3 filings per year. Thus, the rates of resort to DMMA were similarly low in both cities and considerably lower than the rate of court filings for divorce by women of other religions.[34]

In Chennai only 42 percent of the cases filed under the DMMA in the decade for which I have data were pursued to judgment. The rest were dismissed, usually because the petitioner had stopped making the required court appearances, whether because she had reconciled with her husband, had convinced him to divorce her by *khul'*, had been divorced by *talaq*, could no longer afford to pay her advocate's fees or had simply become discouraged. All of the women who stayed the course did eventually succeed in obtaining a court-ordered divorce, but in most cases only after months, if not years, of successive court appearances. Furthermore, in the final settlement they almost always waived their rights to *mahr* and *'iddat* expenses. The DMMA specifies that both are immediately payable upon divorce but, at least in Chennai, judges seemed reluctant to grant a contested divorce under the act. Instead, they endeavored to gain the husbands' consent, even if it meant persuading the wife to agree to a dis-advantageous financial outcome. The implicit model for a court divorce thus appeared to be the Islamic *khul'*.

Maintenance

Maintenance cases are more plentiful than any other kind of case on the dockets of the family courts. As I have discussed above, insofar as MPL is concerned, the key legal issue – which arose upon passage of the MWA in 1986 – is whether and by what means a divorced woman can obtain financial support from her former husband. Although the Supreme Court decreed in 2001 that within three months of divorcing his wife a man must not only pay her *mahr* and *'iddat* expenses but must also provide for her future subsistence needs, the lower courts have been slow to implement this ruling. Many Muslim women have been unable to take advantage of this more recent interpretation of the MWA because their lawyers are unaware of its significance and do not realize the law's potential to ensure a divorced Muslim woman a secure financial future (see Vatuk 2013b). As one Delhi lawyer – himself a Muslim – told me, when a divorced Muslim woman comes to him for help, his strategy is to treat her file for maintenance under section 125 CrPC as if she were a married woman. If the husband contends that he has divorced her, the advocate will argue that the divorce never occurred or that it was not legally executed. If the husband then proceeds to divorce her according to the more recently established judicial guidelines, he can at least be ordered to pay maintenance from the time the couple first separated until the effective date of the new divorce. Like other Delhi lawyers and court officials whom I interviewed in 2005, this gentleman had never filed a case under the MWA and was not even sure how to go about doing so.

In Hyderabad I found a somewhat different situation. Some Muslim lawyers there had been filing suits under the MWA for years and had been able to get several of their clients substantial lump-sum payments under the 'reasonable and fair' provision of that law. Between 1995 and 2005 a total of 224 suits had been filed under the MWA in the Hyderabad Mahila Court, the magistrate's court that dealt mainly with cases of crimes against women. Most of the MWA petitioners sought *mahr* and/or *'iddat* expenses and the return of wedding gifts given by each spouse's family. Many had also submitted claims for 'reasonable and fair provision'. Some of these cases dragged on for years. Of the cases filed in the previous decade, 30 percent were still pending, and 15 cases for five or more years. Forty percent had been dismissed for one reason or another. In only 25 percent of the cases had a judgment been pronounced by the time I left the field and in almost every one of these the husband had been ordered to pay some amount to his former wife, though not always all that she had petitioned for.

Whereas the MWA provides that a divorced woman unable to support herself can ask a magistrate to order one or more of her adult children or natal relatives to maintain her, such cases are extremely rare. I found not a single example during my investigations. However, the final option provided in the MWA – asking a magistrate to order the Wakf Board[35] of one's home state to disburse a monthly stipend – is being increasingly availed of by poor women. A woman's right to do so, even if she has not first filed against any of her kinsmen, was firmly established in a 1996 Supreme Court ruling (*The Secretary, Tamil Nadu State Wakf Board*). Some state boards have been more responsive than others to the requirement that they provide financial assistance to poor divorcées when ordered to do so by the courts. But there is a clear upward trend in the numbers being helped in this way. For example, when I was in Hyderabad in 2005, the Andhra Pradesh State Wakf Board was maintaining only four destitute divorced women. But by March 2012 the number it reported providing with monthly stipends had risen to 320.

A knowledge gap between the higher and lower courts

The practical impact of precedent-setting High Court and even Supreme Court decisions is not as strong as it might be, in part because high courts in one state are not bound to follow the rulings of those issued by others. Furthermore, lower court judges are frequently oblivious to the precedents that have been set by those courts or do not fully understand their implications and therefore do not follow them when making their own decisions on cases that come before them. As Subramanian has observed, with reference to the limited impact of the *Danial Latifi* judgment: 'The knowledge of judges and lawyers in the lower courts is uneven about such recent landmark judgments and some lower courts continue to restrict maintenance for Muslim divorcees to a three-month period' (2008: 649). Likewise, with respect to the issue of instantaneous unilateral divorce, Agnes remarks: 'despite the plethora of judgments [denying the validity of divorce by triple *talaq*], ... many lawyers and some trial court judges continue to endorse the view that ... Muslim women can be deprived [thereby] of their legal right of maintenance' (2011: 64).

Even after the Supreme Court has definitively ruled on such issues as triple *talaq*, cases addressing these same theoretically settled issues continue to be brought before the high courts of various states. But, of course, the vast majority of negative verdicts never even get to be overturned by appeals courts because few women have the knowledge or the wherewithal to pursue their cases beyond the level of the originating court that dismissed them.

Conclusion

I have presented here an outline of the way legal pluralism operates in practice in India with respect to some of the key issues in Muslim personal law. I have shown that the state-sponsored judiciary does not hold a monopoly on the privilege of administering MPL. It takes no active role in facilitating or regulating male-initiated Muslim divorce: a Muslim man may freely divorce extrajudicially and is also empowered to grant this privilege to his wife, if he chooses to accept her offer of financial compensation. A Muslim woman's options outside of the civil courtroom are more limited than a man's, but before resorting to a suit for divorce she too has the choice of either trying to persuade her husband to release her extrajudicially or getting the *qazi* of a shari'a court to declare her marriage void, on the grounds that the marital relationship has become so strained that it is impossible for her to continue to 'observe God's limits' – that is, to remain chaste.

Although the vast majority of marital and family issues that arise among Muslims are handled outside of the official judicial system, there is no lack of cases involving issues of MPL, either in the lower courts or in the various high courts and in the Supreme Court of India. In the lower courts, women greatly predominate among the Muslim plaintiffs, for reasons that I have outlined above. The vast majority of these women are seeking maintenance awards against their husbands or ex-husbands. A smaller number are seeking a divorce. In both the Supreme Court and the high courts, however, Muslim appellants are predominantly male. But there too the main issues being adjudicated relate in one way or other to the maintenance of separated or divorced wives. Such cases have led to a number of far-reaching and game-changing decisions being issued by various high courts and by the Supreme Court of India on the main contentious issues of MPL in India today – not only maintenance for divorced Muslim women, but also unilateral divorce by triple *talaq* and polygamy. Regrettably, the practical impact of these judgments, in terms of actually improving the conditions under which Muslim women experiencing marital problems labor, has been weaker than one would like. This seems to be because too many of the lawyers and judges working in the lower levels of the judicial system are either unaware of, fail to understand the implications and potentialities of, or simply ignore the precedents set by the higher judiciary. The remedy for this might be a more robust system of continuing education for those in both professions. But that is something easier to recommend than to put into place.

64 *Sylvia Vatuk*

Notes

1 My research in Chennai was funded by a US Department of Education, Fulbright-Hays Senior Research Fellowship and a sabbatical leave from the University of Illinois at Chicago. The 2001 Hyderabad research was undertaken with the support of an American Institute of Indian Studies Senior Fellowship and a semester-long research leave from the College of Liberal Arts and Sciences of the University of Illinois at Chicago, while my 2005–06 research on maintenance for divorced Muslim women was again funded by the American Institute of Indian Studies. I am grateful for the valuable assistance provided at different times during these years by R. Saraswathy, Rafia Anjum, Rina Ambikeshwar, H. Rayees Fathima, Muhammad Ayyub, Bhavana Avaneendra, Mahfooz Nazki and Shahkar Mehdi.

2 Merry, in fact, insists that legal pluralism is not characteristic only of societies of a particular type, such as those that have been under colonial domination at some point in their history, but that 'plural normative orders are found in virtually all societies' (1988: 873).

3 A couple can opt out of being governed by one of these religion-specific codes by marrying in a non-religious, civil ceremony under a separate secular marriage law, the Special Marriage Act 1954 (SMA). Furthermore, a couple married in a religious ceremony has the option of registering their marriage after the fact under this act, in order henceforth to be governed in matrimonial and other family matters by the SMA, rather than by the personal law code that formerly applied to them. This device is often used by Muslims who wish to leave a larger proportion of their property to a chosen heir than he or she would otherwise be entitled to under Islamic inheritance laws.

4 To be more precise, the choice of law code depends upon the religious rite under which the individual's marriage was solemnized. Normally, of course, this would be the religion into which he or she was born.

5 The most recent census figures available on the religious distribution of the population show that 80.5 percent are Hindu, 13.4 per cent Muslim (available online at http://censusindia.gov.in/ Census_Data_2001/India_at_glance/religion.aspx). However, fewer than 5 percent of judges in the lower courts are Muslim. The 2006 Sachar Committee Report on the status of Muslims concludes that their poor representation in the judiciary is not due to discriminatory hiring practices but is rather a consequence of the fact that Muslims have, on average, markedly lower levels of educational achievement than upper-caste Hindus; the latter are disproportionately well-represented at this level of the system. (available online at http://minorityaffairs.gov.in/sites/ upload_files/moma/files/pdfs/sachar_comm.pdf, pp. 173–74, 372 accessed 10 October 2010). There are relatively more Muslims in the higher levels of the judiciary, but not nearly in proportions equivalent to those found in the population as a whole. The Supreme Court of India currently has three Muslim justices out of twenty-five (12 percent) (available online at http://doj.gov. in/?q=node/24). Most of the 21 high courts also have two or three Muslim justices. But since these courts are invariably larger than the Supreme Court, the percentage of Muslims is consistently lower than it is in the latter body. For example, among the 51 justices of the Madras High Court, three are Muslim (6 percent) (available online at www.hcmadras.tn.nic.in/prejudge.htm). The Kerala High Court, with 30 justices, likewise has three Muslims (10 percent) (available online at http://highcourtofkerala.nic.in/prjudges.html), the Andhra Pradesh High Court has three out of thirty-two (9 percent) (available online at www.andhranews.net/state/whoswho/hc.asp), the Delhi High Court two out of thirty-five (6 percent) (available online at http://delhihighcourt.nic.in/ cjsittingjudges.asp?currentPage=1) and the Calcutta High Court only one out of forty-two (2 percent) (available online at http://calcuttahighcourt.nic.in/judges.htm, all websites accessed on 15 October 2012).

6 The AIMPLB is a self-appointed body of 251 clerics who represent most of the major Muslim sects in India. It was set up in 1973 'to protect the Muslim Personal Law' and has become the most prominent, vocal and influential organization of its kind in the country. See www.aimplboard.org/ index.html (accessed 19 May 2007).

7 For a review of some of the recent literature on this new kind of dispute resolution body see Vatuk 2013b.

8 This is even true in Family Court, where the law specifies that, except under special circumstances, litigants are not entitled to legal representation (The Family Courts Act 1984, Chapter IV, Section 13). The original purpose of this provision was to enable the parties to come before the judge in person and to argue their own cases in their own ordinary language, rather than in the specialized language of the law. However, few litigants have the necessary knowledge and skills to negotiate, without the help of an advocate, the complicated and lengthy process of filing and pursuing a legal case. Therefore most family courts adapt to the realities of the situation by being, in practice, quite flexible on this point. It is, of course, also in the interest of members of the legal profession that they should be so: this provision doubtless contributes to the receptivity of family court judges to pleas for permission to be represented by counsel.

9 The reasoning behind this *fatwa* was that a woman is prohibited by shari'a law from having sexual relations with both a father and his son.

10 Most feminists and feminist-oriented women's organizations have backed away from their former advocacy for a UCC and now prefer instead to promote 'legal reform from within' the various minority communities. This shift came about largely in response to the politicization of the issue by the Hindu right, whose demand for an end to the current system of personal laws is perceived to be part of a broader anti-Muslim agenda with which feminists are very loath to be associated.

11 *Vishwa Lochan Madan vs Union of India*, Writ Petition (Civil) No. 386/2005. See Redding 2010 for an extended discussion of the issue.

12 For a marriage to be valid under shari'a law, a man must give his bride a gift of money or valuables, the amount to be recorded in the marriage contract. In India the *mahr* is rarely handed over at the time of the wedding and it is seldom paid to the wife even later, during the couple's married life. Legally, it becomes due immediately upon divorce or widowhood but, in practice, few women ever receive it.

13 Such regulations are already in effect, though not necessarily consistently enforced, in some states.

14 This law replaced the similar Child Marriage Restraint Act 1929 (CMRS), as amended in 1978. In 2002 the AIMPLB was party to an unsuccessful petition to the Supreme Court that challenged, on the cited grounds, the earlier law's applicability to Muslims (Report 2002). It has also weighed in recently to the same effect on some cases involving under-age Muslim brides (see, for example, IANS 2012).

15 Available online at http://legalapproach.net/legal.php?nid=218 (accessed 24 October 2012).

16 One of the key issues arising out of this conflict of laws revolved around women's inheritance: customary law rarely allowed daughters to inherit property, particularly agricultural land. So during negotiations over the wording of the bill, large Muslim landowners, particularly in north-western India, who wished to preserve their custom of restricting inheritance to males, insisted upon inserting an exception for the inheritance of agricultural land (Gilmartin 1988). Recently, several southern states have amended the act so as to remove this exclusion, but it is still in effect in the rest of the country. In 2005 a petition signed by large numbers of individuals and women's groups, asking that this passage also be deleted from the central act, was presented to the Prime Minister (available online at http://groups.yahoo.com/mukto-mona/message/28242, accessed 10 October 2012). The AIMPLB has also indicated that it favors the change. However, as of December 2012, the Parliament had taken no action on the matter.

17 Available online at www.helplinelaw.com/docs/THE_MUSSALMAN_WAKF_VALIDATING_ACT, _1913 (accessed 24 October 2012). Not only in India, but also elsewhere in the Muslim world, dedicating one's property to a private, family trust (*waqf alal aulad*) was – and is – a popular device for ensuring a secure financial future for one's descendants. By bypassing those provisions of the Muslim laws of inheritance that lead inevitably to the fragmentation of property, it allows one to keep it intact for the benefit of later generations (see Powers 1990).

18 For more details about the discussions and controversies that led up to the passage of this act, see Masud 1996 and De 2010. The latter author cites and examines much of the relevant case law that preceded it.

19 Specifically, any relatives who stand to inherit from her in the event of her death.

20 The government office charged with the regulation and management of Muslim religious endowments.

21 Under this section any man who neglects or refuses to maintain his wife can be ordered by a magistrate to pay her a monthly allowance. The inclusion of a 'divorced wife' under the definition of 'wife' was strongly opposed from the outset by Muslim religious leaders, who contended that in Islam a husband's financial responsibilities for his wife end when she completes her *'iddat*.

22 This belief has, in fact, proved to be correct.

23 Agnes analyzed statistically 243 reported cases in which maintenance of a divorced Muslim woman was at issue and describes 67 of these in more detail. In 52 cases (78 percent), the petitioner was the husband, appealing a lower court judgment in which he was ordered to pay maintenance under section 125 CrPC. Only a few cases had been originally filed under the MWA (2001: 12–13, 104, 100–01).

24 Some within the Muslim clerical leadership became concerned that through such judicial activism the original intent of the law was being subverted. As Agnes notes, 'In response to the generous interpretations of the Act, Syed Shahabuddin ... moved a Private Members Bill (Bill No. 155 of 1992) ... to amend the Act and restrict its scope in clear terms to maintenance only for and during the iddat period' (2000: 105).

25 I do not have space here to go into detail concerning the reasoning behind such judgments and the points of Islamic law that were drawn upon in their support, but see Agnes 2001 for a detailed analysis of some of those decisions. See also Subramanian (2008: 645–49).

26 Although reliable recent statistics are lacking, most scholars agree that the incidence of polygamous marriages among Indian Muslims is quite low and is in any case no higher than among non-Muslims, even though the latter can be charged with the crime of bigamy (under section 494 of the IPC) if they marry another woman during the subsistence of a prior marriage. But, since bigamy is a non-cognizable offence – i.e. the state will take notice only upon a formal complaint by the first wife or her parents – the actual likelihood of prosecution is minimal.

27 In all of these cases the petitioners demanded that not only polygamy but also other gender-discriminatory provisions of MPL, such as male-initiated unilateral divorce, be declared unconstitutional.

28 The petition also asked that the MWA and certain sections of Hindu and Christian personal laws be declared unconstitutional.

29 This is a legal remedy designed to compel a spouse who has left the matrimonial home to return to it and, in the formulaic phrase repeatedly encountered in court documents: 'restore to the petitioner the comforts and bliss of married life.' In Hindu and Christian personal law, women as well as men can – and do – file for restitution, but only men have access to this relief under MPL. In an unusual recent case, however, a Muslim woman applied for, but was denied, a restitution order by the Bombay Family Court. On appeal, the Bombay High Court ordered the case re-heard (Deshpande 2010). Its ultimate outcome is unknown.

30 This translation, by a highly respected Indian Islamic scholar, was originally published in the 1930s.

31 The precedent most frequently cited in this regard is a 1960 Allahabad High Court decision, *Itwari vs Smt. Asghari.*

32 The rest sought a variety of remedies, including declarations as to the validity of a marriage or a divorce, child custody or the retrieval of personal property in the possession of a husband or parent-in-law. I exclude here the very numerous filings for execution of previously issued court orders, mainly pertaining to maintenance awards that had not been complied with.

33 Even if granted, such an order is unenforceable: there is no legal way to compel a woman to return to her marital home against her wishes.

34 In Chennai I found that Hindu and Christian women were three times as likely as were Muslim women (in proportion to their respective numbers in the city's population) to seek a divorce under their respective codes of personal law. Most of the difference is doubtless explained by the fact that Hindu women lack the same options for out-of-court divorces that are available to their Muslim sisters. Indian law does recognize the validity of so-called customary divorces in castes or tribes that have a longstanding traditional procedure for dissolving marriages extrajudicially. But what proportion of the population is in a position to avail themselves of this option is not known.

35 The government agency charged with the supervision of Muslim endowments.

Cases cited

Aboobacker vs Rahiyanath, 2008 (3) KLT 482.

Abdurahiman vs Khairunnessa, I (2010) DMC 707 Ker.

Ahmedabad Women Action Group (AWAG) vs Union of India, AIR 1997 (3) SCC 573.

A. S. Parveen Akthar vs Union of India, 2002 INDLAW MAD 327.

A. Yousuf Rawther vs Sowramma, AIR 1971 Ker 261.

Danial Latifi & Anr. vs Union of India, 2001 (7) SCC 740.

Itwari vs Smt. Asghari, AIR 1960 All 684.

Jiauddin vs Anwara Begum, 1981 (1) GLR 358.

Mohd. Ahmed Khan vs Shah Bano Begum & Ors., 1985 AIR 945.

Pathayi vs Moideen 1968 KLT 763.

Rukia Khatun vs Abdul Khalique Laskar, 1981 (1) GLR 375.

Sarabai vs Rabiabai, 1905 ILR 30 (Bombay) 537.

Sarla Mudgal, President, & Ors. vs Union of India, 1995 (3) SCC 635.

The Secretary, Tamil Nadu Wakf Board & Anr vs Syed Fatima Nachi, 1996 INSC 770.

Shamim Ara vs State of U.P., 2002 (7) SCC 518.

Vishwa Lochan Madan vs Union of India, Writ Petition (Civil) No. 386/2005.

Bibliography

Agnes, F. (2000) *Law and Gender Inequality: the Politics of Women's Rights in India*, New Delhi: Oxford University Press.

——(2001) *Judgment Call: an Insight into Muslim Women's Right to Maintenance*, Mumbai: Majlis.

——(2011) *Family Law*, Vol. I., New Delhi: Oxford University Press.

All India Muslim Personal Law Board (2005) *Nikahnama*, Delhi: AIMPLB.

Anderson, M. (1990) 'Islamic law and the colonial encounter in British India', in C. Mallat and J. Connors (eds), *Islamic Family Law*, London: Graham and Trotman.

De, R. (2010) 'The two husbands of Vera Tiscenko: apostasy, conversion, and divorce in late colonial India', *Law and History Review*, 28(4): 1011–41.

Deshpande, S. (2010) 'HC relief for Muslim woman seeking conjugal rights', 12 April. Available online at http://article.timesofindia.indiatimes.com/2010–04–12/India/28143668_1_family-court-hc-relief-muslim-women (accessed 15 November 2012).

Fuller, C. (1994) 'Legal anthropology: legal pluralism and legal thought', *Anthropology Today*, 10(3): 9–12.

Galanter, M. (1981) 'Justice in many rooms: courts, private ordering, and indigenous law', *Journal of Legal Pluralism and Unofficial Law*, 19(1): 1–25.

Galanter, M. and Krishnan, J. (2003) 'Debased informalism: Lok Adalats and legal rights in Modern India', in E.G. Jensen and T.C. Heller (eds), *Beyond Common Knowledge: Empirical Approaches to the Rule of Law*, Stanford, CA: Stanford University Press.

Gilmartin, D. (1988) 'Customary law and shari'at in British Punjab', in K. Ewing (ed.), *Shari'at and Ambiguity in South Asian Islam*, Berkeley: University of California Press.

Griffiths, J. (1986) 'What is legal pluralism?', *Journal of Legal Pluralism and Unofficial Law*, 24(1): 1–40.

Hidayatullah, M. and Hidayatullah, A. (eds) (1990) *Mulla's Principles of Mahomedan Law*, 19th edn, Mumbai: T.N. Tripathi.

Holden, L. (2008) *Hindu Divorce: A Legal Anthropology*, Aldershot: Ashgate Publishing Ltd.

Hussain, S. (2007) *Shariat Courts and Women's Rights in India*, New Delhi: Centre for Women's Development Studies.

HVK (Hindu Vivek Kendra) (2002) 'SC admits petition on child marriage act', July 22. Available online at www.hvk.org/articles/0702/172.html (accessed 19 December 2002).

IANS (2012) 'Indian Muslims split over wedding age ruling', June 8. Available online at http://two-circles.net/2012jun08/indian_muslims_split_over_wedding_age_ruling.html (accessed 30 October 2012).

Kirmani, N. (2011) 'Beyond the impasse: "Muslim feminism(s)" and the Indian women's movement', *Contributions to Indian Sociology*, 45(1): 1–26.

—— (2009) 'Claiming their space: Muslim women-led networks and the women's movement in India', *Journal of International Women's Studies*, 11(1): 81–2011

Kozlowski, G. (1985) *Muslim Endowments and Society in British India*, Cambridge: Cambridge University Press.

Kügle, S. (2001) 'Framed, blamed and renamed: the recasting of Islamic jurisprudence in colonial South Asia', *Modern Asian Studies*, 32(2): 257–313.

Larivière, R. (1991) 'Matrimonial remedies for women in classical Hindu law: alternatives to divorce', in J. Leslie (ed.), *Rules and Remedies in Classical Indian Law*, Leiden: E.J. Brill.

Lemons, K. (2010) 'At the margins of law: adjudicating Muslim families in contemporary Delhi', unpublished PhD thesis, University of California, Berkeley.

Mahmood, S.T. (1980) *The Muslim Law of India*, Allahabad: Law Book Company.

Masud, M.K. (1996) 'Apostasy and judicial separation in British India', in M.K. Masud, B. Messick and D. Powers (eds), *Islamic Legal Interpretations: Muftis and their Fatwas*, Cambridge, MA: Harvard University Press.

Merry, S. (1988) 'Legal pluralism', *Law and Society Review*, 22(5): 869–96.

Metcalf, B.D. (2006) 'Imrana: rape, Islam and law in India', *Islamic Studies*, 45(3): 389–412.

Moore, E.P. (1998) *Gender, Law, and Resistance in India*, Tucson: University of Arizona Press.

Pearl, D. and Menski, W. (1998) *Muslim Family Law*, London: Sweet and Maxwell.

Powers, D.S. (1989) 'Orientalism, colonialism, and legal history: the attack on Muslim family endowments in Algeria and India', *Comparative Studies in Society and History*, 31(3): 535–71.

——(1990) 'The Islamic inheritance system: a socio-historical approach', in C. Mallat and J. Connors (eds), *Islamic Family Law*, London: Graham and Trotman.

Redding, J. (2010) 'Institutional v. liberal contexts for contemporary non-state, Muslim civil dispute resolution systems', *Journal of Islamic State Practices in International Law*, 6(1): 1–25.

Reddy, S. (2005) 'Imrana: her story', July 18. Available online at www.outlookindia.com/article.aspx?227975 (accessed 3 October 2012).

Schneider, N.C. (2009) 'Islamic feminism and Muslim women's rights activism in India: from trans-national discourse to local movement – or vice versa?' *Journal of International Women's Studies*, 11(1): 56–70.

Subramanian, N. (2008) 'Legal change and gender inequality: changes in Muslim family law in India', *Law and Social Inquiry*, 33(3): 631–72.

Tamanaha, B.Z. (1993) 'The folly of the "social scientific" concept of legal pluralism', *Journal of Law and Society*, 20(2): 192–217.

TNN (2001) 'SC asks woman to approach Parliament on talaq', 9 September. Available online at http://articles.timesofindia.indiatimes.com/2001-09-08/delhi/27225619_1_talaq-muslim-women-polygamy (accessed 9 November 2012).

——(2006) 'SC rejects PIL against triple talaq', 5 November. Available online at http://articles.timesofindia.indiatimes.com/2006-05-11/india/27828933_1_triple-talaq-muslim-women-pil (accessed 9 November 2012).

Vatuk, S. (2001) 'Where will she go? What will she do? Paternalism toward women in the administration of Muslim personal law in contemporary India', in G.J. Larson (ed.), *Religion and Personal Law in Secular India: a Call to Judgment*, Bloomington: Indiana University Press.

——(2003) 'Muslim women in the Indian family courts: a report from Chennai', in I. Ahmad (ed.), *Divorce and Remarriage among Muslims in India*, New Delhi: Manohar.

——(2005) 'Moving the courts: Muslim women and personal law', in Z. Hasan and R. Menon (eds), *The Diversity of Women's Lives in India*, New Brunswick, NJ: Rutgers University Press.

——(2008a) 'Divorce at the wife's initiative in Muslim personal law: what are the options and what are their implications for women's welfare?' in A. Parashar and A. Dhanda (eds), *Redefining Family Law in India: Essays in Honour of B. Sivaramayya*, London and New Delhi: Routledge.

——(2008b) 'Islamic feminism in India: Indian Muslim women activists and the reform of Muslim personal law', *Modern Asian Studies*, 42(2–3): 489–518.

——(2009) 'A rallying cry for Muslim personal law: the Shah Bano case and its aftermath', in B.D. Metcalf (ed.), *Islam in South Asia in Practice*, Princeton, NJ: Princeton University Press.

——(2013a) 'Islamic feminism in India: Indian Muslim women activists and the reform of Muslim personal law', in F. Osella and C. Osella (eds), *Islamic Reform in South Asia*, Cambridge: Cambridge University Press.

——(2013b) 'The women's court in India: an alternative dispute resolution body for women in distress', *Journal of Legal Pluralism and Unofficial Law*, 45(1):76–1103.

Venkatesan, J. (2007) 'Register all marriages: Supreme Court', *The Hindu,* October 26. Available online at www.thehindu.com/2007/10/26/stories/2007102656810100.htm (accessed 13 November 2008).

Yusuf Ali, A. (1983) *The Holy Quran: Text, Translation & Commentary*, Lahore: Sh. M. Asghar.

4   Family Law in Pakistan

Using the secular to influence the religious

Nausheen Ahmed

Introduction

General Zia ul-Haq's period of martial law in the 1980s is remembered for the widespread introduction of Islamic law. The law of evidence was changed,[1] certain Islamic criminal laws were introduced including the infamous Hudood Ordinances,[2] and the powers of the Federal Shariat Court were strengthened. During this period, as political parties were not allowed to operate in the country, the main opposition to these legal changes came from women's rights groups, which argued that Pakistan had been envisaged as a homeland for Muslims but not as a religious state. Legal developments however belie this argument. Article 2 of the 1973 Constitution of Pakistan confirmed that 'Islam shall be the State Religion of Pakistan'. Later, in the 1980s, the legal structure started moving toward that of a theocratic state. In 1985, under Presidential Order no 14 of 1985, Article 2A (the Objectives Resolution) was inserted into the Constitution. The Article stated, 'wherein the Muslims shall be enabled to order their lives in the individual and collective spheres in accordance with the teachings and requirements of Islam set out in the Holy Quran and Sunnah'. Shariat benches were set up in the high courts and in the Supreme Court, which were later replaced by the Federal Shariat Court in 1980.[3]

Whilst the women's movement denotes the Zia years as being particularly negative for the rights of women and minorities, in reality women and minorities have always experienced differential rights in the Indian subcontinent. During the colonial period, whilst matters of commerce were governed by codified British laws, family matters were governed by the personal law of each community. Muslims were therefore subject to what scholars called Anglo-Mohammadan law, which was compiled and then applied in India by the British court system and British judges.

After independence, Pakistan continued to apply the Muslim Personal Law (Shariat) Application Act 1937, the Dissolution of Muslim Marriages Act 1939 and the Child Marriage Restraint Act 1929. This was followed by codification of family laws through the Muslim Family Laws Ordinance in 1961. Zia ul-Haq's Islamization did not touch issues related to family law, but it extended Islamic laws to criminal and, in some cases, revenue matters, e.g. banking. It also emphasized the role of Islamic provisions in law-making and in judicial review.

The purpose of this chapter is to review the codified Muslim family laws and then analyse the position taken by the family and superior courts in Pakistan when interpreting these laws from 1961 onwards. The chapter also looks at attempts to reform these laws in the mid-1990s and the impact of such attempts.

The Muslim Family Laws Ordinance

Muslim family laws were codified on the basis of the recommendations made by the Commission on the Status of Women in Pakistan (the Rashid Commission) in 1956. The Rashid Commission was formed as a response to the protests by the All Pakistan Women's Association (APWA) when the then Prime Minister Muhammad Ali Bogra took an additional wife in the presence of his first wife. According to activist lawyer Asma Jahangir, '[the report] was not really effected to benefit and advance women's rights. Rather it was, in essence, a means of responding to the situation and an attempt to save the Prime Minister from public embarrassment' (Jahangir 1998: 97).

The mandate of the Commission was to review, within the parameters of Islam, the laws governing marriage, divorce, maintenance and other ancillary matters. The members of the Commission were not, even within themselves, unified as to which interpretation of Islam should be followed and when the final report was published it contained a dissenting note by the only *'alim* sitting on the Commission. The problems experienced by the Commission in agreeing on interpretation are not unique and have been experienced in other Muslim jurisdictions when religious laws were codified.

These problems are linked to the brevity of Qur'anic injunctions, making it difficult to arrive at a unified and monolithic interpretation that could be translated into clear legal principles. The report explained that whilst 'Islamic law either actually derives its principles and sanctions from Divine Authority as revealed in the Holy Qur'an or clear Injunctions based on the Sunnah', the Qur'an, however, dealt mostly with basic principles and provided answers to the questions that arose at the time of Revelation (Report of the Commission 1956: 1198). Consequently, the injunctions in the Qur'an dealing with family laws covered only a few pages. These were then clarified and adapted by the Prophet, responding to changing circumstances that arose during his lifetime. The report stated that 'as nobody can comprehend the infinite variety of human relations for all occasions and for all epochs, the Prophet of Islam left a very large sphere free for legislative enactments and judicial decisions even for his contemporaries who had the Holy Quran and the Sunnah before their eyes' (ibid.: 1199).

The Commission thus expressed an incontrovertible fact about Islamic provisions in the Qur'an and Sunnah, i.e. that these provisions are open to interpretation. Since the death of the Prophet, Islamic scholars have filled this interpretative space thanks to the Islamic concept of *ijma'* and *ijtihad*.

The Commission relied heavily on the conservative Hanafi school of interpretation, which was widely used in the subcontinent because it had been the basis of Islamic law administered by the colonial courts. Therefore, the question of a total ban on polygamy and unilateral repudiation (*talaq*) was avoided. Despite this cautious approach, the report was criticized by religious scholars and was not implemented until 1961, when a military government adopted certain sections of the report and enacted the Muslim Family Laws Ordinance (MFLO).

Whilst the MFLO was criticized by religious groups as being radical in its approach, at the same time it was criticized by women's groups for containing lacunas that allowed for discrimination. On balance, however, the MFLO marked an important first step in the strengthening of Muslim women's rights in the area of family law. It protected the rights of women by ensuring that marriages and divorces were registered and the rights arising from marriages and divorces were enforceable through the court system. A second or subsequent marriage was made subject to the existing wife's consent; divorce required reference to an arbitration council and did not become effective on pronouncement, thereby providing for a reconciliation period. In matters of inheritance, orphan children were entitled to inherit a share of their grandparents' property.

Interestingly, family laws are administered by a court system based on common law, which evolved during colonial times. After independence, special courts were set up to expedite the resolution of matrimonial and family disputes, and procedures were simplified.[4] Family courts were able to frame special procedures and deviate from the rules provided in the Civil Procedure Code and the Qanun-e-Shahadat Order of 1984. Appeals against the decision of the family courts were to be submitted to a district judge or the High Court. The family laws were administered through a hierarchy of courts in which Muslim law was applied, but the procedural methodology used was based on common law rules and concepts. Therefore, the adversarial method was used and judges applied precedent.

Registration of marriages and divorces

One of the most important features of the MFLO was the requirement to register marriages and divorces. Classical Islamic law did not require either writing or a religious ceremony to constitute a valid marriage. It did however require a public proposal and an acceptance (Mulla, Mahmood and Mahmood 2009: para. 252), recognizing therefore that a Muslim marriage was in the nature of a civil contract. Section 5 of the MFLO built on this principle but required, additionally, a written document registered with a *nikah* registrar. The Ordinance also prescribed the form of the *nikahnama* and the manner in which the marriage was to be registered. The written *nikahnama* had certain important characteristics:

- Both parties were required to sign it and therefore the consent of the woman to the marriage was essential. Later case law decided that a Muslim adult female could contract her marriage without the consent of her male guardian.[5]
- The husband was required to state on the form whether this was his first marriage and, if not, whether permission of the first wife had been obtained.
- The *nikahnama* was a public document. The law required that four copies of the *nikahnama* be prepared, one to be kept by the *nikah* registrar, a second held by the municipality and then one each for the parties contracting the marriage.
- Being a civil contract, conditions could be stated therein. Generally, a dower amount was specified as being the amount payable by the husband to the wife at the time of marriage. Payment of dower could be deferred to a later date.

The courts generally upheld the requirement of the MFLO to have a registered mar-riage contract,[6] however some divergence from this view was seen, especially in the period after 1979 when the absence of a valid marriage could result in prosecution and conviction for adultery under the Hudood Ordinances. Thus, the courts held that: 'in Islamic Law, contract of marriage need not be proved through a written document. If a nikah is not registered then either two witnesses can be produced in support of the factum of nikah or a man or woman (i.e. the husband or wife) may together certify the factum of the marriage'.[7]

The written *nikahnama* was said to be an attempt to make marital practices more transparent and accountable (World Bank 2005: 29) and provide unprecedented protec-tion to women. However, the requirement for a written *nikahnama* did not lead to major improvements. Two reasons for this were cited by the World Bank Report, i.e. first, that the written law conflicts with customary practices and is therefore not followed; second, authorities rarely hold parties accountable for not fulfilling requirements. There-fore, even though a penalty was specified in section 5 of the MFLO, which stated that any person involved in the non-registration of a marriage would be punished by simple imprisonment for a term which could extend to three years or with a fine which could extend to one thousand rupees, or both, there are no recorded cases of prosecution under this provision. Further, the courts themselves declared that registration of *nikah* was not a legal requirement for a valid marriage.[8] Even if a *nikah* was not registered with the Union Council, it would not mean that it had not been performed or that it had become illegal.[9] The effect of section 5 was said to be that a person who did not report his marriage to a *nikah* registrar could be held liable under section 5 (4) of the MFLO. However, the *nikah* would not become invalid due to its non-registration.[10]

Divorce

A similar approach is evident in cases of divorce. Under classical Islamic law, divorce can be effected by the husband through a declaration either orally or in writing. Section 7 of the Ordinance followed the Islamic form but required certain additional steps. These are:

- The oral pronouncement of *talaq* should be followed by notice in writing to the Chairman of the Union Council and a copy sent to the wife.
- Such pronouncement would not become effective until the expiration of 90 days from the date on which the notice was delivered to the Chairman of the Union Council.
- The Union Council is required to attempt reconciliation proceedings.

The objective of Section 7 was to protect women from the effects of a 'unilateral, instantaneous and unwritten *talaq*' (Balchin 1994:80). It allowed the parties to recon-cile and live together as a married couple without any further proceedings within the 90-day period. By providing opportunities for reconciliation, the MFLO deviated from tradition by 'effectively making all forms of divorce revocable' (Balchin: 1994: 203). During this period the Union Council was also required to facilitate reconciliation. However, this was rarely done. If reconciliation was not attempted or if it was not successful, the divorce took effect 90 days after receipt of notice by the Chairman of the Union Council.[11]

As in the case of registration of *nikah*, case law is mixed as to whether a divorce takes effect even if the provisions of section 7 of the Ordinance are not complied with. In a number of cases it was held that notice of divorce under section 7 was a mandatory requirement.[12] However, there are also judgments in which it was held that any divorce pronounced orally or in writing by a husband could not be made ineffective or invalid in shari'a because notice had not been given to the Chairman and that this failure to give notice to the Chairman would not affect the validity of a subsequent marriage.[13]

As mentioned above, the courts have been careful to uphold marriages or divorces even if they have technical deficiencies so that the woman would not fall within the mischief of the adultery law. However, this may not be the only explanation. There also continues to be unease about provisions that are not considered Islamic according to the judge's understanding. Since an oral pronouncement of divorce is considered by Hanafi jurisprudence as a valid divorce (Mulla, Mahmood and Mahmood 2009: para. 311), the requirement for written notice and a 90-day reconciliation period was in certain cases considered contrary to the provisions of Islam, and as a consequence the codified law was not strictly applied.[14]

The tendency on the part of certain judges to ignore statutory norms and to adhere to strict Islamic principles was also evident in the treatment accorded in some cases to *halala* (the reunion of a divorced couple after an intervening marriage of the wife with a third person). In classical Islamic law the requirement of *halala* was meant to be a deterrent to a hasty decision by a man to divorce his wife. A plain reading of section 7(6) of the MFLO (which deals with *halala*) would be that an intervening marriage would only be required if the man had exercised his right of divorce three times under section 7 of the MFLO. Section 7(6) was, however, ambiguously worded and the courts have not expressed a view as to whether divorce was defined within the parameters of the MFLO or those of classical Islamic law that refers to three types of divorce. In a case decided in 2003,[15] the Peshawar High Court commented that the MFLO had to a great extent 'trammelled and curtailed the arbitrary power of the husband to divorce his wife'. It had abolished the practice of the triple *talaq* and prescribed only the *talaq-e-ahsan* (a single pronouncement of divorce). Prior to the MFLO coming into force, it was forbidden for couples divorced by any mode of *talaq* other than *talaq-e-ahsan* to remarry unless the wife married another man after the divorce. Before remarriage the parties had to prove that the impediment to their marriage was removed by an inter-mediate marriage, consummation and dissolution, otherwise their marriage was not considered valid. The judge added, 'the plain reading of this section, though, implies that all kinds of *talaqs* have been made revocable without an intervening marriage and it may be that its repugnancy to such extent could validly be agitated on the touchstone of the Quranic behest and the traditions of the Holy Prophet'.[16]

This issue was, however, not decided by the court as the case in question involved dissolution of marriage by a family court. The court decided that in case of divorce through a family court it was not obligatory for the wife to marry a third person before entering into a marriage with her first husband. In a more recent case it was decided that 'since the reunion of the parties after decree of *khula* was a result of a fresh contract, the judgment and decree had no restraining effect upon remarrying'.[17]

A pronouncement of *talaq* under classical Islamic law or under section 7 of the MFLO did not require cause to be stated. It was therefore an unfettered right granted to the husband. Under classical Islamic law the wife did not have a corresponding right. To alleviate the problems faced by women wishing to divorce, Islamic scholars developed the legal fiction of the delegated right of divorce (*talaq-i-tafweez*). The MFLO took the important initiative of incorporating this concept on the *nikah* form. According to the principles of classical Muslim law (Mulla, Mahmood and Mahmood 2009: para. 314), although the power of pronouncing divorce belongs primarily to the husband, he can delegate this power to his wife or to a third person, either absolutely or conditionally and either for a particular period or permanently. The person to whom the power is delegated can pronounce the divorce.[18] In the event that a woman receives this right in her *nikahnama*, then under section 8 of the MFLO she is entitled to exercise the right of divorce without recourse to the Family Court. Her right would be exercised in the same way as that of a man who wished to divorce his wife under section 7(1) of the MFLO and would be effected by sending a notice in writing to the Chairman of the Union Council and a copy to the husband.

Sadly, the clause dealing with *talaq-i-tafweez* is regularly deleted from the form, as traditionally it is felt that it is a bad omen to consider matters of divorce at the time of entering into the marriage. In the absence of this right, the majority of women are required to approach the Family Court either for a dissolution of marriage under the Dissolution of Muslim Marriages Act 1939 or for a *khula*, which will be discussed below. Whereas, for a talaq or *talaq-i-tafweez* the party is not required to provide justification for terminating the marriage, under a dissolution or a *khula* the woman is required to show cause.

The consent of the husband is not required either for dissolution or *khula* as the marriage is terminated by a decree of the court. Further, a woman seeking termination of her marriage by *khula* would also have to give up her right to dower. In line with the classical concept that Muslim marriage is a civil contract, the woman would provide consideration for the termination of the matrimonial contract. This return of consideration is irrespective of the length of the marriage and of the cause for termination. Thus, a woman seeking *khula* due to cruelty or infidelity would still be required to renounce her right to dower. Customarily, in Pakistan the payment of the dower is deferred and therefore it is an important monetary consideration at the time of dissolution of the marriage.

Grounds under the Dissolution of Muslim Marriages Act 1939

The grounds for termination of marriage are detailed in the Dissolution of Muslim Marriages Act (DMMA) 1939. These include a husband failing to perform his marital obligations without reasonable cause for a period of three years, or treating his wife with cruelty, either physically or by conduct, or taking an additional wife, or having more than one wife and failing to treat them equitably in accordance with the injunctions of the Qur'an.[19] The Act also recognized the 'option of puberty', which can be exercised by a girl to end a marriage that was contracted by her guardian when she was a minor. In order to prove grounds, evidence has to be produced. This would be time-consuming and difficult, subjecting both parties to cross-examination. A minority view has been expressed by the courts that, in the event cause is shown, the woman would not be required to forgo the dower she had received at the time of her marriage.[20] The wife would lose her dower if she sought dissolution of marriage under *khula* but not if she raised other grounds under the DMMA.

Generally, however, *khula* and dissolution are understood almost synonymously and invariably the woman is made to give up her right to dower when she asks for dissolution of marriage. On the issue of dower, the courts have been careful to exclude bridal gifts and other benefits exchanged at the time of marriage.[21] In a recent case, the court decided that where the evidence indicated that termination of marriage was due to the misconduct of the husband then the husband would become disentitled to the return of the dower.[22] This was, however, an unusual view and, generally, women are required to pay the dower amount to their husbands when seeking a *khula*.

Grounds under *khula*

Shaheen Sardar Ali points out that the courts have taken differing views on the requirement to show grounds for the grant of khula (Sardar Ali and Naz 1998: 107). In Khurshid Bibi's case, their lordships concurred that the consent of the husband was not a requirement for grant of *khula* if the court was satisfied that the parties could not live together.[23] In 1993 the High Court noted that 'a woman is not a chattel and there is no method by which she could be forced to live with her husband if she herself has acquired a hatred for him'.[24] In other cases it was suggested that once the woman demands a *khula* the courts are required to grant it without inquiring into the circumstances. Further, consent of the husband is not a condition precedent to this, contrary to the view of classical jurists.[25] In the case of *Ahmed Nadeem vs Aasia Bibi*, the court equated the right of a woman to seek *khula* by giving up her dower to that of the man's right to divorce, i.e. without condition or requirement for showing cause.[26]

This liberal view was, however, subsequently tempered, and the view taken was that the wife did not have an absolute right to 'automatically denounce marital bonds'. The right of *khula* should be controlled and should be dependent upon scrutiny by the court which should satisfy itself about the existence of reasonable circumstances on which the separation was based.[27] The court pointed out that there must be 'intense hatred, serious discord, extreme disliking, strong malice explicitly indicating impossibility of future harmonious relationship between the parties in accordance with limits prescribed by God'. This effectively meant that even for *khula*, grounds would have to be proved and that the exercise of the right of *khula* would be subject to restoration of partial or total benefits received by the wife in connection with the marriage.

Maintenance

After divorce, women have limited rights to maintenance. The wife is entitled to maintenance during the marriage and for three months after divorce (the period of *iddat*). The

MFLO does not provide for post-*iddat* maintenance or division of property at the time of divorce. According to the classical Islamic view, the husband is required to maintain his wife unless she disobeys him without any good cause.[28] A disobedient wife is not entitled to be looked after. Thus a woman who is divorced or files for dissolution of marriage would not be entitled to monetary support from her ex-husband, notwithstanding the number of years that they have been married. To explain the link between performance of marital duties (as an obedient wife) and maintenance, in the *Bibi Mussarat* case the Peshawar High Court stated, 'in Islam, a husband is bound to maintain his wife throughout the period she remains in matrimonial bonds with him. This principle is, however, contingent with two pre-conditions. One, when a wife abandons the conjugal domicile of husband without any valid reason and two when she disobeys her husband without a good cause.'[29] Post-divorce maintenance for the wife has not been discussed in Pakistani case law as it was in the classical *Shah Bano* case in India,[30] however the widely held view is that section 9 of the MFLO refers only to pre-divorce maintenance.

The children of marriage are, however, entitled to maintenance. The father is required to maintain his minor children till such time as they attain the age of majority in case of male children or, in the case of female children, until marriage.[31] According to case law, the children have a right to maintenance even if they are residing with the mother and 'to seek maintenance during minority is an independent legitimate right of a child against his father'.[32] The courts in certain cases have used coercive measures to ensure payment of child maintenance.[33]

Custody

Custody issues are determined under the Guardian and Wards Act 1890 (administered by the family courts).[34] Section 17 of the 1890 Act refers to the 'welfare' of the minor and section 17(2) states that in considering welfare the Court shall have regard to the age, sex, and religion of the minor and the character and capacity of the guardian.

With regard to the custody of minor children, the courts follow two important principles:

- First, whilst the guardianship of a minor child remains with the father, the right of custody of a minor is primarily with the mother.
- Second, when deciding matters of custody the courts must keep in mind the welfare of the minor.

The word 'welfare' has been defined by the courts to include both 'material' and 'spiritual' matters. The Supreme Court of Pakistan stated that 'the overriding and paramount consideration always is the welfare of the minor. Indeed this is the sole consideration that must prevail in the oral analysis and the fact that the father is the lawful guardian of his minor children does not compel the Court to pass an order in his favour unless it is in their welfare to do so.'[35] Therefore, the courts have decided that:

- If a mother has a full-time job this does not necessarily mean that she cannot properly look after the welfare of the minor.[36]

- In fact it may not be in the interest of the minor to live with a stranger (in cases where the father has remarried) when the father is out of the home.[37]
- The Courts can also decide the matter of custody in accordance with the wishes of the children.[38]
- Generally, the poverty of the mother or her inability to maintain her minor children will not be treated as a valid ground for denying her custody.[39]
- Remarriage by the mother in itself does not automatically mean that she would lose custody of any minor children.[40]
- A foreign mother can get custody. In a case decided recently by the Lahore High Court, the custody of the minor daughter was handed over to the mother who had converted to Islam and was a resident in Singapore.[41]

It would seem that the courts have taken an extremely strong position in favour of women when deciding custody of children cases. However, it must be pointed out that this view is in accordance with the court's interpretation of Muslim law which emphasizes the woman's role as a mother and a wife. Islamic provisions state, for example, that 'the Mother has the first right of *hizanat*' (Mulla, Mahmood and Mahmood 2009: para. 352) to the exclusion of everyone else. In contrast, since classical Islamic law denotes that a Muslim wife must show obedience to her husband, in situations of divorce the courts do not take a proactive approach to protecting her rights through dower or maintenance and, as a result, a man can terminate his marriage with ease and minimal personal economic impact.

Challenges to the MFLO

As case law shows, there is constant tension between divergent views of Islamic tenets, and the MFLO has been diluted in its application by the family courts. It has also been subject to assault by the superior courts and by Parliament. Immediately after its promulgation in 1961, a resolution disapproving of the Ordinance was brought before the National Assembly. The 1962/1973 Constitution of Pakistan protected the Ordinance from challenge on the basis that it violated fundamental rights granted in the Constitution. Later in 1978–80, when the Shariat Benches were created in the high courts and the Supreme Court – which were later replaced by the Federal Shariat Court – under Article 203B(c) of the Constitution, certain matters were excluded from the Federal Shariat Court's mandate, including Muslim personal law. This court was given jurisdiction to examine 'whether or not any law or provision of law is repugnant to the Injunctions of Islam, as laid down in the Holy Qur'an and Sunnah of the Holy Prophet'.[42] It was also at this time that a new Article 2A was inserted into the Constitution, which, according to the opinion stated in certain cases and by jurists, had the effect of establishing the supremacy of Islam.

The power of the Federal Shariat Court to review Muslim personal law was curtailed by the definition of law as stated in Article 203B(c) of the Constitution of Pakistani; however, based on the inclusion of Article 2A, the High Court of Sindh attempted to enlarge its jurisdiction to examine whether it could review the provisions of the MFLO to determine whether these were in accordance with the injunctions of the Holy Qur'an and

Sunnah. In an oft-mentioned case decided in 1988,[43] dealing with the validity of a divorce pronounced orally, the single-member bench of the Sindh High Court opined that even those laws that are protected under the Constitution have to conform to a double test: first, they have to be in accordance with the provisions of the Constitution and, second, they must be in conformity with the Holy Qur'an and Sunnah. Because Article 2A had been made a substantive part of the Constitution, the courts were bound to ignore any provision of law that was in their view in derogation of the Holy Qur'an and Sunnah. Therefore the requirement imposed under section 7 of the MFLO that written notice of a divorce had to be sent to the Chairman of the Union Council (with a copy to the spouse) was not considered necessary. This reasoning meant that any protection provided under the Constitution for any law could be negated. The Supreme Court upheld this view in 1992[44] and it stated that 'the legal effects of Article 2A have been thoroughly examined in the Case of Qamar Raza referred to above, and it was held therein that since the contents of the Objectives Resolution have been made a substantive part of the Constitution, the Superior Courts can declare a law ultra vires of the Constitution if it is found to be violative of the Injunctions of Islam'.[45]

These two cases were followed in 2000 by the Balochistan High Court.[46] Whilst the cases of Qamar Raza (1988) and Allah Dad (1992) could be explained on the basis that failure to accept an oral divorce could have criminal consequences for the woman by exposing her to the charge of adultery under the Hudood Ordinances, in the case of Fida Hussain (2000) the question related to maintenance and therefore the decision could not be explained merely on the basis that the presiding judge wished to protect the woman concerned. In that case the court went to the extent of saying that Article 2A of the Constitution puts the Islamic laws 'at a higher level to other general laws of the country'.[47]

The implication of this judgment was that settled law could be invalidated by the mere pronouncement of one judge without any legislative amendment by parliament. In fact, in this single-member judgment, the court had assumed that section 7 of the MFLO was not applicable because it was declared to be repugnant to the injunctions of Islam, on the basis of the Qamar Raza case. The court stated that 'the fact further remains that well-established Islamic Injunctions are not in any way subservient to the general and common law of the land'.[48]

In 1994 the Supreme Court had declared that it could not review the MFLO to determine whether it was consistent with the injunctions of Islam. However, the Federal Shariat Court could do so under Article 203D of the Constitution. This judgment did not refer to the exemption granted under Article 203B (c) of the Constitution.[49] In another case in 1994 the Supreme Court stated that the expression 'Muslim personal law' used in Article 203B(c), which excludes the jurisdiction of the Federal Shariat Court under Article 203D of the Constitution, referred to the personal law of each sect of Muslims based on the interpretation of the Qur'an and Sunnah by that sect. Therefore, the judge argued that all other codified or statute laws that applied to the general body of Muslims would not be immune from scrutiny by the Federal Shariat Court in the exercise of its powers under Article 203D. It was also stated, *obiter dictum*, that a restrictive interpretation would reduce the effective role of the Federal Shariat Court, which could not be the intention of the Constitution.[50]

The MFLO was also challenged directly in the Federal Shariat Court. In 2000 the Court looked at a number of sections of the MFLO. With reference to section 4, which deals with succession, the Federal Shariat Court expressed the view that the recommendations of the Rashid Commission (1956) were 'a futile exercise which had caused confusion in the law of inheritance envisaged for the Muslim Society by mandate of the Holy Qur'an'.[51] It also stated that all other sources of law are subordinate to the injunctions of the Holy Qur'an and Sunnah and could not be used to transgress the limitations imposed by the divine scriptures. In fact, it limited the applicability of *ijtihad* to those situations where there was no Qur'anic injunction and even then it said that any ambiguity has to be clarified with reference first to the Sunnah. The Federal Shariat Court assumed jurisdiction stating that it was not excluded from looking at the MFLO. It said that 'the expression Muslim personal law used in Article 203B (c), ... in our view means the personal law of each sect of Muslims based on the interpretation of Quran and Sunnah by that sect'.[52] 'All other codified or statute laws which apply to the general body of Muslims will not be immune from scrutiny by the Federal Shariat Court in exercise of its powers under Article 203D of the Constitution. Mere fact that a codified law or a statute applied to only Muslim population of the country, in our view, would not place it in the category of "Muslim personal law" envisaged by Article 203B(c) of the Constitution.'[53]

Despite the passage of almost four decades, public opinion, judicial reasoning and religious scholarship remain ambivalent as to whether the provisions of the MFLO should be followed, and this is reflected in individual cases decided by the courts, as well as being the broader view of the law held by the senior judiciary. It has been difficult, therefore, to press for reform of family laws. By necessity the demand for improvement and positive change by women's groups has focused primarily on resisting regressive reform. As the law in this area remains linked to the interpretation of the 'Injunctions of Islam', as a strategy women's groups have not advocated change in substantive law but emphasized procedural reform. This has been considered a less contentious area as it does not require reference to Islamic precepts.

Reform of family laws

Recommendations for reform have concentrated on the cumbersome legal process that results in slow and delayed decisions. Although the West Pakistan Family Courts Act 1964 prescribes that a suit for dissolution of marriage has to be decided within six months from the date of commencement of the suit, in a study published by SACH in 2012 it was pointed out that dissolution of marriage cases were delayed for years, partly due to procedural reasons, but also due to collusion and unethical practices. In many instances, women seeking divorce did not have family support, which made it more difficult for them to access the justice system. The study referred to a case in Rawalpindi in which a 20-year-old girl applied for divorce after only three days of marriage because her husband was a drug addict. The case took three years to be concluded. In the meanwhile the girl suffered a major heart attack due to the pressures that she faced (SACH 2012).

In response to reform efforts, a law was passed in 2002 amending the West Pakistan Family Courts Act so as to improve certain procedural requirements. The amendments provided that a number of matters could be presented through written rather than oral evidence, something that would expedite matters. The Act mandated that female judges should be appointed in the Family Court and in section 3(1) it was stated that 'at least one Family Court in each District shall be presided over by a woman judge'. The Family Court was empowered to attempt reconciliation between the parties during the proceedings. However, if reconciliation failed, then the decree for dissolution of marriage had to be passed 'forthwith'.[54] The effect of this proviso was that the parties could receive a decree of dissolution of marriage even if other matters remained outstanding before the judge. The court was able to enforce its judgments by imposing fines, and the amendments to the Act prescribed that maintenance could be recovered as a debt through the Collector, Land Revenue. The jurisdiction of the Family Court was extended under section 5 (of the Schedule) to include cognizance of offences committed by spouses *inter se*. In a case decided in 2008, the Peshawar High Court assumed jurisdiction over a suit for the partition of property that had been part of the dower given to the wife.[55] In this case the court stated that 'radical changes' had been enacted that widened the jurisdiction of the Family Court.

Conclusion

The changes promulgated under the Family Courts Act 2002 were heralded as positive developments that made it easier for a woman to get a *khula*. The MFLO, however, remained intact. Studies have shown that despite the passage of over 40 years, the MFLO does not enjoy widespread acceptance and many of its beneficial sections are ignored. For example, the Ordinance makes the marriage of any female under the age of 16 illegal and requires that both the bride and groom consent to the marriage. A study based on the Pakistan Rural Household Survey 2004 showed, however, that 31 per cent of rural women were married before the age of 16. With respect to consent, 97 per cent of rural women reported that their parents or other family members chose their spouse and in only 12 per cent of cases was their opinion solicited (World Bank Report 2005: 29). Similarly, the right of *talaq-i-tafweez*, though provided for in the printed *nikah* form, is generally not taken up and the clause is deleted. This leads to the conclusion that reform through law does not necessarily lead to a change in attitudes.

In other areas also there is a lack of implementation. Even though section 6 of the MFLO attempted to restrict polygamy, rather than prohibit it, by requiring that a man who contracts a second marriage must seek the permission of the Arbitration Council and of the existing wife or wives, this provision is not enforced. Under section 6(5) of the MFLO 'any man who contracts a second marriage without the permission of the Arbitration Council is liable to simple imprisonment which may extend to one year or a fine which may extend to Five Thousand Rupees or both'. Instead of prosecuting those not complying, the courts have clarified that those persons who participate in the second marriage in contravention of the law will not be prosecuted.[56]

In a review of the MFLO, it was stated that 'the law being given shape through case law, has highly patriarchal overtones and has, as a result, a discriminately [sic] effect on women and children' (Naz and Zia 2008: 3). As pointed out, 'a woman's personal status within the family directly impacts her status at all other levels, since her rights in the public and private sphere are inextricably linked' (ibid.: 3). Within the private sphere, the ease with which a man can terminate his marriage without cause or personal economic impact means that a woman will always have a secondary position within the family, making illusory other social and political rights granted through the Constitution or other laws.

The family laws and their application in the court system are based on the dominance of a particular model of the family in which specific gender roles are ascribed to men and women. The family is a unit of social control headed by the husband/father and in which the wife is entitled to protection (maintenance) as long as she is not *nashiza* (disobedient). This model does not accept her role beyond that of a wife or mother, so that as a mother she is entitled to the custody of her children but is not entitled to post-divorce division of matrimonial assets or post-*iddat* maintenance. She is not acknowledged as an independent economic unit. In cases where the wife seeks dissolution of marriage (even for cause), the courts expect her to forgo the dower (however meagre) on the basis that she is not keeping to her part of the marriage contract. Thus, a husband is not obligated to maintain his wife beyond the three-month *iddat* period and, considering that very few women in Pakistan work, she remains dependent on her family for support or is then forced into another marriage. There are no recorded cases in which the court has taken cognizance of physical cruelty meted out to a woman and considered criminal prosecution. The family is considered part of the private sphere which requires minimal interference by the organs of state. As pointed out by Mary Eaton, 'by supporting the dominant model of the family the court is contributing to the cultural reproduction of society and thereby, to the continued subordination of women' (Eaton 1986: 97). A woman's personal and financial security are compromised under family law.

Whilst the view with respect to the role of the women within the family finds its parallel globally, in Pakistan the additional complexity is that the courts use Islamic principles to define the concept of the family. These Islamic principles could work either in favour of women or could have the opposite effect, depending on what particular interpretation the judge relies on. Thus, whilst under Islamic jurisprudence a woman was said to be independent and to have the right to acquire and hold property, her role within society was also defined and restricted primarily to the home. She was entitled to the same social and legal status that was due to the man 'except in certain specified spheres which distinction had been created by Allah not to lower the prestige of a woman but for a smooth and proper running of the Society'.[57] It should be noted here that when discussing the status and role of women judges refer to Islamic principles, which are said to represent divine will. As a result, it is difficult for rights activists to put forward an alternative point of view on women that does not correspond to the traditional reading of those principles. According to another case, the wife was required to be obedient and 'build up gaiety and happy social life'. The court decreed that '[the] righteous woman guards the sanctity of the bond of marriage and protects her and her husband's chastity and virtues, guards her honour for him and to be faithful to him [sic]'.[58] We have thus seen that the courts have a conservative attitude, ignoring in many instances the letter of the law in favour of other considerations, especially Islamic teaching as interpreted by the judges hearing particular cases.

Unfortunately, the provisions of the MFLO have not received support at a state level. As pointed out above, the state does not take action in cases the provisions of the MFLO are contravened. Therefore, as Shaheen Sardar Ali points out, in the area of family law codified law is mixed with religious edicts and customary law as applied by the courts and 'cultural norms and religious rules are just as potent a force, if not more, as legislative enactments' (Sardar Ali and Naz 1998: 107).

This inter-mixing of law, custom and tradition ensures that women continue to experience differential rights. In the cases where a right has been granted under statute, for example with respect to *talaq-i-tafweez*, due to lack of awareness, the cumbersome legal system and inadequate family support, it is difficult for women to exercise the right in practice. In other cases, like those concerning division of property or the right to maintenance after *'iddat*, the law has not kept pace with global developments. More importantly, whilst the women of Pakistan continue to fight a rearguard action to protect the MFLO, it has not been possible to demand progressive amendment to the Ordinance.

Secular reform is an urgent requirement in the area of substantive family law as is other beneficial legislation, e.g. on domestic violence. In fact, if the state and legal institutions continue to mix religion with law, reform is unlikely. There is a much higher probability that the existing rights granted under the MFLO will face further attacks and that women's groups, whilst continuing to defend the Ordinance, will not have a chance to move beyond this to press for more radical change.

Notes

1 The Qanun-e-Shahdat Order 1984. According to its preamble, it was enacted to 'revise, amend and consolidate the law of evidence to bring it in conformity with the Injunctions of Islam as laid down in the Holy Quran and Sunnah'. Its controversial portion, from a gender perspective, is Article 17(2)(a) which states that 'in matters pertaining to financial or future obligations, if reduced to writing, the instrument shall be attested by two men, or *one man and two women* so that one may remind the other, if necessary' (emphasis added).

2 The Hudood Ordinances were promulgated in 1979. Of these, the Offence of Zina (Enforcement of Hudood) Ordinance 1979, which made adultery a crime, impacted significantly on women, increasing the female prison population drastically.

3 Set up under Presidential Order I of 1980.

4 West Pakistan Family Courts Act, 1964.

5 *Hafiz Abdul Waheed vs Mrs. Asma Jahangir* PLD 2004 SC 219.

6 PLD 2012 (Balochistan) 133; PLD 1969 (Dacca) 47.

7 *M. Bashir vs The State* 1984 PCrLJ 1892.

8 *Shaukat Hussain vs Civil Judge Multan* 2006 YLR 349.

9 *Ghazanfar Abbass vs Additional District Judge – Jhang* 2001 YLR 644.

10 *Aftab Ahmed vs Judge Family Court* 2009 MLD 962 and *Sair Khan vs The State* PLD 2000 FSC 63.

11 *Mst. Farida Parwin vs Qadeeruddin Ahmad Siddiqui* PLD 1971 Kar. 118 and *Syed Ali Nawaz Gardezi vs LT-Col.Muhammad Yusuf* PLD 1963 SC 51.

12 *Syed Ali Nawaz Gardezi vs LT-Col Muhammad Yusuf* PLD 1963 SC 51, *Abdul Manan vs Safuran Nessa* 1970 SCMR 845, *Muhammad Salahuddin Khan vs Muhammad Nazir Siddiqui and Others* 1984 SCMR 583, *Ghulam Nabi vs Farrukh Latif* 1986 SCMR 1350, *Malik Javid Ali and another vs Abdul Kadir and another* 1987 SCMR 518.

13 *Allah Dad vs Mukhtar* 1992 SCMR 1273; *Mst. Zahida Shaheen vs The State* 1994 SCMR 2098; *Muhammad Sarwar and another vs The State* PLD 1988 FSC 42; and *Qamar Raza vs Tahira Begum* PLD 1988 Kar 169.

14 *Shoukat Ali, Mst. Nasim vs The State* 2004 Shariat Decisions (SD) 190; *Ms. Parnian Arooj vs Mehmood Sadiq & Others* PLJ 2011 Lahore 336.

15 *Fazli-e-Subhan vs Sabereen* PLD 2003 Pesh 169.

16 Ibid., p. 170.

17 *Attiq Ahmed Khan vs Noor-ul-Saba* 2011 CLC 1211.

18 *Dr. Qambar Murtaza Bokhari vs Mst. Zainab Bashir* PLD 1995 Lah 187 and *Aklima Khatun vs. Mahibur Rahman and others* PLD 1963 Dacca 602.

19 Section 2, Dissolution of Muslim Marriages Act, 1939.

20 *Mst. Sadia Sultan vs Additional District and Sessions Judge Hafizabad* 2012 PLD Lah 98.

21 *Shakeel Saood Khan vs Rizwana Khanum* 2012 PLD Lah 43.

22 *Shamas Ali vs Additional District Judge, Sambrial* PLD 2012 Lah 183; *Inam-ul-Islam vs Hussain Bano* PLD 1976 Lah 1466; *Shakeel Saood Khan vs Rizwana Khanum* 2012 PLD Lah 43. In these cases the judges held that if the divorce is due to the conduct of the husband he is not entitled to the return of dower unless the wife volunteers it.

23 *Mst. Khurshid Bibi vs M. Amin* PLD 1967 SC 97. The court also said that claiming more than the dower itself in lieu of *khula* was abominable on the part of husband but, nevertheless, if he insisted it was permissible.

24 *Ahmed Nadeem vs Aasia Bibi* PLD 1993 Lah 249.

25 *Shah Begum vs District Judge Sialkot* PLD 1995 Lah 19 and *Rafiq Hussain Shah vs Imtiaz Bibi* 1990 CLC 30.

26 *Ahmed Nadeem vs Aasia Bibi* PLD 1993 Lah 249.

27 *Zeb Sar vs Mst. Kosar* PLD 2004 Pesh 15.

28 *Kashif Akram vs Mst. Naila and 3 others* 2011 MLD 571. The judge held that the wife could not claim maintenance during her stay at her parents' house because she had deserted her husband without any lawful cause.

29 *Mst. Harran Bibi vs Abdul Khaliq* PLD 1981 Lahore 761 and *Mst. Bibi Musarrat vs Sarfaraz* 1990 CLC 1908.

30 *Mohammad Ahmed Khan vs Shah Bano Begum & Others* 1985 AIR 945.

31 *Mansoor Tariq Khan vs Nafeesa* 1999 CLC 305 and *Ghulam Khan vs District Judge – Gujrat* 1990 SCMR 136.

32 *Muhammad Yusuf vs Shazia Bibi* MLD 1992 SC 235.

33 *Miskeen Ahmed vs Mst. Sajida* 2012 CLC 160. The West Pakistan Family Courts Act 1964 did not specify any particular procedure to enforce its orders. The court said that it was entitled to take punitive steps even though they were not specifically mentioned.

34 Section 5 of the Family Courts Act 1964.

35 *Feroz Begum vs Muhammad Hussain* 1978 SCMR 299.

36 *Mst. Abida Bibi vs Abdul Latif* 2002 CLC 1416 and *Dr. Aisha Yousuf vs Khalid Muneer* 2012 PLD Kar 166. The mother's plea was that she, being a doctor by profession, had got a job in Dubai and would like to take the minor with her. The judge said: 'Female has absolute right to roam in search of career and livelihood wherever she found same more apt and could not be deprived of custody of children if she wanted to served abroad.'

37 *Masroor Hussain vs Additional District Judge* Islamabad 2011 CLC 851.

38 *Aneela Khan vs Tahir Saeed* 2005 CLC 859.

39 *Mst. Akbar Bibi vs Shaukat Ali* 1981 CLC 78.

40 *Rukhsana Malik vs Abdul Aziz* 2004 PLD Lah 801.This case pertained to minor sons and the court said that the same principle may not apply in the case of minor daughters because 'philosophy in Islam is to keep stranger away from females'. However, the court said that each case with regard to minor girls would be decided on its own facts. And *Mst Jasmine Bibi vs Mehmood Acuter* YLR 2004 Lah 641.

41 *Aya Sasaki vs Zarina Akhtar* 1999 CLC 1202 and *Peggy Collins vs M. Ishfaque Malik* 2010 PLD Lah 48. The judge in the *Peggy Collins* case held that 'mere professing of Muslim faith by him [the father] and mere incidence of his birth in Pakistan might not suffice all by themselves to conclude that welfare of the minor would lie in living with him rather than in living with a Christian mother with French origin whose credentials are blotless, whose antecedents were clean, whose

proven love and care for the child had dragged her in foreign land facing untold trial and tribulations and whose courage, fortitude and character might be better suited for imbibing [sic] good moral, social and human values in the minor's personality'.

42 Article 203D of Constitution of Pakistan 1973.
43 *Qamar Raza vs Tahira Begum* PLD 1988 Kar 169.
44 1992 SCMR 1273.
45 Ibid., p. 1279.
46 *Fida Hussain vs Mst. Najma* PLD 2000 Quetta 46
47 Ibid., p. 51.
48 Ibid., p. 51.
49 *Pakistan Railways vs M. Anwar Bhatti* 1994 SCMR 681.
50 *Dr. Mahmood-ur-Rehman vs Government of Pakistan* PLD 1994 SC 607. However the Supreme Court itself has expressed conflicting views; see *Kaniz Fatima vs Wali Muhammad* PLD 1993 SC 901 and *Zaheeruddin vs The State* 1993 SCMR 1718.
51 *Allah Rakha vs Federation of Pakistan* PLD 2000 FSC 1, p. 42.
52 Ibid., p. 27.
53 Ibid., p. 28.
54 Proviso to Section 10(4) of West Pakistan Family Courts Act, 1964, inserted by Ordinance of 2002.
55 *Sifat Aizdi vs Dr. Saima Bashir* PLD 2008 Peshawar III.
56 *Mst. Robina Ashraf and 5 Others vs Shagufta Fardous* 2009 P.Cr.L.J. 1189.
57 *Abdul Waheed vs Asma Jahangir* PLD 1997 Lah 301 p. 361.
58 *Malik Tanveer Khan vs Mst. Amber Liaqat* 2009 CLC 1210.

Bibliography

Anderson, R.M. (1996) *Islamic Law and the Colonial Encounter in British India*, Los Angeles, CA: Muslim Women's League, Occasional Paper 7. Available online at www.wluml.org/node/5627 (accessed 2 November 2012).

Balchin, C. (1994) *A Handbook on Family Law in Pakistan*, 2nd edn, Lahore: Shirkat Gah.

Eaton, M. (1986) *Justice for Women? Family, Court and Social Control*, Milton Keynes and Philadelphia, PA: Open University Press.

Jahangir, A. (1998) 'The Origins of MFLO: reflections for activism', in F. Shaheed *et al.* (eds), *Shaping Women's Lives: Laws, Practices & Strategies in Pakistan*, Lahore: Shirkat Gah.

Khaled, A. (1999) *Muslim Law: the Latest Assault on Society*, Los Angeles: Muslim Women's League. Available online at www.mwlusa.org/topics/marriage&divorce (accessed 2 November 2012).

Mahmood, M. (2012) *The Code of Muslim Family Laws*, 12th edn, Lahore: Al-Qanoon Publishers.

Mulla, D.F., Mahmood, M. and Mahmood J. (2009) *D.F. Mulla's Principles of Muhammadan Law: with Survey of Case Law from the Superior Courts, 1906–2008*, Lahore: Al-Qanoon Publishers.

Mumtaz, K. and Shaheed, F. (1987) *Women of Pakistan. Two Steps Forward, One Step Back?* Lahore: Vanguard Books.

Naz, R. and Zia, M. (2008), *MFLO in Pakistan: critical issues*, Lahore: Aurat Publication and Information Service Foundation. Available online at www.af.org.pk/newsletters.htm (accessed 15 December 2012).

SACH (Struggle for Change) (2012). *Report 2012*. Available online at www.unic.org.pk (accessed 2 November 2012).

Sardar Ali, S. and Naz, R. (1998) 'Marriage, dower, and divorce. Superior courts and case law in Pakistan', in F. Shaheed *et al.* (eds), *Shaping Women's Lives: Laws, Practices & Strategies in Pakistan*, Lahore: Shirkat Gah.

Shah, A. (2012) *Encyclopedia of Family Laws*, Lahore: National Law Book House.

Sheikh, Z. (2012) *The Constitution of The Islamic Republic of Pakistan 1973*, 4th edn, Karachi: Zain Sheikh.

Shirkat Gah (2000) *Women's Rights in Muslim Family Law in Pakistan – 45 Years of Recommendations vs. the FSC Judgment (January 2000)*, Special Bulletin, Lahore.

Vishwanath, T. (2005) *Pakistan: Country Gender Assessment. Bridging the Gender Gap: Opportunities and Challenges*, Washington, DC: World Bank.

5 The Enforcement of Personal Status Law by Egyptian Courts

Monika Lindbekk

Introduction

Over the course of the twentieth century, the Egyptian state enacted personal status laws designed to turn marriage into a more permanent bond than envisioned by traditional Islamic jurisprudence by, among other things, curbing men's right to repudiation. It was also believed that providing women with greater rights, including that to petition for judicial divorce, would strengthen the marital bond (Kholoussy 2010: 95–96, 2005: 317–50).

This contribution deals with court practice in matters of personal status with particular emphasis on how gender hierarchy is reproduced and challenged, and attempts to situate this in a context of nation-state formation. Relying on discourse analysis of a sample of marriage and divorce cases and interviews with judges, the chapter argues that contemporary Egyptian judges articulate a dual discourse on marriage. On the one hand, they employ a strategy designed to retain men as heads of families while, on the other hand, disciplining them into more moral subjects by giving legal force to ethical injunctions of the Qur'an that according to *fiqh* are only sanctioned in the hereafter. While marriage is reinforced as a hierarchical institution privileging men, this discourse is intertwined with and partly challenged by another discourse, which is inspired by the western-derived ideal of affective ties as the basis of conjugality. A heightened emphasis on emotions like amity in marriage is, among other things, reflected in legislation and court rulings that grant women divorce from emotionally unsatisfying marriages. With regard to both strategies, judicial decisions are legitimated with reference to shari'a in novel ways.

The tension between the two ideals is an indication of the complexity and contradictory nature of Egyptian personal status law enforcement, an area where contemporary judges exercise considerable discretionary power. In order to better understand the interplay between the two ideals, I will examine a sample of judicial decisions in the field of marriage and divorce from Egypt's Supreme Constitutional Court, the Court of Cassation, and family courts in Cairo.[1] The sample of cases addressed is too small to fairly represent Egyptian personal status law in its complexity. Yet, the aim of the analysis is to outline some predominant positions as well as points of ambiguity in the adjudication of disputes. I begin by briefly examining important personal status reforms in the twentieth century and concomitant developments in the judicial system. The following sections deal with the adjudication of marriage and divorce cases in courts; I end by discussing challenges to marriage and divorce legislation in the wake of the 2011 revolution.

The legal framework: Egypt's laws of personal status

This section explores the development of Egyptian personal status codes. The objective of marriage, according to *fiqh*, is sexual satisfaction and reproduction (El-Alami 1992). Underlying the classical rules of Islamic jurisprudence is an unequal construction of gender that is reflected in the permission given to the man to take up to four wives and to divorce at will, while the wife has a limited right to obtain a dissolution of marriage. Following the formation of a modern Egyptian state in the nineteenth century, a centralized and hierarchical legal system was developed with the parallel promulgation of law codes based on European models. Increasingly, the welfare of the Egyptian family came to be considered central to the welfare of society as a whole and the family – re-conceptualized as the unit of the nuclear family (*al-usra*) – became an object of state administration (Asad 2001).

In the twentieth century the process of codification extended to the field of family with the adoption of a series of personal status laws that aimed to advance perceptions of general interest (*maslahat al-ʿamma*) through marriage registration requirements, by curbing marriage of minors, men's right of repudiation and polygamy, while expanding women's rights to judicial divorce. These legal developments took place through a selective process in which doctrines from the classical Islamic law schools were combined and fused into new legal rules. A further development took place in 1955 with the state's establishment of a unified legal system. Hence, Egyptian family law today is found in legal codes determined by the state and implemented by the modern judicial apparatus of the state, and judges are trained in modern law schools and are not familiar with traditional Islamic jurisprudence.

A growing concern over divorce appears to be part of a new hegemonic definition of marriage influenced by the ideal of companionate marriage and where divorce, male polygamy, and serial marriage are increasingly blamed for threatening the well-being of the nation-state (Hasso 2010). The putative increase in divorce rates, which many attribute to the adoption of the so-called *khulʿ* law in 2000, by which a woman may obtain judicial divorce on condition of the forfeiture of all her financial rights, has been perceived by the population at large as the product of 'a family crisis'. This development must also be considered in relation to the increase in women's education and participation in the workforce, providing them with more independence. The widespread perception of an increase in female-initiated divorce is clearly shared by a judge of the Cairo Appeal Court who in 2008 used the court as an arena to address the media:

> The court beseeches the media to solve the problems of the Egyptian family which threaten to destroy the integrity of Egyptian society, the family being its cornerstone. External influences, represented by the international conference on population and development, the Beijing world conference on women, the Nadim Center, Bahai's,[2] secularists, and exiles, push Egyptian society toward disintegration. Eventually, the

situation has become dire, which is what the 21st state seeks.[3] In the past, divorce was a hated thing, the mention of which was harmful to Egyptian families and unbearable for women, but now it has become part of culture and its sentiments, something which no girl fears and no woman flinches from. Where are we headed? Oh God, we complain to you of our weakness and our humiliation before ourselves and the entire world. God be my witness!

(Cairo Appeal Court, personal status circuit, case no. 1997,
judicial year no. 124, 21 July 2008)

The judge's plea illustrates that judicial practice cannot be viewed in isolation from discourses and practices centered on the family and changing socio-economic circumstances. Although personal status laws promulgated in the twentieth century sought to make marriage a more permanent bond than envisioned in classical Islamic law, the law codes nonetheless reify a hierarchical relationship between the spouses. While the laws are at times ambiguous and contradictory, they define women as persons (*askhas*) whose status in the family is not autonomous. The normative concept in the construction of the spousal relationship in Egyptian law remains the *fiqh*-based notion of the husband's duty to maintain his wife in exchange for her duty of obedience. Women do not have an equal right to divorce as it is defined as a prerogative of the husband. The laws also codify men's right to take up to four wives.[4] While this legal discourse reinforces marriage as a hierarchical institution privileging men, it is enmeshed with another discourse: judges also say that marriage should be characterized by Qur'anic values such as amity (*mawadda*) and mercy (*rahma*) which are conceptualized in a romantic way as strong emotional ties between spouses rather than in terms of sexual relations.[5] In this contribution I argue that the discourse idealizing love and deep affection between spouses may both support male privilege and challenge it.[6]

A constitutional amendment in 1980 designated the principles of Islamic shari'a as the foremost source of legislation, an article that has been retained in Egypt's post-revolutionary Constitution. In practice it is primarily personal status legislation that is reviewed for consistency with the principles of shari'a. While the majority of interviewed judges claim that the personal status laws are derived from shari'a, understood as the manifestation of divine commands, several judges doubt the legitimacy of some controversial laws. This is an interesting aspect of some rulings concerning judicial divorce, through *khul'* in particular. However, regardless of the attitude to certain controversial provisions, it is important to bear in mind that the judges' approach is largely guided by orientation to procedural correctness and legal relevance, reflecting their bureaucratic resistance to the possibility of being overruled (Dupret 2007).

The sources of law used by family court judges include statutory legislation and precedence. Article 3 of law no. 1 from 2000 instructs the judge to employ the predominant opinion of the Hanafi school in the absence of a textual provision. The Egyptian judiciary in general is not well acquainted with traditional Islamic jurisprudence and is uncertain as to how to deal with it. Therefore it generally avoids using it or refers to it via one of the acknowledged works of modern jurisprudence or the esteemed decisions of the Court of Cassation. Egyptian judicial practice is also influenced to a considerable extent by local custom because the laws allow judges to exercise considerable discretionary power. Instead of finding a clear hierarchy between sources, a study of court decisions gives the impression of sources that intersect and interplay although legislation – with its alleged origin in Islamic sources – usually taking precedence over other sources of law.[7]

Marriage – what is in a name?

According to medieval Islamic jurists, marriage is not a sacrament, but has a contractual basis that is sometimes likened to a sale (*bay'*) whereby the husband purchases the right of sexual access by payment of the dower (Coulson 1964: 221). The classical jurists defined the marriage contract in terms of physical gratification, procreation and preservation of lineage (El-Alami 1992: 10). Egyptian law does not include a provision providing a holistic definition of the marriage contract. Nonetheless, the courts have taken an active role in defining the essence and purposes of marriage. The Arabic words most commonly used by judges to signify marriage are *'aqd nikah* (literally, contract of sexual intercourse) and *zawaj* (marriage). Unlike medieval jurists, Egyptian judges refrain from the analogy of a contract of sale and instead privilege the religious dimensions of marriage by redefining the marriage contract as an 'eternal contract' (*'aqd abadi*) and a 'pact' or 'covenant' (*mithaq*), words which lend the marriage contract a lasting and spiritual nature and distinguish it more sharply from other contracts.[8]

In addition, while a prime purpose of marriage remains sexual gratification, a conceptual shift in the meaning of marriage has taken place, with a change of emphasis from procreation to amity and mercy as essential elements of ideal marriages.[9] In the words of one judge '[t]he best marriage is that which brings to humans a good spouse and a trusted cave (*kahf amin*) to which a person may resort in the face of troubles in order to be protected by its shadows'.[10] This is strongly reminiscent of the normative ideals of companionate marriage propagated by colonial administrators and Egyptian nationalists since the nineteenth century (Abu-Lughod 1998). I therefore argue that contemporary Muslim judges' redefinition of marriage may be situated within the context of modern nationalist discourses where the nuclear family was reconfigured as the cornerstone of the nation, and marriage as the foundation of the family.

Establishing marriage

By adopting the preponderant doctrine of the Hanafi school, Egyptian judges state that the validity of the marriage contract is determined by the following conditions (*shurut*) or pillars (*arkan*):

- the offer and acceptance by competent parties, whether oral, written or by gesture;
- the absence of temporary or permanent impediments;[11]
- the presence of two male Muslim witnesses who are adult, free and of sound mind;[12]
- the groom's compatibility with the bride in terms of social status.[13]

According to these requirements, a marriage does not have to be registered with the state authorities in order to be valid. However, the twentieth century witnessed unparalleled penetration of the Egyptian family by the state. Egypt enacted legislation that required the formal registration of marriage and precluded courts from hearing disputes from marriages lacking an official marriage certificate.[14] The standardized marriage contract may be considered as having developed into a 'technology of governance' making it more difficult to marry outside the state's legal system (Hasso 2010; Kholoussy 2010). Yet, the authority of the state and its ability to regulate marriage continues to be undermined by the prevalence of unregistered marriages, the so-called customary marriages (*zawaj 'urfi*). Many of these marriages comply with the above-mentioned conditions and pillars of marriage, such as the consent of both parties to the marriage and the presence of witnesses, and are, hence, valid from a religious perspective, but they are in a sense relegated to a legal limbo because rights and duties arising from such marriages cannot be enforced through the courts. However, personal status law no. 1 from 2000 introduced an important change in this regard by allowing women to petition the court for divorce, on condition that they provide some form of written evidence proving their marriage (Berger and Sonneveld 2010: 74). A ruling of divorce in relation to an unregistered marriage has the effect of terminating the relationship without the financial or legal rights attached to a registered marriage, thus underscoring the inferior nature of that relationship from a legal point of view while mitigating its negative effects.[15]

Judges have adopted different methods of establishing that there is a marriage when it has not been registered. The analysis of family court records indicates that most judges refuse to grant a divorce on the basis of failure to provide a document that fulfills the above-mentioned requirements of validity.[16] However, these intricate rules do not always govern what evidence is required to prove the existence of a marriage. Relying on the term 'any writing' in Article 17 from the 2000 law, judges occasionally also accept written tokens of love, such as letters, as proof of marriage.[17] Judging from the material analyzed, courts also take varying positions on the importance of written evidence. For instance, some judges of the Cairo Appeal Court consider circumstantial evidence, such as cohabitation and the existence of a child, as sufficient to prove the existence of a 'marital relationship' (*alaqa zawjiya*) in the absence of documentation.[18] These judicial practices have been criticized as accommodating sexual practices that do not comply with the conditions for the validity of a marriage according to the authoritative doctrine of the Hanafi school.[19]

Legal capacity to contract marriage

The offer and acceptance of marriage by competent parties is a condition for a valid marriage contract. Because Egyptian law makes no specific provision about requirements on this issue, courts generally refer to the dominant opinion of the Hanafis. According to this, it is a condition that the parties to the marriage contract have reached puberty and are of sound mind. Otherwise, they should be represented by a guardian who has the right to conclude a marriage on their behalf.[20]

In classical Islamic law there are no rules on the a minimum age for marriage (El-Alami 1996: 6). Similarly to the case of unregistered marriages, Egypt has discouraged the practice of early marriage by denying judicial relief in cases where the spouses are not old enough to have received an official marriage certificate (Esposito

2001: 52). In 2008, the Egyptian legislature adopted a substantive child law that forbids the registration of marriage for males and females below the age of 18.[21] The law also prescribes punishment for notaries who fail to comply with the law. Although the average age of marriage among Egyptians has increased, it is important to note that the marriage of female minors continues, especially in Upper Egypt (Fargues 2003: 263). Moreover, customary marriages are frequently contracted in order to circumvent restrictions on the the minimum age of marriage.

Unlike the view taken in relation to unregistered marriage contracts, the Cairo Appeal Court has not been prepared to use indirect procedural methods to accommodate the entrenched practice of marriage among minors. Its judges have stated adamantly that the legal age of 18 constitutes a main principle and is to be protected at all costs.[22] By invoking the concept of public policy, the Appeal Court has placed the legal rule forbidding registration of marriage of minors among the fundamental elements of a national legal order from which there should be no deviation.[23] However, the law is not implemented by all family courts in the country. These discrepancies lead to conflicting legal practices.[24]

It is also far from exceptional that adult women are instructed by their male guardians in the choice of their spouse (Deif 2004:16). In spite of the widespread practice of intervention by male guardians, cases in which women have been coerced into marriage rarely reach the courts, perhaps due to rules of procedure and evidence and to social pressure. This is perhaps due to rules of procedure and evidence, along with social pressure that prevent such cases from reaching the courts. Moreover, other legal methods might offer a more expedient exit from an undesired union. The positions of judges differ with regard to whether an adult woman is fully competent to conclude marriage, as shown in rulings where judges elaborate on the pillars and conditions that determine whether a marriage is valid. Applying the preponderant opinion within the Hanafi school, most judges appear to hold that that an adult woman has the right to marry without the intervention of a guardian.[25] Some judges nevertheless deny women full legal competence and require that a woman's guardian concludes the marriage on her behalf in order for acceptance to be legally valid even if she has reached puberty.[26] Moreover, although the preponderant Hanafi view acknowledges the right of an adult and rational woman to conclude her own marriage, judges restrict her legal capacity through reference to another Hanafi precept that empowers judges to annul a marriage if the woman's guardian is able to demonstrate that she independently concluded marriage with a groom who is not her equal or who did not present her with a dower compatible with her social status.[27] Thus, whereas statutory legislation has attempted to curtail marriage of male and female minors, the extent of an adult woman's legal competence is subject to the discretionary power of judges.

The dower

The dower (*mahr*) was an important legal institution in classical *fiqh* where it was a sum of money or other valuable given by the husband to the wife in order to obtain sexual union (Coulson 1964: 221). Although Egyptian law does not regulate the dower in any comprehensive way, it is an integral feature of the standard marriage contract as spouses are not allowed to completely waive it. In contemporary legal practice, the dower is not considered a condition or pillar of a valid marriage, but is regarded as a legal obligation. Contemporary Egyptian judges avoid the analogy of a sale transaction and characterize the dower as 'an obligation on the part of the husband underscoring the honour of marriage'.[28] Although the marriage is valid without dower, owed dower becomes a debt incumbent on the husband. The legal institution of the dower is customarily divided in two parts: a *muqaddam al-sadaq* (prompt dower), which is paid at marriage, while a *mu'akhkhar al-sadaq* (deferred dower) is paid at the husband's death or divorce. The dower should be recorded in the marriage contract, which contains a specific space for the dower agreed upon in advance by the parties. The dower may take two forms: 'specified dower' (*al-sadaq al-musamma*) or 'appropriate dower' (*mahr al-mithl*). A specified dower is usually agreed upon at the time of marriage and recorded in the marriage contract, whereas appropriate dower refers to a dower that has not been specified but is determined by judges according to the bride's social status and other factors.

In relation to prompt dower there is a trend toward token dower in urban areas. Frequently, a symbolic amount, ranging from one pound to fifty piasters, is registered as the prompt dower in the marriage contract. This is partly because husbands are reluctant to register a higher amount in the marriage contract as they do not want to pay taxes to the notaries who charge between one and five percent of the amount registered (Sonneveld 2009: 88). In addition, many parents consider education an asset that compensates for a low dower (Shaham 1997: 29). Contributing to the declining importance of prompt dower, a future wife and her family increasingly prefer to ask for engagement presents in the form of jewelry (Sonneveld 2009).[29]

Although the dower always has to be included in the standardized marriage contract, it is considered meaningless among some upper-middle-class couples in view of women's increasing education and economic independence. One such couple told me that they considered the dower to be a safeguard for women who are dependent on men and a sign of status and materialism, like other customs such as throwing extravagant weddings. While their marital contract states that 'the dower is specified', in reality no monetary amount was agreed upon. 'Our dower is our trust and our love for each other', said the husband. When they decided that they wanted to marry, the couple opened a joint savings account where both deposited money in preparation for conjugal life.[30]

The decision not to specify the dower in the marriage contract may be opposed, however, by the notary, who is entitled to claim a certain percentage of the *mahr*. The relative paucity of disputes concerning the prompt dower in the material I analyzed could possibly be attributed to its low value and that to the fact that the family courts increasingly refer disputes over its real value to civil courts. However, although the prompt dower appears to have become less relevant in urban areas, it may still be a substantial sum. In one case before the family court of Misr Al-Gedida, the husband sought to prove that he had paid his wife, after the consummation of the marriage, the agreed upon prompt dower of L.E 50,000 (one-quarter of an apartment).[31] Among the poor and uneducated families in Cairo's slum areas a considerable prompt dower may constitute an important source of revenue.

Whereas the prompt dower appears to have taken on a more symbolic role in urban areas, the deferred dower still constitutes considerable amounts, something that raises the level of financial obligations incumbent on the husband in the event of divorce. In addition to deterring a husband from rash divorce, it may signify social status. Judges also presume that divorce is harmful to the wife and that the dower is a means to provide her with a measure of economic security.[32] The only provision that can be found in Egyptian law with regard to dower is Article 19 of law no. 25 of 1929, amended by law no. 100 of 1985. According to this article, the burden of proof falls on the shoulders of the wife in case of a dispute over the amount of the dower. Underscoring the bureaucratic rationality characterizing regulation of marriage, the judges usually resolve disputes over the amount of dower by basing their decision on the sum stated in the official marriage document.[33] If the woman is unable to establish her claim, the court accepts the amount that the husband states under oath, provided this amount is appropriate to the wife's social status.[34] The social prestige attached to a considerable deferred dower is further supported by the number of judicial disputes where husbands claim that the deferred dower registered in the marriage contract is higher than the dower actually owed by the husband to his wife, the so-called secret dower (*mahr al-sirr*).[35] Finally, if the groom is not compatible in terms of status and did not pay the wife an appropriate dower, the wife's guardian may request the annulment of the marriage.[36] The analysis of Egyptian legal practice indicates that the deferred dower varies tremendously, reflective of status and social class, ranging from L.E 300 to L.E. 600 000.[37]

Clauses in the marriage contract

While the amount of dower is subject to much negotiation and usually is stated in the contract of marriage, the issues of *whether* stipulations are to be included in the marriage contract and *which* conditions are controversial. According to Amira Sonbol (2005), marriage was seen as more of a civil contract until the beginning of the nineteenth century when there was 'a shift to privileging the religious at the expense of the contractual … toward achieving homogeneity and bureaucratic rationality'. In 2000, a new standard-format marriage contract was adopted which allows more flexibility as it contains a blank section of seven lines for the inclusion of negotiated conditions (Al-Sharmani 2008: 9). Among stipulations usually specified are the following:

- the wife's right to a certain amount of marital alimony;
- the wife's right to a monthly salary if divorced without her consent;
- the husband's need to obtain the wife's consent in order to marry a second wife;
- the wife's right to divorce if the husband takes another wife;
- the husband's delegation of the right to repudiation to his wife;
- the wife's right to the conjugal house in the event of divorce regardless of whether the former spouses have minor children;
- the wife's right to the furnishings of the conjugal house in the event of divorce;
- stipulations that the wife does have the right to pursue education, work, and travel without the husband's permission;
- stipulations that the wife does not have the right to work after marriage and receipt of a monthly compensation in return for leaving work if she was working prior to marriage.[38]

Above in the chapter it was shown that Egyptian judges distinguish sharply between the marriage contract and other contracts. It is a peculiar characteristic of the Egyptian marriage contract that while the inclusion of certain conditions is permitted, they remain largely unenforceable through the courts. This was most clearly articulated by a judge who stated: 'Marriage is not a contractual matter which may be dissolved if one of the two parties does not honor contract stipulations, except with one notable case.'[39] The exception is that a husband may delegate his right of repudiation to the wife in the marriage document or a subsequent document so that she can divorce him. While it is hard to ascertain how prevalent this practice is, the impact of the wife's authorization to divorce her husband represents a fascinating reversal of the legal active/passive dichotomy that dictates the enforcement of divorce law: men repudiate, while women are repudiated. When the wife exercises the delegated right to divorce her husband, the resulting repudiation will be considered either revocable or irrevocable depending on the formulation of the delegation.[40]

However, some judges choose to regard the marriage contract as no different to other contracts and apply civil law to it. This happened in a case where the wife and husband from the area of Nasr City had stipulated in the marriage contract her right to L.E 100,000 and a monthly salary of L.E 5,000 if she was divorced against her will. She petitioned the court claiming that she had been subjected to moral pressure from the husband and his family to agree to the repudiation. The court referred to the principle of the sanctity of contracts that is codified in Article 147 of the civil code, but since it found no evidence of coercion it refused to grant her request.[41] Although the views of judges differ, legal development over the last century stands in stark contrast to the situation in Ottoman Egypt where wives were entitled to judicial divorce if conditions included in the contract were breached (El-Bendary 2000). This shows that contemporary Egyptian courts treat the marriage contract as fundamentally different from other contracts where courts endorse the principle of sanctity of contracts and regard conditions as binding.

Dissolution of marriage

Through textual analysis of court practice I have shown that contemporary Egyptian judges define marriage as an eternal contract or pact. This must be seen in relation to attempts by Egyptian legislators and courts to restrict divorce and make marriage a more permanent bond than envisaged by classical jurists. I have also shown that judges articulate a dual legal discourse about marriage, where asymmetric gender relations co-exist with compassion and love. As will be shown in the forthcoming discussion, this is also evident with regard to the dissolution of marriage, where judges attach novel significance to the religious, moral and affective dimensions of conjugal life. Legislation and judicial decisions during the twentieth century sought to curtail the husband's right of repudiation by the enforcement of ethical injunctions and to expand women's rights to judicial divorce. While this discourse reaffirms asymmetrical gender roles, Qur'anic values of mercy and amity have attained a more prominent place in legal discourse in recent years. This will be demonstrated with reference to judicial divorce through *khul'*, where these values have been translated into legal rules that challenge male authority.

Repudiation *(*talaq*)*

According to classical Islamic law, a Muslim man may divorce his wife at will without offering any justification. The repudiation acquires legal effect upon the pronunciation of a formula, without notifying the wife or recourse to court, and witnesses are not necessary for its validity (Coulson 1964: 46). Repudiation *(talaq)* has been institutionalized in Egyptian law as an inherent right of the husband and has been justified on the basis of a presumed superior male rationality.[42] Whereas traditional authorities viewed repudiation as an entirely extrajudicial process, legislation and court rulings during the twentieth century subjected the man's right of repudiation to some constraints by the requirement of registration and by making repudiation contingent upon the husband's intention to divorce. The emphasis on intention represents a departure from the interpretations of Hanafi doctrine where repudiation takes effect upon the correct pronouncement of a formula and is detached from a notion of a personhood capable of voluntary behavior (El-Alami 1996: 22; Esposito 2001: 53).

These judicial attempts to counter abuse were followed in 1985 by an important legal amendment that obliged men to pay their ex-wives a so-called *muta'* compensation in addition to maintenance during the waiting period, as well as outstanding dower if they had been unjustly divorced. The effect of the amendment has been to subject the husbands' motives behind repudiation to judicial scrutiny and to punish husbands guilty of what the Court of Cassation calls 'despotism in repudiation' *(talaq al-mustabidd)*.[43] In 1993 the Supreme Constitutional Court (SCC) issued a judgment that established the conformity of the amendment with the principles of shari'a. According to the court, the basis of the obligation to pay *muta'* compensation was the Qur'anic injunctions to treat divorced wives with kindness and with the 'chivalry demanded by shari'a'.[44] The consequence of this and similar judicial developments related to the dissolution of marriage is a closer fusion between law and the ethical dimensions of marriage than that which existed in traditional Islamic jurisprudence, where Qur'anic injunctions urging men to treat women equitably were only given sanction in the hereafter. Simultaneously, the state's construction of male powers has been linked with the attempt to limit a man's powers through a moral discourse centered on chivalry.[45]

Judicial divorce due to discord *(*tatliq al-shiqaq*)*

According to the SCC, repudiation is an inherent right of the husband vested in him by God.[46] However, the court has argued, Islamic shari'a also emphasizes equilibrium *(muwazana)* between husband and wife in the context of dissolution of marriage. The wife has the right to petition the judge to obtain judicial divorce through the use of a legal fiction where the state, represented by the judge, takes the husband's place and divorces the wife in his stead.[47] Egyptian legislative reforms at the beginning of the twentieth century concentrated on providing judicial relief to Madhabi *fiqh* to abused wives whose husbands inflicted intentional injury *(darar)* on them by adopting the Maliki doctrine.[48] This section deals with an important but under-researched amendment enacted in 1985 regarding judicial divorce due to discord *(shiqaq)*. While state legislation and court practice left the husband's right of repudiation intact, I argue that this provision and the so-called *khul'* law were significant steps in the direction of greater equality for women in the initiation of divorce.

Based on Maliki doctrine, law no. 25 of 1929 provided that if the wife's request for divorce on the basis of *darar* was refused and she later repeated her complaint but failed to establish injury, the courts were empowered to appoint arbitrators and rule for divorce if the arbitrators failed to resolve the discord. However, the 1929 law departed from Maliki doctrine by not allowing courts to dissolve a marriage if they found that the blame for the discord chiefly lay with the wife (Coulson 1964). In law no. 100 of 1985, the legislature adopted the rules of the Maliki school and authorized the judge, following arbitration, to impose repudiation, even if he determined that the wife was at fault, in return for her payment of compensation and forfeiture of some or all her financial rights (Article 11).

Although the lawmakers did not explicitly define this type of judicial divorce as an application of the principle of *al-khul'*, it was considered as such.[49] The 1985 amendment targeted a specific category of women, namely the 'quarrelsome wife' (*al zawja al-mushakesa*). The explanatory memorandum states that the rationale behind the amendment was to discourage such a woman from harming her husband as a stratagem to compel him to repudiate her without paying him compensation.[50]

The adoption of Maliki doctrine represented a departure from the majority of the classical law schools according to which a *khul'* can only be effected with the consent of both spouses (Arabi 2001: 15). The amended provision was contested by a divorced husband before the SCC in 1995 on the basis of its purported contradiction with the principles of shari'a. The husband relied on the argument that this provision was unconstitutional because only husbands are allowed by Islamic law to impose repudiation and, in his view, the provision in question amounted to a transfer of the husband's right of repudiation to the wife. In 1997 the SCC issued a ruling confirming the constitutionality of the amendment.

Alongside the alleged juristic foundation of the reform in the Maliki school, the judges of the SCC defended the law by articulating a model of marriage that is based on amity (*mawadda*) and mercy (*rahma*). According to the Court, if amity becomes replaced by rancor (*shahna*), the institution of marriage weakens because rancor is incompatible with the true nature (*haqiqa*) of marriage. The SCC upheld men's right to *talaq*, but sought to discipline husbands by deploying an ideal of a virtuous Muslim subject, conceptualized as a 'champion of chivalry'. Analogous to the justification for *muta'* compensation to wives who are unjustly divorced, the court argued that a husband's unwillingness to repudiate his wife when the marriage does not exhibit the qualities of mercy and amity amounts to despotism (*istabad*) toward the wife and that the judge in such cases should exercise *talaq* on behalf of the husband.[51] Thereby, the SCC confirmed the constitutionality of an avenue for women to obtain divorce in court from emotionally unsatisfying marriages in a manner that challenged the gendered and asymmetrical nature of Islamic divorce law in Egypt in a fundamental respect.

Although the lawmakers envisaged the 1985 amendment as a way to discourage quarrelsome women from abusing their husbands, it is noteworthy that family courts when assessing the financial consequences of divorce due to discord only mete out compensation in exceptional cases. According to an interviewed judge, the wife rarely or never pays compensation to the husband because she is considered the weaker party under personal status law and should be protected. As he stated: 'Hence the judges are sympathetic to their pleas.'[52]

Judicial decisions concerning divorce due to discord provide an opportunity to analyze prevalent ideas about proper gender roles in marriage. Egyptian court records show that the provision on *shiqaq* paves the way for women who wish to pursue divorce. However, a wife's very insistence may have a negative impact on the assessment of her financial rights following divorce, as shown in a decision handed down by the Cairo Court of Appeal in November 2008.[53] This judgment was based on the report by the arbitrators, who suggested granting divorce to the wife, but-depriving her of half her financial rights as she was not keen to continue conjugal life and refused reconciliation. While women may benefit from being considered by judges as the weaker party under personal status law, it serves as a reminder of the disdain that some judges have for women who actively pursue divorce, as is also apparent in the appeal of the judge to the media that was noted at the beginning of this chapter.

Judicial divorce through khul'

As shown in the previous section, judicial divorce through *khul'* was implicitly addressed by the legislators in the 1985 amendment that adopted the Maliki view regarding divorce due to discord. It is also worthy of note that *khul'* was mentioned explicitly in Articles 6 and 24 of the ordinances on the organization and procedures of the shari'a courts in 1931. However, the legislators did not specify the rules governing female-initiated divorce.[54] A case that originated in the city of Mansoura provides insight into variations on the precise definition of *khul'* contained in the 1931 ordinance. In 1998 a dispute broke out between a husband and wife after he defamed her and her family. This inspired in the wife emotions of resentment and hatred, whereupon she offered to return the dower to her husband and lodged a petition for judicial dissolution by *khul'*. In November 1998 the first instance court of personal status in Mansoura granted her a divorce from her husband through judicial *khul'* without the husband's consent. Not pleased, the former husband appealed the decision to the appeal court of Mansoura where the order for judicial *khul'* was overturned. The appeal court based its ruling on an understanding of *khul'* as a contract (*'aqd*) that cannot take legal effect without the husband's consent. The wife later appealed to the Court of Cassation, which in 2005 resolved the long-standing controversy. According to the Court, Articles 6 and 24 of the 1931 ordinances provided wives the right to file a claim for judicial *khul'*. The Court of Cassation then proceeded by presenting two interpretations of *khul'* – one as a contract of divorce based on mutual agreement, the other as a form of judicial dissolution. If mutual consent is not reached, the judge has the right to impose a judicial decision of *khul'* on the husband.[55] Not incidentally, the 2005 ruling of the court was issued after the passage of law no. 1 in 2000 in which the two definitions of *khul'* were expressly codified in Article 20. Although the Court of Cassation referred to the 1931 ordinances, the court clearly interpreted the older provisions in light of the 2000 provision. Purportedly drawing on the authority of the Maliki school, the second paragraph of Article 20 of the 2000 law entitles a wife to separate from her husband on the condition that she renounces her outstanding financial rights, restores the prompt dower to her husband and goes through reconciliation sessions. Thereby, the law significantly reduced the discretionary power of judges, compared with the 1985 amendment concerning judicial dissolution due to discord, which allows judges greater flexibility

According to the 2000 law, the wife should explicitly declare in court that she hates living with her husband and that she fears going beyond God's mainstays due to that hatred (*al-bughd*). With this requirement, the provision structures the possible course of action based on an understanding of women as psychological subjects who feel rancor, resentment and hatred. By allowing women judicial dissolution of marriages that do not conform to the emotions of amity and mercy, Egyptian lawmakers and judges – together with other factors – have, during the last three decades, encouraged the understanding of women as more individualized subjects, while undermining male authority.[56]

Implementation of the khul' law by the courts

Article 20 provoked considerable controversy and its religious legitimacy was contested before the SCC on the basis of its contradiction with the principles of Islamic shari'a.[57] Court records from before and after the 2011 revolution show that this provision has become a favored procedure among women from many walks of life who are in pursuit of divorce. However, at first the implementation of the *khul'* law faced resistance and confusion over the exact steps to be followed (Maugiron 2008; Sonneveld 2009). There are still some lingering ambiguities and doubts concerning the legitimacy of the *khul'* law and its Islamic foundation. This appears to be partly related to the fact that personal status laws are composed of elements from different schools of laws, i.e. *madhhabs*. The lawmakers adopted Maliki doctrine in the provisions on judicial divorce, although they instructed judges to apply Hanafi doctrine in the absence of statutory provisions. This appears to have led some judges to deploy traditional doctrines in inconsistent ways to add authenticity to their decision, as illustrated by rulings concerning judicial *khul'*.[58] Paragraph 2 in Article 20 of Law no. 1 of 2000 seemingly adopted the doctrine of the Maliki school that permitted the judge to free the wife from her husband on the basis of the arbitrators' suggestion. Nevertheless, it transpires that in some cases judges routinely cite the preponderant Hanafi doctrine that describes *khul'* as a contract of mutual consent between the spouses or as a sale.[59] This creates an illusion of a mutual process where *khul'* is conditioned by the husband's acceptance.

Egyptian judges occasionally invoke Islamic norms in their judgments in order to reinforce legislation. More rarely, judges do so out of apparent concern about the ethical aspects of this form of divorce. Some judges appear to harbor doubts about the legitimacy of *khul'* in the cases brought before them, and reiterate a warning issued by the Prophet Muhammad to women who opt for *khul'* without good reason: 'a wife who requests divorce without legitimate reason shall be deprived of smelling the scent of paradise.'[60] Here the judge reminded the wife that God is witness and that her actions in the final analysis have a religious significance, and said that judicial *khul'* may be legally valid, but is nonetheless reprehensible. In this way the judge conflated a matter of moral and religious conscience with personal status law. It is worth mentioning that many judges believe that wives who resort to this legal mechanism take marriage lightly (Sonneveld 2010: 101).

Although a ruling of *khul'* does not formally affect a woman's right to custody of her children, analysis of court practice reveals that some judges are prepared to punish women through visitation arrangements if they suspect the wife resorted to judicial divorce through *khul'* for frivolous reasons.[61] The judges do not seem as concerned that a husband might intentionally mistreat his wife so as to force her to seek a divorce that abridges her rights. Further, although rulings of judicial divorce by *khul'* are not formally subject to appeal, according to the 2000 law, some husbands nonetheless appeal them in order to prolong the case, and rulings of *khul'* are occasionally overturned on the basis of procedural reasons.[62]

The Egyptian revolution and calls to amend 'Suzanne's laws'

Women were key players in public demonstrations that led to the ousting of Mubarak, and spent nights in Tahrir Square and in Suez side by side with their fellow male pro-democracy demonstrators. Although the Egyptian revolution did not expressly rally around the advancement of women's rights, it inspired feelings of empowerment that made many women believe the stage was set for a paradigm change in terms of women's citizenship rights. The belief in a trickle-down or spillover effect was shattered by calls from disparate groups, such as Islamists, liberals, associations of men, such as *Thawra al-rigal* (literally: revolution of men), and various media actors, to cancel or amend controversial personal status legislation. These laws are described in pejorative terms as 'Suzanne's laws', the 'laws of shame' and 'the most dangerous laws'. Two of the main elements of the criticism are leveled against the top-down procedure of their adoption by the *ancien regime*, and the prominent role played by the former president's wife, Suzanne Mubarak, in their adoption. The former first lady is frequently described as an agent of the UN and of Western women's rights organizations. In addition to being passed in an undemocratic way, existing laws are accused of contradicting the shari'a. Accordingly, the laws are described as threatening the Egyptian family – considered to be the basic unit of society – and, hence, the social order with collapse (Lindbekk 2011).

Among the most contested reforms is the Law no. 1 of 2000 on *khul'*, the debate over which has not abated since its introduction in 2000. Above, we saw a judge using the court to call on Egyptian media to protect the Egyptian family against female-initiated divorce. In 2011 a family court judge by the name of Abdalla Baga launched a campaign to amend Egypt's laws relating Muslims – Copts and Jews are entitle to follow their own laws and have their own judicial system – with the aim of bringing about greater stability (*istikrar*) to the family. A main goal of his proposal is to make the consent of the husband a prerequisite for a valid *khul'* divorce, in order to curtail female-initiated divorce, which he blames for a perceived increase in the divorce rate. Moreover, he believes that: 'The man owns the right of repudiation. Judicial dissolution through *khul'* places men and women on an equal footing in effecting repudiation.' According to his suggestions, judicial divorce should only be granted to women in response to 'real injury' (*darar haqiqi*), meaning cases where the husband has intentionally subjected the wife to objective harm.[63] With this proposal, the judge is challenging the legal discourse regarding judicial divorce through *khul'* that has been elaborated by the legislators, the SCC and the Court of Cassation over the past three decades.

From when Egypt's first freely elected parliament convened in January 2012 until it was abruptly dissolved in June 2012, several proposals dealing with the minimum age of marriage, judicial divorce through *khul'*, child custody and visitation rights after divorce were submitted by MPs to the Committee of Proposals and Complaints. While the Cairo Appeal Court had protected the legal age of 18 as an essential norm, this legal provision came under fire from Islamists sitting in the parliament. Since the Islamist-dominated parliament was dissolved by Egypt's SCC in June 2012, in terms of legislative steps none of these law proposals reached further than the Committee of Proposals and Complaints. A proposal to 'cancel *khul'*' was swiftly rejected by the Committee. Although the law proposals were neither enacted into law nor discussed by the People's Assembly, they provide an opportunity to analyze important discursive strategies. The fact that the proposal to cancel *khul'* was so swiftly refused indicates that a combination of factors has tipped the scale in favor of legal stability, at least for the time being. These factors include the political priorities of the transitional period, lack of experience and legal knowledge among MPs, combined with the support of al-Azhar and prominent members of the Ministry of Justice for the current personal status laws. Whereas the possibility that controversial provisions will be repealed cannot be ruled out, existing norms offer significant institutional and ideational resistance to future challenges (Lindbekk 2012).

Conclusion

We have seen that some judges doubt the legitimacy of the *khul'* law and frown upon female-initiated divorce for what they deem to be frivolous reasons. Meanwhile, adjudication of divorce due to discord shows that judges usually rule in the wife's favor on the basis of the principle of protection of the weak. This illustrates that judicial practice in matters of personal status is multilayered. In disputes brought before the courts, judges also attach considerable significance to the religious, ethical and affective dimensions of conjugal life. By doing so, they articulate a dual discourse on marriage. On the one hand, judges conceptualize marriage as a hierarchical institution, stressing asymmetrical gender roles where brides and wives are subjected to male authority. Yet, as we have seen, this ideal is intertwined with another discourse oriented toward an ideal of conjugal ties based on emotions of amity and mercy. The two dominant discourses are also reflected in legal practice with regard to dissolution of marriage. Although Egyptian judges construct repudiation as an intrinsic right of the husband, his authority has been curtailed in a manner designed to discipline male subjects by promoting intentionality and a notion of manhood that includes chivalry. While this legal-ethical discourse reinforces marriage as a hierarchical institution privileging men, judicial divorce by *khul'* demonstrates that increased emphasis on emotional bonds between spouses may both support male privilege and undermine it. With regard to both dimensions of judicial practice in matters of personal status, judges occasionally deploy interpretations of Islamic shari'a to validate their assertion of authority.

Notes

1 This study is based on cases from three family courts in Cairo and the Cairo appeal court (circuit of personal status) collected from the period 2008–10. It also examines a sample of decisions handed down by the Court of Cassation from 1985–2007, as well as three decisions issued by the Supreme Constitutional Court in 1997, 2002 and 2007. For further details on the system of courts involved in adjudicating cases of marriage and divorce, see Nathalie Bernard-Maugiron's chapter in this book.

2 El Nadim Center is an Egyptian NGO rehabilitating victims of violence. The Bahai's are a religious sect subjected to persecution in Egypt.

3 I.e. Israel.

4 See the Chapter by Bernard-Maugiron.

5 See the Romans' sura, verse 21.

6 Similar arguments have been advanced by Ali (2006) and Kholoussy (2005: 324).

7 See also the Chapter by Bernard-Maugiron in this book.

8 See the report by the commissioners' body in constitutional case no. 201, judicial year 23, p. 22; Supreme Constitutional Court, case no. 145, judicial year no. 18, 3 June 2000. See also Cairo Appeal Court, case no. 1084 and no. 1475, judicial year no. 125, 3 December 2008. See also El-Alami 1992: 12.

9 See Cairo appeal court, personal status circuit, case no. 1620, judicial year no. 126, 26 January 2011.

10 Case no. 835, 22 November 2009, Al-Marg family court.

11 For a thorough treatment of the issue of temporary and permanent impediments to marriage in traditional Islamic jurisprudence according to the Hanafi school, see El-Alami 1992.

12 Case no. 637, 2009, Ain Shams family court, 31 December 2009. The court did not refer to the school of Hanafi, but to a ruling by the Court of Cassation (case no. 194, judicial year 1963, 19 October 1998). The witnesses can also be one man and two women. Case no. 1020, 28 January 2010, Misr Al-Gedida.

13 Some courts mention the husband's compatibility in term of status as a condition of validity without elaborating the factors by which compatibility of status is determined. See case no. 637, Ain Shams family court, 31 December 2009.

14 See Article 99 of law no. 78 on the organization of shari'a courts from 1931. See also Court of Cassation, case no. 767, judicial year 74, 16 April 2007.

15 Cairo appeal court, case no. 4460, judicial year no. 125, 5 January 2010.

16 See for instance, case no. 1020, 28 January 2010, Misr Al-Gedida family court; case no. 10, 28 January 2010, Misr Al-Gedida family court. If one of the spouses is a non-Muslim belonging to the 'people of the book', one of the witnesses may be likewise. Case no. 10, 28 January 2010, Misr Al-Gedida family court.

17 Interview with Judge A.B., 13 March 2012, Judges' Club, Cairo.

18 Cairo appeal court, case no. 4460, judicial year no. 125, 5 January 2010.

19 Al-lagna al-islamiya al-'alamiya l-l-marra wa al-tifl 2012: 16.

20 Case no. 1014, 2009, 28 January 2010, Misr Al-Gedida family court. For a more extensive discussion on legal competence, see El-Alami 1992.

21 Prior to the promulgation of the child law in 2008, law no. 78 from 1931 prohibited notaries from registering marriages of males and females under the ages of 18 and 16 respectively.

22 Cairo appeal court, case no. 8487, judicial year no. 126, 17 February 2010.

23 See also Berger 2001: 88.

24 This issue was raised by the claimant in case no. 186, 25 May 2009, Al-Aiat family court. See also, case no. 637, 31 December 2009, Ain Shams family court.

25 Case no. 637, 2009, 31 December 2009, Ain Shams family court. The same transpired in case no. 1014, 2009, 28 January 2010, Misr Al-Gedida family court.

26 Case no. 300, 28 June 2008, Misr Al-Gedida family court.

27 Case no. 637, 2009, Ain Shams family court, 31 December 2009. See also Shaham (1997: 44).

28 Case no. 353, 12 July 2008, Misr Al-Gedida family court, and case no. 241, 28 June 2008, Misr Al-Gedida family court.

29 Further, the costs of marriage are increasingly shared among the bride, the groom, the bride's family and the groom's family (Singerman 2007: 15).

30 Interview with K.N. in Cairo, 13 March 2010.

31 Case no. 977, 3 January 2009, Misr Al-Gedida family court. For more on the issue of dower and consummation of marriage, see Kholoussy (2010: 33) and Shaham 1997: 31.

32 Cairo appeal court, no.1554, 5409 for the judicial year 123, 19 March 2008. On the different functions of the dower, see Fredriksen 2011.

33 Cairo appeal court, no.1554, 5409 for the judicial year 123, 19 March 2008.

34 See Cairo appeal court, case no. 6560, judicial year 125, 7 May 2009.

35 Cairo appeal court, case no. 7191, judicial year no. 125, 3 September 2008.

36 Case no. 637, 2009, Ayn Shams family court, 31 December 2009. See also, Shaham (1997: 44).

37 Cairo appeal court, case no. 2358, judicial year no. 123, 21 February 2007. Cairo appeal court, case no. 12017, judicial year 126, 14 July 2010.

38 Interview with marriage registrar in Dar al-Salam, Cairo, 11 April 2012.

39 Interview with judge in Talat Harb Street, Cairo, 16 June 2012.

40 Court of Cassation, case no. 88, judicial year no. 63, 28 January 1997.

41 Cairo appeal court, case no. 3068, judicial year 124, 23 April 2008.

42 Supreme Constitutional Court, case no. 82, judicial year no. 17, 5 July 1997.

43 Court of Cassation, case no. 26, judicial year no. 50, 29 January 1985. See also, Coulson (1969: 95).

44 Supreme Constitutional Court, case no. 8, judicial year 8, 15 May 1993 and Court of Cassation, case no. 6, judicial year 63, 10 March 1997. See also, the explanatory memorandum of law no. 100 from 1985, 'Al-muta' l-l-mutalaqa ba'da al-dukhul'.

45 See Lindbekk 2009. Coulson (1969: 95) refers to these and similar legal developments as a 'resurgence of legal moralism'.

46 Supreme Constitutional Court, case no. 82, judicial year no. 17, 5 July 1997.

47 Report by the commissioners' body in constitutional case no. 201, judicial year 123, p. 20.

48 See Nathalie Bernard-Maugiron's chapter for a more extensive treatment of the judicial implementation of Article 6 in law no. 25 from 1929 concerning judicial divorce due to injury (*darar*).

49 See report by commissioners' body in constitutional case no. 201, judicial year 123, p. 32. Khul' is a type of separation, usually initiated by the wife, where she pays the husband a sum of money in exchange for release from the marriage contract.

50 Explanatory memorandum of law no. 25 from 1929, part 2, 'Al-shiqaq bayna al-zawgin wa al-tatliq l-l darar'. See also, the report by the commissioners' body in constitutional case no. 201, judicial year 123, p. 32.

51 Supreme Constitutional Court, case no. 82, judicial year no. 17, 5 July 1997. See also, report by the commissioners' body in this constitutional case.

52 Interview with judge on the Court of Cassation, 22 March 2012, Adli Street, downtown Cairo.

53 Cairo appeal court, case no. 12301, judicial year no. 124, 5 November 2008.

54 According to Article 6 from the 1931 ordinances on the organization and procedures of the shari'a courts, these courts were authorized to rule in cases of 'repudiation (talaq), khul' and mubara'. Article 24 requires that claims related to *talaq*, *khul'* and *mubara'* be lodged before the court in the constituency where the wife resides.

55 Court of Cassation case no. 485, judicial year 69, 3 January 2005.

56 See Hasso (2010: 16) on subjectivities and practices encouraged by transnational Islamic discourse and practices and neo-liberal globalization.

57 Constitutional case no. 20, judicial year 23, 15 December 2002. See also Supreme Constitutional Court, case no. 99, judicial year 24, 19 April 2007. The SCC confirmed the constitutionality of the provision by drawing on the authority of the Maliki school although prominent Islamic scholars and others argued that the second paragraph of Article 20 from law no. 1 of 2000 is not in conformity with Maliki doctrine (Maugiron 2008: 248; Moussa 2005: 22). A committee of

judges charged with preparing the constitutional case copied several passages from the legal reasoning adopted by SCC in its 1997 ruling on judicial divorce due to discord into a report confirming the constitutionality of Article 20. In doing so, the committee contributed to a degree of institutional stickiness surrounding the issue of judicial divorce through *khul'*. See the report by the commissioners' body in constitutional case no. 201, judicial year 123.

58 Dupret (2003: 130) refers to such processes as a form of 'over-validation'.
59 Case no. 701, 23 February 2008, Misr Al-Gedida family court.
60 Case no. 651, 24 March 2007, Misr Al-Gedida family court.
61 Cairo appeal court, case no. 8210, judicial year 124, 21 July 2008.
62 In 2005, the al-Giza family court cancelled a ruling of judicial divorce through *khul'* previously issued by the same court because the wife had notified the husband of her claim at the wrong address. See case no. 28, 27 November 2005, al-Giza family court and Cairo Appeal Court, case no. 417, judicial year 123, 6 December 2010.
63 Interview with Abdalla Baga, Judges Club, Cairo, 13 March 2012.

Bibliography

Abu-Lughod, L. (1998) 'The marriage of feminism and Islamism in Egypt: selective repudiation as a dynamic of postcolonial cultural politics', in L. Abu-Lughod (ed.), *Remaking Women: Feminism and Modernity in the Middle East*, Cairo: The American University in Cairo Press.

Alami, D. El- (1992) *The Marriage Contract in Islamic law*, Arab and Islamic Law series, vol. 6, London: Brill.

Ali, K. (2006) *Sexual Ethics and Islam: Feminist Reflections on Qur'an, Hadith and Jurisprudence*, Oxford: Oneworld Publications.

Al-lagna al-islamiya al-'alamiya l-l-marra wa al-tifl (2012) *Al-ifsad al-tasrhri'i fi magal al-usra*, Cairo: International Islamic Committee for Woman and Child.

Arabi, O. (2001) *Studies in Modern Islamic Law and Jurisprudence*, The Hague: Kluwer Law International.

Asad, T. (2001) 'Thinking about secularism and law in Egypt', Leiden: Isim. Available online at https://openaccess.leidenuniv.nl/bitstream/handle/1887/10066/paper_asad.pdf?sequence=1 (accessed 11 May 2012).

Bendary, A. El- (2000) 'Conditional surrenders', *Al-Ahram Weekly*, 13–19 January 2000. Available online at http://weekly.ahram.org.eg/2000/464/spec3.htm (accessed 7 June 2012).

Berger, M. and Sonneveld, N. (2010) 'Sharia and national law in Egypt', in M. Otto (ed.), *Sharia Incorporated. A Comparative Overview of the Legal Systems of Twelve Countries in Past and Present*, Leiden: Leiden University Press.

Berger, M. (2001) 'Public Policy and Islamic Law: the Modern Dhimmī in Contemporary Egyptian Family Law', *Islamic Law and Society*, 8(1): 88–136.

Coulson, N. (1964) *A History of Islamic Law*, Edinburgh: Edinburgh University Press.

——(1969) *Conflicts and Tensions in Islamic Jurisprudence*, London: The University of Chicago Press.

Deif, F. (2004) 'Divorced from justice', *Human Rights Watch*, 16(8): 1–12.

Dupret, B. (2003) 'A return to the shariah?' in John L. Esposito (ed.), *Modernizing Islam: Religion in the Public Sphere in Europe and the Middle East*, London: Hurst & Company.

——(2007) 'What is Islamic law? A praxiological answer and an Egyptian case', *Theory of Culture and Society*, 24(2):79–100.

——(1996) *Islamic Marriage and Divorce Laws of the Arab World*, London: Kluwer Law International.

Esposito, J. (2001) *Women in Muslim Family Law*, New York: Syracuse University Press.

Fargues, F. (2003) 'Terminating marriage', in Nicholas Hopkins (ed.), *The New Arab Family*, Cairo: Cairo University Press.

Fredriksen, K.J. (2011) 'Mahr (dower) as a bargaining tool in a European context: a comparison of Dutch and Norwegian judicial decisions', in R. Mehdi and J. Nielsen (eds), *Embedding Mahr in the European Legal System*, Copenhagen: DJØF Publishing.

Hasso, F. (2010) *Consuming Desires: Family Crisis and the State in the Middle East*, Palo Alto, CA: Stanford University Press.

Kholoussy, H. (2005) 'The nationalization of marriage in monarchical Egypt', in A. Goldschmidt, A. Johnson and B. Salmoni (eds), *Re-envisioning Egypt 1919–1952*, Cairo: The American University in Cairo Press.

——(2010) *For Better, For Worse: the Marriage Crisis that Made Modern Egypt*, Palo Alto, CA: Stanford University Press.

Lindbekk, M. (2009) 'Polygyni i Egypt mellom regjering og disiplinær makt', *Babylon – Nordisk tidsskrift for Midtøstenstudier*, 2: 92–101.

——(2011) 'A revolution in Egyptian family law?' *Babylon – Nordisk tidsskrift for Midtøstenstudier*, 10(2): 22–35.

——(2012) 'The political controversy surrounding family law in post-revolutionary Egypt', paper presented at the Middle East Conference held at the University of Oslo, 7–8 May.

Maugiron, N. (2008) 'The judicial construction of the facts and the law', in B. Dupret, B. Drieskens and A. Moors (eds), *Narratives of Truth in Islamic Law*, London: I.B. Tauris.

Moussa, J. (2005) 'The Reform of *shari'a*-derived divorce legislation in Egypt: international standards and the cultural debate', *University of Nottingham Human Rights Law Commentary*. Available online at www.nottingham.ac.uk/hrlc/documents/publications/hrlcommentary2005/divorcelegislationegypt.pdf (accessed 16 April 2012).

Shaham, R. (1997) *Family and the Courts in Modern Egypt*, Leiden: Brill.

Sharmani, M. Al- (2008) 'Family court in Egypt', American University in Cairo, Social Research Center. Available online at www.pathwaysofempowerment.org/Familycourts.pdf (accessed 4 August 2012).

Singerman, D. (2007) 'The economic imperatives of marriage: emerging practices and identities among youth in the Middle East', Working Paper, vol. 6, Dubai: Wolfensohn Centre for Development and Dubai School of Government.

Sonbol, A. (2003) 'Women in shari'a courts a historical and methodological discussion', *Fordham International Law Journal*, 27(9): 25–56.

——(2005) 'History of marriage contracts in Egypt', *Hawwa*, 3(2): 159–96.

Sonneveld, N. (2009) *Khul Divorce in Egypt: public debates, judicial practices, and everyday life*, PhD dissertation, University of Leiden.

——(2010) 'Khul' divorce in Egypt: how family courts are providing a "dialogue" between husband and wife', *Anthropology of the Middle East*, 5(2): 100–120.

Tucker, J. (1998) *In the House of Law: Gender and Islamic Law in Ottoman Syria and Palestine*, Cairo: The American University in Cairo Press.

6 Courts and the Reform of Personal Status Law in Egypt

Judicial divorce for injury and polygamy

Nathalie Bernard-Maugiron

Introduction

From the twentieth century onward, Egyptian lawmakers strived to reinstate a balance between men and women in their access to marriage dissolution.[1] Among other reforms, they limited the male prerogative to end marriage unilaterally[2] and expanded women's grounds to file for judicial divorce. The right to divorce was elaborated in three stages: first of all, laws in 1920 and 1929 allowed divorce for various forms of harm;[3] then, in 1979 and 1985 the law dealt with the particular case of divorce due to damage caused by the husband's polygamy; finally, a law adopted in 2000 introduced a judicial procedure for the breakup of marriage without harm (*khul'*). These reforms were introduced as a result of an internal renovation process and were made legitimate by reference to shari'a principles, as disclosed by the explanatory memorandums to the laws.

If the codification process led to improvements in women's status, implementation of the reforms could not however be achieved without the active support of judges. Whatever the grounds, but in particular in cases of requests for divorce based on injury or polygamy, judicial divorce requires the assessment by a court of the nature and the degree of harm suffered by the wife, and judges enjoy a great deal of discretion in making their decisions. If no specific provision in the law can be found on a particular point, Law No 1/2000 further stipulates that the judge shall follow the most prevalent opinion within the Hanafi school.[4] This means that if a legal provision exists, the judge has to apply it; however, if the law is silent, it will be up to the court to seek, identify and implement non-codified Islamic shari'a norms.

Different courts may be involved in requests for divorce. At first, family courts will decide on the substance of the case.[5] These courts were established in 2004 to bring relief to an over-burdened judicial system by consolidating all aspects of a divorce dispute into a single case and thereby speeding up the legal process.[6] Each court is run by a panel of three judges and their decisions, except in *khul'* cases where the ruling of the judge is final,[7] can be appealed before appeal courts. Since 2004, rulings in family law cases are no longer challengeable before the Court of Cassation.[8] The rulings of the Court of Cassation mentioned in this chapter were issued before the entry into force of that law. Finally, the law providing women with the right to file for divorce in cases of polygamy was challenged before the Supreme Constitutional Court for unconstitutionality, as was the *khul'* law. The Court had to decide whether the provisions violated Article 2 of the Constitution, according to which 'Egypt is an Arab state, its official language is Arabic and shari'a is the main source of legislation'.

Although Egyptian judges have demonstrated liberalism by fighting for compliance with the rule of law and for the independence of the judiciary (Bernard-Maugiron 2008), they are often perceived as being rather conservative in the field of family rights. An analysis of court rulings of different branches of the Egyptian judiciary involved in requests for divorce for injury and polygamy, however, shows that this perception may not be accurate.

Egyptian courts and divorce due to injury

Divorce for injury (*darar*) was introduced by Law No 25/1929, with certain conditions. When granting divorce due to injury, the Court of Cassation and lower courts gave general definitions of injury, but the interpretation of what constitutes an injury varied according to the social class of the spouses.

A broad definition of injury

According to Article 6 of Law No 25/1929, if a wife alleges that she suffered an injury caused by her husband and that the injury is such that it makes the continuation of the marriage relationship between persons of their social class impossible, she may file for divorce. She will be granted an irrevocable divorce, provided maltreatment is established and the judge fails to achieve a reconciliation between the couple.

The explanatory memorandum to the law emphasizes that this ground for divorce was inspired by the Maliki School. The Hanafi school of law, traditionally applied in Egypt for more than four centuries, only acknowledges a husband's impotency[9] and apostasy as grounds for the legal annulment of a union. That school does not consider any injury that the husband causes the wife a reason for divorce because this could be dealt with by other means, such as reprimanding the husband, putting him in jail or releasing the wife from her duty of obedience. As the memorandum reminded people: 'No opinion in the Abu Hanifa doctrine provides women with the means to exit marriage or foresees any way to bring the husband back to the right path. Each one can harm the other out of vengeance.' This discord between spouses 'is a source of harm which hurts not only the spouses, but also their offspring, parents, and in-laws. ... [T]he welfare commands the adoption of Imam Malik's doctrine in case of discord between spouses.'[10]

It is the wife's responsibility to prove to the judge that the injury inflicted upon her by her husband renders the continuation of the marriage relationship impossible. She will have to convince him of the validity of her claim by proving that her husband mistreated her and that his behaviour caused her so much harm that continued cohabitation is impossible. The judge will, on an *ad hoc* basis, have to characterize the facts under review and decide whether they fit into the definition of harm within the meaning of Article 6.

Trial courts are bound by the rulings of the Court of Cassation, but the definition that the Supreme Court gave to injury is so broad that is leaves them with almost full discretion. The Court of Cassation decided to consult the legal literature of the Maliki school to interpret the concept of injury because the explanatory memorandum to Law No 25/1929 stated that the provision was based on that school. This decision of the Court may appear surprising because, according to Law No 1/2000, where the law is silent the judge should refer to the prevalent opinion in the Hanafi school. However, reference to the Hanafi school makes little sense because that school, as we have seen, does not recognize injury of a wife as grounds for divorce.

The Court of Cassation defined injury as damage caused by the husband, by either words or deeds, to his wife, and which is inappropriate for people of their status and is considered by customs (*fi al-'urf*) to be abnormal, harmful treatment, and that the wife complains she cannot stand anymore because it makes continuation of a life together impossible.[11] In their decisions, courts of merits (trial courts) usually refer to this definition of injury, though they often do not refer to the same rulings.[12]

The Court of Cassation decided that the wife is entitled to sue for separation if her husband harms her, whether through violence in words or actions, or by abandoning her bed.[13] The wrongful action does not need to have occurred several times: once is enough.[14] The fact that the wrong has stopped at the time of examination of the case does not matter, as long as it occurred in the past.[15] It is not clear in the Court of Cassation rulings whether harm must be intentional or whether unintentional harm is sufficient.[16] The Court of Cassation has recognized, on the basis of a Qur'anic verse, the right of the husband to punish his wife by beating her, but the husband may resort to this means only after having tried, by way of exhortation and desertion of her bed, to convince her to obey him. Beating should only be used by the husband if absolutely necessary to discipline the wife, and is considered as a detestable permissible act (*halal makruh*). The Court of Cassation established that lower courts should evaluate, on an *ad hoc* basis, whether beating is justifiable or not.[17]

The Court of Cassation considered as injury various kinds of behaviour on the part of the husband. It considered the abandonment of the wife by a husband[18] and his abstention from marital intercourse as damage[19] because the wife was 'suspended', neither living with her husband like a proper wife, nor being divorced. The Court's view was that the absence of a husband renders his wife vulnerable to seduction and there is a risk of her committing infidelity. In one case a wife, insulted by her husband who threw her out of the marital home in her nightdress and broke her furniture, was granted a divorce.[20] The Court decided that if the wife returns to the conjugal residence after having suffered damage she is not deprived of her right to claim divorce on the basis of harm.[21] However, sterility of the husband is not enough to justify a divorce because procreation is not the sole purpose of marriage and the absence of children does not prevent a couple from feeling mutual tenderness and compassion.[22]

Wives often refer to several types of harms, including polygamy and its effects, in their request for divorce based on injury. For instance, a wife was granted a divorce for injury because her husband failed to pay her maintenance,[23] confiscated her salary and married another wife without her agreement.[24] Another wife was granted divorce because her husband expelled her from the marital home, entered a polygamous union and stopped fulfilling his financial duties toward her.[25]

A family court granted a divorce to a wife on the grounds of injury because her husband had beaten and insulted her, and accused her of being a liar and a thief.[26]

In another case, a court of first instance in Giza decided to grant a divorce to a wife who had been beaten and insulted by her husband, who married a second wife and stopped providing for her financially.[27] The decision was confirmed by the Cairo Appeal Court. The Mansoura court of first instance granted a divorce to a wife whose husband abandoned her, married another wife and tried to tarnish the first wife's reputation by reporting her to the police.[28] Other grounds of divorce for injury include the non-payment of the dower, abusive behaviour, taking control of the wife's private property, inducing her into prostitution or causing her humiliation. The legislature also provided special grounds for divorce where the husband is imprisoned[29] and where the husband suffers from a serious and incurable defect, if this defect makes life together harmful to the woman.[30] The wife could not, however, invoke this last ground were it present before marriage and she was aware of it, or if such a disease appeared after marriage but she accepted it, expressly or tacitly.[31]

Definition of injury based on social status

The husband's wrong must be such as to make marriage relations between persons of that status impossible. The Court of Cassation repeatedly stated that the criteria was subjective and not objective, and could change according to the environment of the spouses, their level of education and their social milieu.[32] The Court added that adjudication on the substance of the case and the assessment of the criteria was left to the discretion of the judge.[33]

Lower court judges therefore have to decide what kinds of ill-treatment should be considered unbearable and to what kinds of people. The definition therefore relies on the presumption that the ability of women to endure a certain threshold of violence depends on their rank within society. Moderate physical violence could be deemed acceptable for poor or illiterate rural women, on the assumption that violence is widespread and natural in lower social strata, while it would be considered excessive and unacceptable in upper social classes, where wealthier women are well-educated and expected to be accustomed to better treatment.

To assess the level of abuse and violence women can tolerate, judges will take into consideration what they perceive to be the accepted norms of the community in which the spouses live. Their appreciation of the wrong will therefore vary according to their subjective assessment of the environment, the culture, the socio-economic background, the profession and the social status of the couple. Very few cases give a detailed account of this assessment process by the lower court judge.

For instance, in one case the Court of Cassation held that when considering the environment to which the two parties belonged, the lower court judge had correctly characterized as harmful, the behaviour of a husband who assaulted his wife in the street, broke her necklace, soiled her clothes while passers-by congregated to watch what was going on.[34] In another case, the Court of Cassation confirmed a decision of the lower court judge who had considered the attempt by a husband to prevent his wife from entering the house and insulting her in from of two men as damaging because the two spouses came from a respectful family, both enjoyed an advanced level of education, came from a high social status where people are not used to such treatment. This behaviour, the court decided, should be considered as damage to the honour of the wife and a wrong that is not acceptable to people of her status.[35]

In another case, a court of first instance took an opposite view and rejected a request for divorce from a wife who claimed that she felt ashamed because her husband had been jailed. The court argued that the wife belonged to a social stratum where it is not a disgrace for a wife to have her husband in prison. The court noted the fact that the wife had waited six months before applying for divorce: if the husband's conviction had really been shameful for the wife, why had she not sued for divorce immediately?[36] Another court of first instance turned down a request for divorce from a wife who claimed that her husband had beaten her. Although the court heard the testimony of several witnesses who supported the wife's claims, it took the view that as the wife belonged to a lower social class where such behaviour does not constitute a detriment that would make continuing in the marriage impossible, she should not succeed in her claim for divorce.[37]

If a court takes into consideration the social standing of the person harmed when it is assessing prejudice, this may reinforce stereotypes and lead to different standards and discrimination on the basis of class, as well as contradictory rulings and a lack of certainty for women who have been injured.

Burden of proof

The burden of providing evidence of injury rests on the wife's shoulders. The Court of Cassation allows judges to use their discretion when deciding on the veracity of the evidence and does not require them to justify the decisions they take, including those relating to witnesses' testimony and giving precedence to one witness over another.[38]

The burden of proof is very difficult to meet. To substantiate the injury she allegedly suffered, the woman must bring witnesses to court. The Court of Cassation has ruled that the principles of the Hanafi school, and not those of the Maliki school, should be applied to determine whether the witnesses are acceptable.[39] Pursuant to the prevailing opinion in the doctrine of Abu Hanifa, the Court of Cassation requires the testimony of two men, or two women and a man.[40] They must be Muslims,[41] because a non-Muslim cannot testify in support of a Muslim.[42] The testimonies relating to the alleged injury should be first-hand evidence and not hearsay (*tasammu'*) evidence.[43] Testimony about overhearing a marital dispute without witnessing the physical or verbal abuse will not be acceptable as proof. If the wife fails to bring witnesses, her request for a divorce will be turned down.[44]

The need for witnesses represents a huge barrier for wives to obtain divorce on the basis of injury. Physical violence and psychological abuse often take place in the bedroom, far from outsiders. Besides, women may be reluctant to disclose intimate details of their private lives and, in particular, of sexual abuse, and witnesses may be reluctant to testify in court. The Court of Cassation has decided that a wife can establish harm using documentary or other types of evidence, for example documents that prove her husband stole her properties;[45] letters from a father to his son in which he accuses his wife of having betrayed him and of having lost her morals;[46] or the fact that the husband has received a criminal conviction for assault and battery.[47] A medical certificate or a police report can also prove that a husband beat his wife.[48]

Divorce for polygamy

Egyptian law allows a wife to sue for divorce in case of polygamy, if she can prove she suffered a significant wrong or harm because of her husband's new marriage. This provision has been used in Egyptian courts, including the Supreme Constitutional Court.

Evolution of the statutory provisions

In 1979, President Sadat issued a far-reaching reform amending laws No 25/1920 and 25/1929 that had remained unchanged for more than half a century. Among the new provisions introduced was a requirement whereby a husband marrying another wife without the first wife's (or first wives') consent could be considered as harming the first wife, who could be granted automatic divorce by the judge, provided so requested within a year from the day she first knew about his marriage.[49] The simple fact that a husband married another woman was thus presumed harmful to the first wife (or earlier wives), and a wife could obtain a divorce without needing to prove the harm. The explanatory memorandum referred to Maliki and Hanbali precedents, a Qur'anic verse (4: 35) and the saying attributed to the Prophet – 'la darar wa la dirar' (no harm, no injury) – to justify this new provision.

The provision led to heated debate in the press and was challenged as constituting an indirect restriction on polygamy, whereas there should not be a presumption of injury because polygamy is legal and religiously legitimate. Many judges refused to apply the provision and attacked the law as being unconstitutional, considering it to be contrary to the shari'a. The Supreme Constitutional Court had to assess a considerable number of petitions claiming that the law was unconstitutional. Law No 44/1979 was finally declared unconstitutional in 1985, but due to procedural error and not on substantive grounds. The decree had been passed by the President while Parliament was suspended. It was argued now that this procedure could not be resorted to when seeking to amend laws dating back to 1920 and 1929, which had the consequence of invalidating Sadat's decree.[50]

Law No 100/1985, adopted two months after the decision that Law No 44/1979 was unconstitutional, authorized a wife to divorce her husband for polygamy even if the marriage contract did not stipulate that he may not marry another,[51] but required the wife to prove that her husband's remarriage had caused her physical or moral harm of a type that made continued marital life between them difficult.[52] The explanatory memorandum emphasized that the provision did not seek to restrict the husband's right to polygamy, but was intended to provide a remedy for the first wife who was injured by her husband's remarriage. It also referred to the Maliki school, the same *hadith* and the same verse as did the earlier law, as well as to the Hanbali school and the *fiqh* elaborated in Medina.

The new provision removed the presumption of injury. A wife no longer has an automatic right to divorce her polygamous husband, but has to prove that she suffered a physical or moral injury. She has a one-year grace period from the date she first knew of her husband's remarriage to request divorce, unless she has consented explicitly or tacitly.[53]

Although Law No 100/1985 mentions polygamy as a possible source of harm, the situation is close to that which was prevailing under Law No 25/1929: a woman is entitled to sue for divorce for the harm inflicted by her polygamous husband, but the burden of proof lies on her to substantiate the harm suffered. The judge enjoys wide discretion in the evaluation of evidence that is provided by witnesses. The harm must result from the remarriage of the husband and should be of a type that would make continued conjugal relations 'difficult' between people of their status, whereas the condition for divorce for injury is that a continued life together would be 'impossible'. Law No 100 departs from Law No 25 when it states that the wife will lose her right to petition the court for divorce after one year and that the damage may be physical or moral. The appreciation of the damage will depend on the social strata of the spouses. This provision was challenged before the Supreme Constitutional Court on the basis of having violated Article 2 of the Constitution.

The Supreme Constitutional Court rules that divorce for polygamy is constitutional

In 1994 the Supreme Constitutional Court (SCC) refused to considerer that a wife's right to request divorce in case of polygamy had violated the shari'a.[54] A bigamous man, whose first wife had asked for a divorce on this ground, referred this provision to the constitutional judge, asking the Court to declare it unconstitutional as it jeopardized the shari'a right to marry up to four women.

In a ruling based on a basic principle established for the first time in 1993,[55] and systematically repeated in all its decisions dealing with the conformity of laws with Article 2 of the Constitution, the constitutional judge made a distinction between absolute and relative principles of the Islamic shari'a. In his opinion, only the principles 'whose origin and significance are absolute' (*al-ahkam al-shar'iyya al-qat'iyya fi thubutiha wa dalalatiha*), i.e. which represent incontestable Islamic norms, be it because of their source or their meaning, must be applied. They are fixed, they cannot be subject to interpretative reasoning (*ijtihad*) and cannot evolve over time. They represent the fundamental principles and the fixed foundation (*thawabit*) of Islamic Law.

Relative rules (*ahkam zanniyya*), conversely, can evolve over time and in different places, are dynamic, give rise to different interpretations and are adaptable to the nature of, and the changing needs in, society. It is up to the person in authority (*wali al-amr*), i.e. the legislator, to interpret and establish the norms related to such rules, guided by his individual reasoning and in the interest of the shari'a. Such an interpretative effort should be based on reasoning and will not be limited by any previous opinion.[56]

After having referred to this distinction, the SCC argued that whereas the man's right to have more than one wife was guaranteed by a Qur'anic verse, immutable in time and space,[57] polygamy was not obligatory. Moreover, the right to marry up to four women was granted in respect of each individual's needs and its exercise was subordinate to fair and equal treatment of all wives. Law No 100/1985 had not forbidden the practice of polygamy, the SCC argued, which indeed would have violated an absolute principle in the shari'a, but had only referred to objective grounds, taking into consideration the physical and moral suffering of the first wife that would render it impossible to maintain an amicable life between the couple. In addition, the wife's request for divorce was not based merely upon dislike of her husband – she had to prove that she had been harmed by the second marriage – and the judge had a discretionary power to assess the wrong and had to try to effect a reconciliation between the spouses. Accordingly, the SCC refused to consider that the provision had violated Article 2 of the 1971 Constitution.

In 2004 the SCC applied the same distinction when considering the constitutionality of the 2000 *khul'* law.[58] The law makes it possible for a wife to go to court to obtain an automatic dissolution of their marriage, and the judge is without power to turn down the request, even when husband opposes it. A declaration by a wife that she detests living with her husband, that continuation of married life between them has become impossible and that she fears she would transgress the 'limits of God' due to this hatred[59] if she were compelled to remain with him, is sufficient. She neither has to justify her request by proving injury, nor substantiate its accuracy. As compensation for the husband, however, she has to forfeit her alimony (*nafaqa*),[60] her financial compensation (*muta'*),[61] return to him the dower she received at the time of marriage,[62] and give up the deferred part of the dower (*mu'akhkhar al-sadaq*).[63] This procedure, which allows women to buy their way out of the marriage in exchange for financial compensation, was known in Egyptian law prior to 2000. However, at that time the procedure of *khul'* took place before a civil state officer rather than before a judge and was contingent on the husband's express agreement and was a type of amicable separation agreement or joint application for divorce.[64] The revolutionary nature of the 2000 law was the fact that it did not require the agreement of the husband for *khul'*.

In its 2004 decision the SCC declared that *khul'* did not contradict the rules of the shari'a. It stressed that the woman's right to resort to *khul'* and to set herself free in exchange for repudiation figured in a Qur'anic text and was therefore an absolute principle and, as such, uncontestable. However, the details of the procedure to follow for *khul'* had not been provided by the Sacred Text. This led Islamic scholars to give their own interpretations. Some of them held that the husband's agreement was required for the woman to divorce through *khul'*. Others, however, deemed that it unnecessary for the couple to be in agreement. The statutory provision was founded on the Maliki school's authorization for the wife to resort to *khul'* in case of necessity, if she could no longer bear to live with her husband. This was a logical solution, argued the SCC, which in no way contradicted the rules of the shari'a. One cannot force a woman to live with a man. The challenge of unconstitutionality was rejected.

The definition of injury

According to the Court of Cassation, the definition in Law No 100/1985 requires that the harm occasioned by the second marriage be real, not illusory, actual, not imagined and proved, not assumed.[65] If a husband takes another wife, the first wife can request divorce only if she can prove that she suffered such a physical and moral harm that it is difficult to continue cohabitation. The mere hatred she feels toward her husband or her repulsion toward him because of his marriage to another are not sufficient grounds to justify dissolution of the marriage.[66] The purpose behind the second marriage does not need to be legitimate.[67]

The Court of Cassation quashed a ruling by a first instance court that had granted divorce to a wife who claimed she was full of sadness and jealousy and felt depressed because of her husband's marriage to another woman. The Court deemed that these feelings were not sufficient to prove damage that was independent from the marriage itself. Jealousy is a natural feeling between a man's two wives, the Court argued.[68] The mere psychological suffering engendered by the new marriage is not considered as harm within the meaning of the 1985 law.

Even before the laws of 1979 and 1985, a wife could be granted a divorce in a case of polygamy, if she could prove injury within the definition of Article 6 of Law 25/1929, for example, by proving that the husband did not treat his wives in the same way (a condition for polygamy to be valid is that the husband treats all his wives in the same way), desertion by her husband of the conjugal bed, or the cessation of financial provision by the husband.[69] For example, the Court of Cassation confirmed a judgment by a first instance court that had granted a wife divorce on the ground that if polygamy is allowed by the shari'a, the husband has to be fair. In that case, the husband had abandoned his first wife for more than two years and had stopped providing for her financially, which was unfair.[70] A wife who cannot prove that her husband's second marriage has been detrimental to her may request a divorce for injury, on the basis of Article 6 of Law 25/1929.[71] The wife could also be granted a divorce on the ground of the absence of her husband.

A husband taking his new wife to the marital home was considered to constitute a moral and physical harm justifying divorce for polygamy.[72] A wife was also granted a divorce because after marrying again, her husband had abandoned her and stopped providing her with maintenance.[73] In a 1999 decision the Cairo Appeal Court confirmed the decision of the Giza first instance court[74] to divorce a wife because she suffered physical and moral harm due to the second marriage of her husband who expelled her from the matrimonial home in order to house his second wife, stopped providing for her financially, beat and insulted her and repudiated her before taking her back.[75] Judges also granted a divorce to a wife whose husband was refraining from cohabitation and from sexual intercourse after having married another wife;[76] to a woman for abandonment by her husband for more than ten months and for the husband's non-provision of her maintenance and that for her children after his remarriage;[77] and to a wife whose husband had brought his new bride to the marital home after having expelled the earlier wife from it.[78]

Conclusion

If the provisions of Egyptian personal status law are marked by their Islamic inspiration, the Egyptian legislator, supported by judges, has been able to reform Islamic law to proceed with its – limited – adaptation to the modern needs of society and with its improvement of the legal status of women within the family. Lawmakers referred to the shari'a to legitimate the provisions they were adopting and presented their reforms as the products of an internal renovation process legitimized by reference to shari'a principles. To bypass the often rigid rules of Hanafism, the reformers referred to rulings from other schools or reputable authorities, in particular the Maliki *mudhhab*. This enabled the reforms to be presented as taking place within the shari'a and avoided strong attacks from the conservative religious circles.

Personal status law reform in Egypt has however been limited in its scope and constrained by the political context, the survival of patriarchy and the role played by conservative and religious opposition. Experience shows that it is not easy to amend these laws because of resistance by society and conservative religious groups. Amendments to family law are unpopular in the Egyptian patriarchal society and therefore they are politically costly. Although further reforms are needed to improve the status of women within the family, Egyptian women reformists now rather fear for their vested rights after Islamist parties won the 2012 parliamentary and presidential elections. The *khul'* law, in particular, known as one of the 'Suzanne laws', is the target of Islamist groups who attempt to discredit it by associating it with the wife of the ousted president and claiming that these laws were designed to break up Egyptian families and impose Western values.

If the Egyptian legislature has allowed women to obtain a divorce on grounds of various grievances, women's requests for divorce remain subject to the judge's discretion. Judges are an important element in the process of social regulation and in the evolution of family practices. Far from simply being 'the mouth of the law', the judge interprets the legal norms and exercises creative discretion. This is the case even in a field traditionally presented as pertaining to Islamic law, such as personal status law. In the period analysed, Egyptian judges paid little attention to Islamic law and hardly mentioned shari'a norms. When they could not find a provision in the current personal status laws, or in a ruling of the Court of Cassation, they referred to the Hanafi school, although they did so in very few instances.[79] Reference by judges to Islamic law had legislative authorization: Article 3 of Law No 1/2000. As for the SCC, it used different means to limit the place of the shari'a within the Egyptian legal system. Lower judges interpreted injury rather broadly, and wives managed to obtain a divorce for a wide range of harms. Courts are quite open to women and ready to examine their cases with sympathy, but they exercise their discretion on the basis of the social status of the couple. They seem to take social factors more into consideration than religious ones. Their alleged conservatism vis-à-vis women and requests for marriage dissolution might be explained by the fact that, until the beginning of 2007, not one woman sat in Egyptian ordinary courts and the SCC was the only court that included a woman, and she was only nominated in 2003.[80]

Even if judges are not the main obstacle to women's access to divorce, wives face a huge number of social and economic difficulties in using the rights to which they are entitled in divorce matters. The prevailing opinion is still that the family, as the basic unit of society, must be preserved and protected even at the expense of the woman's personal feelings. A wife fighting to break up a marriage will be considered responsible for destroying her home, even if her request is the result of bad treatment inflicted upon her by the husband. She will be stigmatized and sometimes rejected by her own family. Financial difficulties are added to social criticism. Lawsuits involve financial burden, whatever the type of dissolution, and women will face economic difficulties in most cases, in particular, in collecting child support because a great number of ex-husbands do not pay alimony or maintenance and litigation against them continues for years. Most women do not have any independent source of income and will depend on the financial support of their family and relatives in order to survive. A faithful assessment of access to judicial divorce for injury and polygamy must take all of these issues into consideration.

Notes

1 This article deals only with personal status law for Muslims. For personal status law for non-Muslims see Bernard-Maugiron 2011. Cases from the Court of Cassation, the Supreme Constitutional Court, appeal courts, courts of first instance (until 2004) and family courts (after 2004) were looked at. Most of the cases were after after the 1970s.

2 The legislature put up many barriers to repudiation. However, it neither went as far as abolishing it, nor demanded that the repudiation be pronounced before the judge and justified by legitimate grounds. A simple, blame-free, unilateral declaration by the husband before a civil servant remains enough to break spousal bonds.

3 Law No 25 of 1920 regarding Maintenance and some Questions of Personal Status and Law No. 25 of 1929 regarding certain Personal Status Provisions.

4 Art. 3 of Law No 1 of 2000 that reasserted Art. 280 of the 1931 Sharia Courts Regulations, repealed by that same law.

5 Shari'a courts that ruled in Muslim personal status matters were abolished by Laws No 461 and No 462 of 1955 and their powers transferred to the ordinary courts in which there are judges dealing specifically with personal status cases.

6 Law No 10 of 2004 Establishing Family Courts. Family courts were annexed to the more than 200 summary courts and eight appeal courts in which there are judges dealing specifically with personal status cases.

7 Art. 20 of Law No 1 of 2000.

8 Law No 10 of 2004, Art. 14. The explanatory memorandum of the law justified this measure by the special nature of personal status cases and the necessity to rule in as short a time period as possible in order to fix the legal status of some of the most important questions regarding individuals and the family. Only the public prosecution is allowed to bring a personal status case before the Court of Cassation, and only on certain conditions.

9 On the basis of the predominant view in the Hanafi school, the Court of Cassation gives the husband one year to consummate the marriage before undertaking an investigation. See for instance, Court of Cassation, No 20/46, 14 December 1977. To save time and protect privacy, some women prefer to file a request for divorce for injury instead of sexual incapacity.

10 The explanatory memorandum to Law No 25 of 1929 was published with the law itself and can be found in al-Chazli, 1987.

11 Cassation, No 23/57, 28 June 1988, or Cassation, No 369/68, 9 March 2002.

12 See Family Court of Shubra, No 256/2008, 29 July 2008, which refers to Cassation No 99/59, 5 December 1991 and Family Court of Badrashin, No 465/2006, 31 May 2007, which refers to Cassation, No 337/67, 13 October 2001.

13 Cassation, No 15/47, 2 April 1980.

14 Cassation, No 23/57, 28 June 1981, or Giza First Instance Court, No 3322/2000, 29 January 2001, that refers to the case law of the Court of Cassation with regard to injury.

15 Cassation, No 19/48, 21 February 1979.

16 Cassation, No 640/66, 11 June 2001, or Cassation, No 163/59, 19 May 1992, where the Court stated that injury must be willful; and Cassation, No 19/48, 21 February 1979, where the Court

decided, on the basis of the Maliki school, that the wife was injured even if the husband did not intend to hurt her by abandoning her.

17 Cassation, No 85/66, 10 February 2001.

18 Absence of the husband is considered as a special ground for divorce by Arts 12 and 13 of Law No. 25 of 1929, out of concern for the abandoned wife's honour and chastity. The wife can claim divorce on that ground if the husband's absence is longer than a year without any justified excuse, even if he has left goods or investments that can be sold to provide money for maintenance, or property that she could rent, but the judge shall grant divorce if after a month the husband has not resumed maintenance. The explanatory memorandum defines absence of the husband as his residence in a town other than that of the matrimonial residence, and considers travel for the purpose of study or trade justifiable, as is lack of communication if there are other reasons why the husband cannot be in touch. Absence within the meaning of Art. 6 of Law No. 25 of 1929 does not require that the residence of the husband be in a different city.

19 Cassation, No 50/52, 28 June 1983, or Cassation, No 92/58, 18 December 1990.

20 Port Saïd First Instance Court, No 127/1990, 22 December 1992, confirmed by Cassation, No 398/63, 27 January 1998.

21 Cassation, No 82/63, 28 January 1997.

22 Cassation, No 357/63, 29 December 1997.

23 The husband has an obligation to financially support his wife for the duration of the marriage, even if she has personal resources. Failure to provide maintenance is considered as a special ground for divorce by Art. 4 of Law No. 25 of 1920: if the husband proves his insolvency, the judge shall grant him a period not exceeding one month after which, if he fails to pay maintenance, divorce shall be granted. The husband then retains the right to reinstate his wife during the waiting period if he pays the arrears of maintenance (Art. 6).

24 South Cairo First Instance Court, No 1193/1919, 31 December 1992.

25 Tanta Appeal Court, No 233/26, 7 February 1994, as confirmed by Cassation, No 175/64, 21stApril 1998.

26 Family Court of al-Badrashin, No 806/2006, 28 June 2007.

27 Giza Court of First Instance, No 561/97, 25 August 1997.

28 Mansoura First Instance Court, No 1115/1983, 31st March 1985.

29 The wife can also get a divorce if her husband has been condemned to jail for more than three years, even if he has property that can be rented or sold and from which she could get maintenance. She can ask for divorce after at least one year of separation (Law No. 25 of 1929, Art. 14).

30 The Court of Cassation decided that the list of defects enumerated in Article 9 was not exhaustive. Cassation, No 13/44, 11 February 1976.

31 Law No. 25 of 1920, Art. 9.

32 Cassation, 665/68, 9 March 2002. See also Cassation, No 135/63, 17 March 1997.

33 Cassation, No 96/56, 24 January 1989.

34 Cassation, No 5/46, 9 November 1977.

35 Cassation, No 19/44, 24 March 1976.

36 Sayyida Court, No 355/33, quoted in Ahmed Nasr Al-Guindi, *Mabadi al-Qada fi-l-ahwal al-shakhsiyya*, p. 446.

37 South Cairo Court of First Instance, 1973. Full citation not available.

38 Cassation, No 133/64, 13 April 1998.

39 Cassation, No 15/47, 2 April 1980. In their decisions, lower court judges regularly refer to decisions of the Court of Cassation that establish this principle. Giza Court, No 3322/2000, 29 January 2011, referring to Cassation, No 62/63, 24 February 1997.

40 Cassation, No 15/47, 2 April 1980. See also, Family Court of Badrashin, No 1070/2006, 31 January 2008, where the court refused to grant divorce because only two women had been present when the husband was beating and insulting his wife.

41 Cassation, No 16/38, 5 June 1974, where the request for divorce was rejected because the witnesses were non-Muslim Austrians.

42 Cassation, No 16/38, 5 June 1974.

43 Cassation, No 11/47, 25 April 1979. In Cassation, No 509/65, 26 June 2000, the court refused to grant divorce because the two witnesses had described actions that the wife claimed had taken place but which they had not seen and heard themselves. See also, Family Court of Shubra, No 196/2008, 2 August 2008, where the testimonies did not corroborate her statements.

44 See Shubra Family Court, No 162/2008, where the wife did not bring witnesses to testify that her husband had abandoned her for five years.

45 Cassation, No 11/47, 25 April 1979.

46 Cassation, No 202/62, 25 March 1996.

47 Cassation, No 101/64, 28 December 1998, or Cassation, No 60/8, 14 December 1939.

48 Giza First Instance Court, No 3322/2000, 29 January 2001.

49 Art. 6 bis 1§2 added to Law No 25 of 1929.

50 Supreme Constitutional Court, No 28, 24 May 1985.

51 Spouses can agree on stipulations to add to their marriage contract at the time of marriage, in particular, the right of the wife to repudiate herself whenever she wants or in specific circumstances, for instance, if her husband engages in polygamy. She will retain her financial rights.

52 Law No 25 of 1929, Art. 11 bis 1, as added by Law No 100 of 1985.

53 Any new marriage must be registered and the previous wife must be notified by the public notary. If the husband is already married, he must state the name of his wife and her place of domicile. If the new wife did not know that he was already married, she is entitled to apply for divorce.

54 Supreme Constitutional Court, No 35/9, 14 August 1994.

55 Supreme Constitutional Court, No 7/8, 15 May 1993.

56 Supreme Constitutional Court, No 29/11, 26 March 1994.

57 Sura IV, verse 3.

58 Law No 1 of 2000 Concerning some Rules and Procedures of Litigation in Matters of Personal Status, Art. 20.

59 The law drew its terminology from Surat *al-Baqara* (The Cow), verse 229.

60 This alimony is paid for a maximum of one year after the divorce is issued; see Law No. 25 of 1929, Arts 17 and 18. The alimony is due to the wife, whether the marriage ended by means of repudiation or by a judicial decision. It must cover her food, clothing, housing and medical expenses.

61 Since 1985 (Art. 18 bis 1), the wife is entitled to financial compensation (*muta'*), the amount of which should not be less than two years of maintenance, and should be evaluated according to the husband's financial means, the circumstances of the divorce and the length of marriage. This compensation is only due if the marriage was broken without the wife's consent and without her being responsible for the breakdown. The wife can apply for *muta'* whether the marriage was dissolved through repudiation or judicial divorce (Cassation, No 40/54, 26 May 1987).

62 The husband-groom must pay his bride a dowry – an amount of money that is totally hers. In Egypt the custom is to divide the dowry in two parts; the first part is paid at the time of marriage, while the second is paid when the marriage is dissolved (upon the husband's death or divorce).

63 Other legal rights enjoyed by women – such as her right to custody of the children and to the marital house during the period of custody – were not reappraised by the judges (Law No 1 of 2000, Art. 20 para. 3).

64 Cassation, 28 October 1937, which *defines khul'* as an agreement to obtain final separation in exchange for a financial compensation paid to the husband.

65 Cassation, No 256/61, 8 January 1996.

66 Cassation, No 465/68, 18 March 2002.

67 Cassation, No 225/59, 24 November 1992.

68 Cassation, No 256/61, 8 January 1996.

69 Courts have allowed wives to request both divorce for injury and divorce for polygamy. See Badrashin Family Court, No 1070/2006, 31 January 2008, where the two applications were included in the same claim.

70 Cassation, No 34/48, 13 June 1979.

71 Cassation, No 341/63, 27 October 1997. The court allows wives to request divorce for injury if their request for divorce for polygamy has failed (Cassation, No 553/65, 20 November 2000).

72 Cassation, No 129/59, 5 March 1991.
73 Cassation, No 504/65, 30 October 2000, and Cassation, No 422/64, 29 September 1998.
74 Giza First Instance Court, No 281/1998, 20 September 1998.
75 Cairo Court of Appeal, No 1133/110, 4 February 1999.
76 Cassation, No 114/95, 24 March 1992.
77 Cassation, No 212/63, 5 January 1998.
78 Cairo Court of Appeal, 4 February 1999.
79 For example, Egyptian judges referred to the Hanafi school to allow divorce because of the husband's impotence, to fix the amount of the dower and the way it should be paid, to recognize the wife's right to consent to marriage if she is of majority age, to determine impediments to marriage, and to affirm the existence of the wife's obligation of obedience.
80 The lack of female representation in courts has no legal basis. In fact, neither the Judicial Authority Law nor the State Council Law establishes any discrimination based on gender in the recruitment of judges. It has turned out that, in practice, no woman had ever passed the recruitment examination … In the beginning of 2007, after years of struggle by feminist groups and due to international pressure, 30 women were finally appointed as judges in the ordinary judiciary.

Bibliography

Bernard-Maugiron, N. (2007) 'The judicial construction of the facts and the law. The Egyptian Supreme Constitutional Court and the constitutionality of the law on the khul', in B. Dupret *et al.* (ed.), *Narratives of Truth in Islamic Law*, Cairo and London: CEDEJ-I.B. Tauris.

——(ed.) (2008) *Judges and Political Reform in Egypt*, Cairo: American University in Cairo Press.

——(2011) 'Divorce and remarriage of orthodox Copts in Egypt: the 2008 state council ruling and the amendment of the 1938 personal status regulations', *Islamic Law and Society*, 18(3–4): 356–86.

Bernard-Maugiron, N. and Dupret, B. (1999) 'Les principes de la *shari'a* sont la source principale de la législation. La Haute Cour constitutionnelle et la référence à la loi islamique', *Égypte-Monde arabe*, 2: 107–25.

——(2008) 'Breaking-off the family: divorce in Egyptian law and practice', *Hawwa*, 6: 52–74.

Chazli, Y. Al- (1987) *Personal Status Laws for Muslims with the Explanatory Memorandums*, Part 1, al-Maktaba al-Qanuniyya (in Arabic).

Chemais, A. (2004) 'Divorced from justice: women's unequal access to divorce in Egypt', *Human Rights Watch Report 16.*

Dupret, B. (1995) 'La shari'a comme référent législatif: du droit positif à l'anthropologie du droit', *Revue interdisciplinaire d'études juridiques*, 34: 99–153.

——(2006) 'The practice of judging: the Egyptian judiciary at work in a personal status case', in K.M. Masud, R. Peters and D.S. Powers (eds), *Dispensing Justice in Islam. Qadis and their judgements*, Leiden: Brill.

——(2007) 'What is Islamic law? A praxiological answer and an Egyptian case study', *Theory, Culture and Society*, 24(2): 79–100.

El-Alami, D. (2001) 'Remedy or device? The system of *khul'* and the effects of its incorporation into Egyptian personal status law', *Yearbook of Islamic and Middle Eastern Law*, 6: 134–39.

Fawzy, E. (2004) 'Muslim personal status law in Egypt: the current situation and possibilities of reform through internal initiative', in L. Welchman (ed.), *Women's Rights and Islamic Family Law: Perspectives on Reform*, London: Zed Books.

Guindi, A.N. Al- (1992) *Mabadi al-Qada fi-l-ahwal al-shakhsiyya*, Cairo: al-Qahira al-haditha lil-taba'a.

Lombardi, C.B. (1998) 'Islamic law as a source of constitutional law in Egypt: the constitutionalization of the shari'a in a modern Arab state', *Columbia Journal of Transnational Law*, 37: 81–123.

Naveh, E. (2001) 'The tort of injury and dissolution of marriage at the wife's initiative in Egyptian Mahkama al-Naqd rulings', *Islamic Law and Society*, 9(1): 16–41.

Shaham, R. (1994) 'Judicial divorce at the wife's initiative: the shari'a courts of Egypt, 1920–55', *Islamic Law and Society*, 1(2): 217–57.

Sharmani, M. Al- (2008) 'Recent reforms in personal status laws and women's empowerment. Family courts in Egypt', AUC Social Research Center. Available online at www.pathwaysofempowerment. org/Familycourts.pdf (accessed 15 September 2012).

Singerman, D. (2005) 'Rewriting divorce in Egypt: reclaiming Islam, legal activism and coalition politics', in R. Hefner (ed.), *Remaking Muslim Politics: pluralism, contestation, democratization*, Princeton, NJ: Princeton University Press.

Sonneveld, N. (2007) 'The *khul'* law of 2000: the public debate', unpublished PhD thesis, ISIM, Leiden
——(2011) 'Four years of *khul'* in Egypt: the practice of the courts and daily life', in M. Badran (ed.), *Gender and Islam in Africa*, Palo Alto, CA: Stanford University Press.

Voorhoeve, M. (ed.), (2012) *Family Law in Islam: Divorce, Marriage and Women in the Muslim world*, London and New York: I.B. Tauris.

Welchman, L. (2004) 'Egypt: new deal on divorce', *International Survey of Family Law*: 123–42.
——2007) *Women and Muslim Family Laws in Arab States: a Comparative Overview of Textual Development and advocacy*, Amsterdam: Amsterdam University Press.

7 The Potential Within

Adjudications on *shiqaq* (discord) divorce by Moroccan judges

Fatima Sadiqi

Introduction

Linguistically, the Arabic word *ijtihad* means 'striving, exerting'. Classical Muslim Sunni jurists transposed this meaning to the realm of Islamic jurisprudence and defined *ijtihad* as the exertion of the maximum 'mental energy' to first comprehend and then apply *fiqh* (legal theory) with the aim of discovering the 'law of God' (Sell, 1907; Hallaq, 1984; Karamali, Ali and Dunne, 1994). This 'law of God' is shari'a, defined as the 'all-encompassing law of Islam' that is based on the Qur'an (Muslim's holy book), the Sunna (Prophet Muhammad's sayings and behaviour) and *ijtihad* (Coulson 1964). This complex relationship between shari'a, *fiqh* and *ijtihad* is not stagnant, as Muslim societies constantly change over time and the mutability of shari'a, in particular, has been a point of contention for many centuries, resulting in a rich tradition of legal theory and *ijtihad* in Islam. A characteristic of classical Muslim Sunni jurisprudence is that it reserves the right of *ijtihad* to a few 'ulama' (religious scholars) alone, who are considered well versed in shari'a (divine law) and *fiqh* (human legal theorization).

As for modern jurists, they are in two main categories: (i) conservatives who, while accepting reform and *ijtihad*, tend to prefer classical jurisprudence, and (ii) modernists who while accepting classical jurisprudence as fundamental, refer more to *maqasid al-shari'a* (the goals or spirit of shari'a) in their practice of *ijtihad*. The latter category of jurists may go beyond *fiqh* and consider the sociological, psychological and even human rights aspects of the issues at hand. The 2004 Moroccan Family Law is a good example of modernist *ijtihad* whereby, on the recommendation of the Royal Commission (composed of 'ulama', sociologists, medical doctors and other lay figures and subject to the arbitration of the king in his capacity as *Amir al-mu'minin*), it allows judges and magistrates to practice *ijtihad* in accordance with the foundational principles of the Sunni Maliki school, the various changes that Moroccan society is undergoing, as well as the relevant international conventions that Morocco has ratified.

A good amount of research has been conducted on the influences of modern *ijtihad* on Moroccan family law (see Mernissi 1984; Mir-Hosseini 1993; Sadiqi and Ennaji 2006; Badran 2008; and Ennaji 2011). For example, the fact that both the husband and wife are heads of the family and that both of them can initiate and obtain a legal divorce is a consequence of interpreting *ijtihad* as a flexible instrument that responds to the sociocultural context in which it is used. However, serious work on the practice itself rather than the theory of *ijtihad* used in Moroccan family law is rather scarce. In other words, the issue of how magistrates and judges apply *ijtihad* in Moroccan court adjudications is still poorly studied and under-theorized. This shortfall can be explained: the application of *ijtihad* in courts of law is far from being a straightforward application of *fiqh* or shari'a because, on the one hand, it has to take into consideration the overall political, social and psychological contexts surrounding specific cases and, on the other hand, it often clashes with deeply ingrained attitudes and accepted cultural dogmas transformed into values. This insufficiency needs to be addressed because *ijtihad* in action (where it is most needed) is the ultimate test for *ijtihad* in theory.

In this chapter, I will address *ijtihad* in practice through an analysis of judges' adjudications in five cases of divorce based on discord (*shiqaq*) delivered between 2006 and 2012, i.e. in implementation of the 2004 Family Law. I have used data gathered through personal research and from published works and reports on the topic. The chapter is structured into three sections: (i) the genesis of *ijtihad* in Moroccan family law, (ii) *ijtihad* in practice, i.e. specific cases, and (iii) a synthesis. The overarching aim of this chapter is twofold: first to participate in emerging debates on the practice of *ijtihad* in Muslim societies and second, to highlight the potential that *ijtihad* has as a legal tool, not only with respect to further reform of legal texts in the light of constantly evolving Muslim societies, but also by narrowing the wide gap between the spirit of Islam and its everyday implementation in a rapidly changing world.

The genesis of *ijtihad* in Moroccan family law

The codification of family law in Muslim societies is a social and political undertaking that regulates the lives of citizens from birth to death and carries powerful symbolic meanings (Hallaq 1984; Charrad 2001; Buskens 2003). Understanding the conception and perception of the 2004 Moroccan Family Law in a space-based patriarchy is fundamental for the purpose of gaining insight into Islam and politics in the public sphere of authority, and the status of women in and outside the home.

The genesis of *ijtihad* in Moroccan family law had three main phases: 1957–58, 1993 and 2004. The period 1957–58 witnessed the first codification of the *Mudawwanat al-ahwal al-Shakhsiyyat* or *Moudawana* (Personal Status Code). During this period, a commission of ten male '*ulama*' and jurists, in collaboration with the Ministry of Justice and the royal court, reformulated the precepts of classical Maliki jurisprudence into a modern legal code (Taoufik 1993).[1] Five concepts of *ijtihad* characterize this initial codification of the law: (i) it replaced the practice of *taqlid* (imitation) that jurists applied during colonization, (ii) it replaced Berber Customary Law[2] that was used in some rural parts of Morocco, (iii) it was presented as an Islamic law based on a specific school of *fiqh*, the Maliki school, (iv) it was crafted as stemming from the political and religious authority of the monarch, in his capacity as *Amir al-Muminin*,[3] and (v) it was conceived and engineered as a symbol of national unity, identity and modernity.

A closer look at these concepts of *ijtihad* reveals that they targeted more the form than the substance of the law. For example, by specifying that 'for all matters not covered by this text reference should be made to *al-rajih* (probable), *al mashur* (common) or *al-'amal bihi* (precedent) in the school of Malik', the code defined the classical school of jurisprudence as a fundamental legal reference. This specification crippled the application of *ijtihad*, especially in matters where it was needed: tutorship in marriage (*wilaya*), marriage age, unilateral divorce, and polygamy. The law articles referring to these matters in the first Code were heavily biased against women: for example, a father could oblige his daughter to marry a man of his choice and could give her in marriage at the age of 15 or under. Further, a husband could unilaterally repudiate his wife and marry up to four wives at any one time without the consent of a judge. Indeed, the first codification of family law honed male supremacy by making the husband the sole head of the family and its provider, and relegating the wife's rights to maintenance (*al-qiwama*) in return for obedience (*ta'a*) to her husband.[4]

The Code was legally announced through a royal decree (*dahir*) and sanctioned by the then King Mohamed V, thus becoming a 'sacred' text. Indeed, the overall post-independence historical and sociopolitical climate within which the first Code was drafted and the quasi-absence of a critical mass of educated women facilitated the call for unity among conservatives and modernists, which fact increased the sacrality of the Code and made any resistance to it pointless. However, in the following decades and with the mass education of urban women, this Code started to generate severe criticism as it was detrimental to women's rights and, as such, was a point of contention for the Moroccan feminist movement, with its three sections (academic, activist and political).

The second phase in the genesis of Moroccan family law is May 1993, when *ijtihad* was used to introduce some minor reforms to the Code. This reform was preceded by no less than six failed attempts to amend the Code: 1965, 1970, 1974, 1979, 1981 and 1982.[5] The success of the 1993 reforms was mainly due to the heated sociopolitical context. At the beginning of the 1990s there was a strong and loud feminist movement and human rights civil society, opposed by an equally strong and loud conservative Islamic movement. This opposition culminated in the March 1992 One Million Signature Campaign (led by l'Union de l'Action Féminine) to reform the Code. In September 1992, the king – in his capacity as arbitrator between the two opposing camps – summoned representatives of women's organizations to the royal palace and addressed them in a speech where he underlined the need to use *ijtihad* to revise the Code in an attempt to avoid its political instrumentalization. A commission of 21 members (including one woman) was set up one month later with the task of preparing a draft of a new Code. In May 1993 a selected number of women's rights organizations joined the commission to finalize the draft. In September 1993, King Hassan II announced the new reforms in the form of a royal decree. These reforms attest to the fact that some *ijtihad* was used: a man could divorce only with a court order and had to pay compensation to his divorcee, and a man could marry a second wife only with the consent of the first one.

It is true that these reforms, like the first ones, targeted the form and not the substance of the law, but they were crucial on a symbolic level as they removed the sacrality of the Code and opened the road for more reforms, which is, after all, a major goal of *ijtihad*. Indeed, from 1993 to 2004, loud and vociferous ideological turmoil – the first of its kind in Moroccan history – opposed the modernists and the conservatives (now including Islamists as well as traditionalists) and continued to focus on the Personal Status Code. In 1998 the first-ever socialist-led government came up with a 'plan'[6] to include women in development projects and the reform of the Code. This plan further polarized public opinion, and tension between the women's movement and the Islamists intensified. This ideological escalation culminated in the 2000 showdown of marches that divided Morocco into two camps, with the majority leaning towards the conservative camp.[7] The death of Hassan II and the accession of a new king somehow facilitated the setting up of a new 16-member (thirteen Islamic scholars, two of whom were progressive, and three women) commission in April 2001 with the aim of reforming the Code. However, it was only in October 2003, and following dramatic events, that new substantial reforms were announced by the king in parliament.

The third phase

The 16 May 2003 unprecedented bombings in Casablanca, in which 44 Moroccans and non-Moroccans were killed at the hands of Islamist extremists, created change. Often described in the various local media as a 'slap in the face', the bombings calmed the heated ideological debates and awakened the general public to the looming danger of Islamist extremism. Women, backed by human rights organizations, were among the first to take to the streets to denounce Islamist extremism and call for the acceleration of reforms. As a follow-up, reform discussions in the previously established commission resumed and, in September 2003, a draft of the new reforms was presented to the king. This draft was turned into a bill submitted to parliament in October 2003. Extensive debates ensued before the reforms were unanimously approved and made official in February 2004.

The new Moroccan Family Law is the result of 'serious' *ijtihad* that targeted both the form and the substance of the law for the first time in the history of Morocco. The main changes introduced by the law are the following: (i) the new name 'Family Law', which includes wives, husbands and children, (ii) the improvement of the traditional Maliki *fiqh* language and concepts, through the inscription of equality in the rhetoric of the text, (iii) the announcement of the law in parliament, and (iv) the definition of marriage as an equal partnership between spouses with equal responsibility for the family. The new law also secured several important rights for Moroccan women, including the right to self-guardianship, the right to divorce and the right to child custody. It also placed new restrictions on polygamy, raised the legal age from 15 to 18 and made sexual harassment punishable by law. Most importantly, it introduced divorce for discord (*shiqaq*).

In the previous Personal Status Code, a woman could file for judicial divorce in the following cases: failure by the husband to provide for the family, a husband's incapacitating illness, his continuous violence, his absence for more than one year without any reasonable motive, and neglect of marital duties. However, the problem resided in the difficulty of proving any of these grounds for divorce, in addition to the lack of legal facilitating mechanisms, which rendered the legal processes of divorce almost impossible.

In the new Family Law, the provisions concerning divorce have improved considerably with the introduction of divorce by *shiqaq*, i.e. the possibility for women to sue for divorce motivated by *shiqaq*; and new and easier procedures for all kinds of divorce have been introduced: delays in legal enforcement by the court have now narrowed, the amount of maintenance that the wife receives has increased and women can now file for judicial divorce if the husband fails to respect the conditions stipulated in the marriage contract. These new provisions replace the previous tedious evidence that women were required to provide in order to obtain a divorce. As these changes are based on new interpretations of the Qur'an, they also include the institutionalization of reconciliation through two mediators (one from each of the two families) before the conclusion of a divorce. The stipulation prescribing that the judge can reconcile the spouses has widened judges' potential to manoeuvre, especially when children are involved. Of course, other factors enter into play: the social status of the wife, her level of education, her geographical origin (urban or rural), etc. Thus, reconciliation works more in rural than in urban areas due to the relatively greater family and social pressure on rural women.

These reforms constitute a modern re-evaluation of women's legal rights and their role in society and grant judges and magistrates greater discretion. They introduce new rights for Moroccan women and constitute a clear departure from the two previous Personal Status Codes while referring to various elements of Islamic law, primarily Qur'anic verses, *hadiths*, and selective elements of *fiqh*. These developments were made possible by the political will of the king and by the efforts of women's rights organizations to use jurisprudential arguments to back their vision. For Mir-Hosseini, the new Moroccan Family Law is 'the most substantive and radical reform of family law achieved by women's activism in any Muslim country' (2007: 1500).

This brief account of the genesis of *ijtihad* in Moroccan family law illustrates that there has been continuity of *ijtihad* in contemporary Morocco, and that *ijtihad* is indeed a powerful tool of change in the legal system. The question that arises at this juncture is: does *ijtihad* allow change on the ground where it matters? It is true that a gap always exists between legal theory and implementation (the theoretical gap), but for how long will the gap exist, granted that gap-filling crucially depends on extra-legal factors such as social and political dynamics? These issues will be addressed in the rest of this chapter.

Ijtihad in practice: specific cases

What I mean by '*ijtihad* in practice' is *ijtihad* as actually applied by judges in court. This type of *ijtihad* is obviously different from *ijtihad* in theory as it is determined by factors such as the personality characteristics of the judge, the setting, and the particular cases he or she addresses. I have selected five cases where women filed for *shiqaq* divorce and where the adjudication of each case provides an example of *ijtihad*. In each of these cases, *ijtihad* was mentioned specifically by the judge who often drew expressly on both the Qur'anic text and on general Islamic principles to justify his/her decision. The first three cases are taken from my own 2009 fieldwork in the region of Fez-Boulmane and the last two from Zeidguy's (2007) fieldwork. I will start by illustrating the cases.

Case number 1 (6 October 2010, File Number 75/135/02, Fez main tribunal)

A relatively young woman living in the Netherlands and whose husband lives in Fez, Morocco filed for *shiqaq* divorce. According to the woman, one of the conditions of her marriage was that her husband was to join her in the Netherlands shortly after their wedding ceremony. However, this never materialized; instead, the husband wanted the reverse: i.e. for his wife to return to Morocco. This tension lasted for four years. The wife stated that if she went back to Morocco she would lose hard-won rights for her and for her children. She was visibly shaken and in tears. When asked by the judge, she stated that she declined any rights arising out of her marriage and that all she wanted was divorce.

Case number 2 (2 November 2010, File Number 75/219/02, Fez main tribunal):

A woman filed for *shiqaq* divorce, underlining the fact that she declined all the rights that she had gained from her marriage. Her main reason for approaching the court was continuous violence perpetrated against her by her husband. She accused him of mistreating and insulting her, then completely neglecting her and her two children, and finally beating her in front of her children. She repeated several times that her life with her husband had become impossible. When the judge summoned the husband and asked him about his opinion, he said that he wanted MAD50,000 (roughly US$5,000) as compensation for his wife seeking recourse to *shiqaq*, that he was very attached to his family and children and that he wanted to continue living with them.

Case number 3 (21 November 2010, File Number 75/221/02, Fez main tribunal)

A man filed for divorce from his wife. He accused her of running away with their three daughters (aged 2, 4 and 6) and settling down in France with them. According to the husband, the wife refused to go back to Morocco. He claimed MAD800 (approximately US$80) for each day of absence, commencing the day she left home. As for the wife, she declared that during her nine years of marriage she noticed that her husband had gradually changed from a peaceful to a violent man. She also said that he failed to secure a house for the family, and added that she left for France because her own parents and two brothers lived there. According to her, she ran away with the children because she felt that their future was not guaranteed if she stayed in Morocco, especially with such an unpredictable husband. She also mentioned that she suffered extreme physical and mental violence at the hands of her husband and that she wanted a divorce. For her, running away was a sacrifice that she was making for the sake of her children. All these allegations were refuted by the husband who accused his parents-in-law of instigating the divorce.

Case number 4 (17 February 2005, File Number 32/277/04, Rabat main tribunal)

A woman filed for *shiqaq* divorce. She lived in the US and her husband in Morocco. Neither of them was willing to join the other. The woman highlighted the fact that her marriage was becoming impossible as emotional attachment and cohabitation were precluded by the situation. Their marriage could not fulfil its legitimate objectives as it had become a source of detriment to them both. The husband accepted the wife's petition.

Case number 5 (31 March 2005, File Number 32/422/04, Rabat main tribunal)

A woman living in France filed for *shiqaq* divorce from her husband. The reason for the petition was that upon her marriage in Morocco she was to send all the necessary documents facilitating her husband's emigration to live with her. However she could not obtain what she wanted in spite of the large sums of money spent and in spite of her frustration and ensuing moral suffering. She also mentioned that her husband mistreated her, that he had not provided a home for them to live in and that he did not help her financially. During the reconciliation session, where the husband was absent in spite of the fact that he was summoned by the tribunal, the wife reiterated her accusations and added that life together with her husband had become impossible due to the deep conflicts that tore them apart, such as a lack of gratitude on the part of her husband in spite of all of her efforts to bring him to France. She underlined that she declined any rights arising out of marriage and that all she wanted was divorce.

Preliminary information on the cases

The preliminary information on all the above five cases can be summarized as follows (i) the court's efforts to achieve reconciliation failed, (ii) the women declined the rights arising out of their marriage, and (iii) the women were granted a divorce. It is also important to note that while the last two cases took place in Rabat (the capital) the first three cases originated in Fez (a rather conservative city). I chose the five cases because they share one common denominator: they involve migration, a recent but fast spreading phenomenon in Morocco.

The fact that in all the cases the court's efforts at reconciliation failed shows that the women were determined to divorce, and the fact that in all the five cases the women declined their rights arising out of their marriage despite the legal guarantees awarded to them[8] shows the extent to which women are subject to social pressure. It should be noted that it is not easy for women to file for divorce as whatever the result, they will lose socially (Sadiqi 2003). More importantly, from the perspective of this chapter, is the fact that in all the five cases the women were granted divorce, which shows the power of the judge in instrumentalizing *ijtihad*. Granting divorce in cases like the above would have been almost impossible before the 2004 Family Law. What then are the main aspects of this instrumentalization?

First, in all five cases the judge had recourse to *ijtihad* and referred to the spirit, rather than the letter, of the sacred texts (the Qur'an and the *hadiths*). For example, in Case 2, the judge prioritized the interests of the wife by safeguarding her rights in the Netherlands that only divorce could guarantee. This was a bold decision on the part of the judge because the husband wanted his wife to return to Morocco. Before the new law, such a wish on the part of the husband would have been amply sufficient to defeat the wife's petition for divorce. Likewise, it is very significant that the reason for divorce was the fact that the wife lived away from the husband, rather than the husband living away from the wife, because the usual practice is that a wife follows her husband and is expected to even relinquish her job to do so. It is important to note that in Case 4 the judge went to the extent of quoting the wife's lawyer who stated that the meaning of the term *shiqaq* is 'large' and may include any situation that renders the survival of marriage difficult and that there is no worse *shiqaq* than the absence of cohabitation between the spouses (Zeidguy 2007). Although in this particular case the husband accepted his wife's petition for divorce, it is remarkable that the judge pronounced the divorce in accordance with the wife's, not the husband's, wishes. Interestingly, in most cases the judges invoked the notions of affection, clemency and mutual respect as criteria for a solid marriage and cited discord and conflict as grounds for divorce. They often quoted the Qur'anic verse: *wa laa tumsikuuhunna dararan lita'tadou* (Don't keep them [women] if they are harmed as you will then wrong them). For example, in Case 3 one would expect the judge to side with the husband, yet he chose to take into consideration the situation of the wife who regarded the continuation of her marriage as impossible. He rejected the husband's demands and granted divorce on the basis of the argument that the new Family Law provides *shiqaq* as an option for both spouses and that in this particular case the rights of the wife would be violated if she remained married.

Along with prioritizing affection, clemency and mutual respect as part of the spirit of shari'a, it transpires from the five cases that, in the eyes of the judges, the bottom line is the protection of family stability whenever it is threatened. This is based on the fact that marriage, according to the new Family Law, is founded on 'mutual consent in view of establishing a legal and durable union between and a man and a woman' (Article 70).

This attitude is reinforced when children are involved. Hence, the judges seem to seek what they refer to as *aqal darar*, the least harm, in so far as family cohesion and the protection of children are concerned, which is another provision of the 2004 Family Law. For example, in Case 4, the judge considered geographical distance between the spouses and the possible consequences thereof as being of greater harm than divorce.

According to Zeidguy (2007), the main factors judges use in their decisions on *shiqaq* divorce depend on their own understanding and appreciation of the term itself. According to the cases that I studied, a plethora of reasons may lead to *shiqaq* divorce within the provisions of the new Family Law. Examples of these reasons include: the failure by the husband to abide by his marriage obligations especially with regard to financial maintenance of the family; the abandonment or ill treatment of the wife; the impossibility of cohabitation (due to incompatibility of personalities, divergence in thought, traditions and way of life, geographical distance, adultery); the difficult temperament of the husband; the repeated *li'an* imprecations by the husband; the abduction of children and pressure on the mother to renounce her rights to her children; the expulsion of the wife with her children and removal of all her belongings; a radical change in the behaviour of the husband for no reason and to the extent that life together becomes impossible; an alcoholic and/or drug-addict husband; a husband trafficking illegal drugs, preventing his wife from visiting her family or from receiving them in her house or denying her a salary that he instead uses to pay debts that are in no way related to the interests of the family; avarice, jealousy, lack of trust; a husband demanding unconventional sexual practices from his wife; or even a wife giving birth to a child in her own family home without the husband coming to see her or paying for the birth expenses.

The various reasons that may lead to *shiqaq* divorce show that the judges make an expansive appraisal of the notion of discord that leads to *shiqaq* divorce. It seems that sometimes judges go even further than discord because some of the reasons mentioned by judges may sound somewhat vague and formulaic, such as the 'ill treatment of the wife renders the life of spouses impossible' or 'the husband does not respect his marriage obligations' or 'the situation has become too complicated'. These arguments have become genuine 'illocutionary acts' or 'performance acts' in the sense of the British philosopher of language John Austin (1975), i.e. they are 'acts of divorce'.

This type of *ijtihad* in practice reveals an openness on the part of the judges with respect to points on which they used to show a great deal of conservatism, as in the case of geographical distance being grounds for divorce in Case 4. In the new Family Law the obligation of cohabitation is stated in Article 51, which addresses the mutual rights and obligations of spouses. Contrary to the previous personal Status Code, where the text was very formulaic in the sense that it mentioned 'cohabitation' with no further specification, Article 51 gives more legal weight to cohabitation, implying fair treatment of the wife (or wives) in the case of polygamy, fidelity and protection of lineage.

Analysis

In the analysis of the above cases, I mainly relied on my knowledge of the Moroccan context, relevant research on the topic addressed, observation, and interviews with some judges and with women who filed for *shiqaq* divorce in the region of Fez-Boulmane, Morocco. My analysis of the cases reveals that the judge is the key factor in *ijtihad* in practice and that his/her decisions are the result of a creative process that depends on five criteria: (i) the overall religious, political and economic context of *ijtihad*, (ii) the specific nature of the case addressed, (iii) the judge's training in *ijtihad*, (iv) the location where the judge adjudicates, and (v) the judge's personal inclination to use *ijtihad*. In other words, creative adjudications depend, first, on a mixture of religious and legal knowledge and, second, on knowledge of the overall context (local, national and sometimes international) in which the judge acts. In the section above, I dealt with the overall religious, political and economic context of *ijtihad* and underscored the fact that it has become common practice in Moroccan courts, while in the following sections I will deal with the remainder of the criteria in light of the cases analysed.

The specific nature of the cases

We have seen that that the five cases studied involve migration in one way or another and that this fact was instrumental in the judges' adjudications. When asked about this, a judge responded that migration entails taking into account the nature of the laws in the host countries, as well as the nature of the rights and obligations in these countries. In Morocco, migration is part and parcel of politics, economy and everyday life.

Morocco has a unique geographical position: situated at the westernmost edge of the Middle East and North Africa (MENA) region, it is at an intersection with the Maghreb, Africa and Europe. It is only seven miles from Europe. The history of Moroccan women and migration is an interesting one. In the 1960s, Moroccan women barely participated in migration, while today they constitute 50 per cent of Moroccans living in Europe and in the Gulf, without counting illegal migration, which is becoming increasingly feminine. In statistical terms, out of approximately 3 million Moroccan migrants in Europe, 900 000, i.e. 37 per cent of them, are women. Migration is not only feminized but also young. In 2003 the Global Development Finance Annual Report took formal notice of remittances as an important source of external development finance for the first time, listing Morocco as the fourth largest remittance recipient among developing countries. In 2012, remittances to Morocco stood at USD 7.014 billion (IOM 2013), of which approximately half is transferred from France. Nonetheless, and despite the high level of remittances, Morocco remains characterized by considerable regional and other inequalities. Emigration potential is very high in north and central Morocco, where Fez is located. Thus overall migration is certainly an issue in *ijtihad* in practice.

The location where the judge adjudicates

The location of the court where adjudications take place is very important. Judges tend to be more flexible and lenient in urban areas where women are supposedly more educated and aware of their rights than in rural areas where women are predominantly illiterate and dependent on their male kin for any court procedure. Whereas rural areas symbolize tradition in Morocco, urban areas symbolize modernity, social opportunity and mobility. Modernity has been concomitant with urbanization in Morocco. Urbanization is a relatively recent phenomenon in the country's history; it started and developed in a rapid way after Morocco obtained its independence in 1956. Although this process brought about a new 'modern' social structure, it deeply disrupted the existing social order and imposed new constraints.

Moroccan urban women started to participate in the household economy in the 1930s. Their work was not an act of militantism, rather it was dictated by poverty as most of these women worked as domestics in French or upper-class Moroccan households or were recruited as low-paid workers doing menial jobs in the fields or in factories. Following Morocco's independence, a growing number of Moroccan urban women were incorporated into the official labour market. Women's rate of economic activity in urban areas increased by 5.6 per cent in 1960, 10.8 per cent in 1971, 14.7 per cent in 1982 to 17.3 per cent in 1994 and reached 30 per cent in 1999; however, and in spite of an increase in women's access to education, their participation in the labour market was only 25 per cent in 2012, probably as a result of the world financial crises (A1 Monitor 2103). Further, the rate of feminization of the labour force (aged 15 and older) grew during independence and reached 33 per cent in 1990 (cf. UNDP 1996). Women's work in industry greatly assisted Morocco's development. The greatest majority of salaried women has been and is still concentrated at the lower and middle sections of the job ladder. Very few women have managed to reach top positions in their jobs (Sadiqi 2003).

In addition to salaried jobs, personal and domestic services have become highly feminized in urban areas. The more urban women take jobs outside the home, the more domestic services are required in households to keep the balance between outside work and daily domestic chores. According to Mernissi (1982), in 1971, a quarter of domestics were children (under 15 years of age). In 1993, this percentage went down by about 10 per cent. According to a 2005 study, around 86,000 girls under 15 work as maids in stark violation of Moroccan and international law (Associated Press 2013). Domestics, who receive small salaries that differ according to the families involved, are not only economically marginalized, they are also marginalized by the law as they are neither included in labour legislation or in social security programmes. Most very young domestics are not paid directly; the money they earn usually goes to their parents.

Given these facts, Moroccan urban and rural women are not given the same choices in the economy as intended by Folbre (1995) in the sense that rural women are, for example, less educated and less likely to earn a salary, and hence they resist patriarchy differently. Urban and economically well-off women often exploit rural and economically weak women. Further, as a social group, urban women are offered more chances to acquire education than rural women, and hence have greater access to language skills and job opportunities than rural women. It is on the basis of this asymmetry in opportunities that rural women are socially categorized as subordinate to urban women.

The most significant arena in which urban women challenge patriarchy is through their writing, work in civil society and activism in feminist associations (Sadiqi, 2003). Urban feminism in Morocco has managed to make its voice heard and has greatly contributed to improving women's circumstances, and urban women's literacy makes them aware of the problems and generally more prone to reflect intellectually on their condition. However, these women often speak and write in the name of 'all' Moroccan women and therefore appropriate the voices of rural illiterate women and reinterpret them as 'the others', the 'weaker' and the 'subordinate'.

The difference between urban and rural women's strategies on resisting patriarchy shows that gender negotiation is sensitive to geographical environment and this is bound to have a bearing on court practice. Generally, urban women use education and class to boost their self-confidence and negotiate, whereas rural women use their manual skills and family bonding. These differences are due to the fact that Moroccan rural and urban women are not affected by the gender bias in the same way and, thus, do not react to it in the same way. As women are more personalized and less anonymous in rural areas, human relations in those areas render gender role subversion more collective (group singing, group lamentation, group visits to saints, etc.), whereas the more anonymous and less personalized human relations in urban areas make gender role subversion relatively more individual.

The judge's training and his/her personal inclination to use **ijtihad**

According to the interviews I conducted with judges, the more trained these judges are the more flexible they are. Trained judges are more aware of their creative prerogatives than non-trained ones. Trained judges often understand that the new Family Law bestows on them a new mission: that of supervising relationships within the family, managing conflict and promoting conciliation, in addition to protecting children's interests. According to the interviewed judges, by understanding this mission they are equipped and empowered to overcome the heavy legacy of conservative jurisprudence that still prevails in the mentalities of most judges. Training also sensitizes judges to universal laws and human rights.

The judge's personal inclination to use *ijtihad* may also depend on gender. For example, Zhor El Horr, one of the few female judges, never fails to be prone to progressiveness when adjudicating family matters. Although one should avoid generalizing here, it is true that female judges are more understanding of women's issues than male judges, as corroborated by the interviews I conducted.

Synthesis

A synthesis of the aforementioned cases and the ensuing analysis highlights three points: (i) the centrality of the judge in practising progressive *ijtihad*, (ii) the importance of training in triggering progressive *ijtihad* in practice, and (iii) the relevance of extra-legal factors, such as migration, in progressive *ijtihad* in practice.

With regard to the first point, judges are indeed central in the practice of *ijtihad*: their particular function in court and society at large makes them social guardians of norms and bestows on them the responsibility of securing respect for the law and, in this capacity, they are a strong symbolic force. At the same time, these same prerogatives often blur the boundary between the religious referential and morality, not only in the minds of the judges themselves, but also in society at large. Therefore, these responsibilities may constitute a major obstacle to the straightforward application of family law, especially as the Moroccan Family Law does not specify the nature of *shiqaq*, leaving it to the judges to gauge the definitions of discord they prefer to adopt in particular cases.

In Arabic the term *shiqaq* means 'fracture', a semantically loaded and elastic concept that leaves the judge with considerable discretion as to its exact meaning. The definition used depends on the adopted reference: traditional Maliki, *fiqh*, *ijtihad*, or ratified international conventions. In today's Morocco, judges are encouraged to adopt the ratified international conventions because whereas in the previous Personal Status Code, Article 297 obliged judges to refer to the Maliki rite and its jurisprudence, the new 2004 Moudawana allows judges to practise *ijtihad* (Article 400 calls for a jurisprudential effort that concretizes the values of Islam: justice, equality and a good conjugal life). In so doing, the enforcement of the new Family Law needs to go beyond the Maliki rite to integrate Islamic values and other sources of reference, such as international conventions ratified by Morocco.[9]

The decisions by judges in the cases mentioned in this chapter are examples of progressive readings of *shiqaq* divorce that promote fairness and also equality between spouses. When interviewed, however, judges did not have the same attitude towards their power to innovate. The judges interviewed were unanimous in acknowledging that the new Moroccan Family Law opens the door to *ijtihad*, and that it is the result of a progressive reading of the Maliki Islamic judicial tradition. They also agree that it aims to safeguard the stability of the family, fight discrimination against women, establish equality between spouses and protect the rights of children. Most judges also acknowledged the existence of discrimination in Moroccan society and welcomed the new Family Law provisions. Another point of convergence is that most of the judges I interviewed noted that a good application of the new Family Law is often hindered by impediments such as the sore lack of training for judges, their lack of specialization, as well as their lack of 'means of implementation'. Most of them also added an additional serious impediment: the crippling dependence of family sections of the justice system on the first instance tribunals.

However, judges diverged on a number of points, the most important of which is the extent to which they should adopt *ijtihad*, especially in matters of marriage age, tutorship (*wilaya*), repudiation, polygamy, absence of guardianship when the mother is not Muslim, the division of common wealth, and the use of other references in case of lacunas in the text. In sum, there are two types of judges: progressive and conservative. Whereas the former are inclined to broader interpretations of the law, are in favour of equality between men and women, invoke the international conventions ratified by Morocco and call for the removal of reserves attached to them,[10] the latter are more inclined to adopt traditional religious references, are not enthusiastic about women's rights and oppose the lifting of reserves in international conventions. The polarized attitudes of the judges are a mirror of polarized attitudes in Moroccan society in matters of divorce, tutorship (guardianship), marriage age and other family issues.

Conclusion

The new 2004 Moroccan Family Law opens wide the gate to progressive *ijtihad* in practice. The future of *ijtihad* and women's rights is in the hands of the judges, hence the importance of their training and adaptability to the changing conditions of women in Morocco. This is 'the potential within' that this chapter has attempted to highlight. The history of religion has taught us that consultation of sacred sources may allow us to gather all sorts of arguments that may support or reject a specific interpretation. Various religious scholars have used the same sources to sanction or condemn slavery, to venerate or burn icons, to ban or tolerate wine. Various societies have, throughout the history of humankind, unearthed sacred citations to justify a specific practice in a specific moment. As Maalouf (1998) observes, it took two or three thousand years for Christians and Jews to apply the biblical saying 'Thou shall not kill' to the death penalty, thereby considering this practice as against God's will; in two hundred years the belief that the death penalty is contrary to religious doctrine will be taken for granted. Sacred texts do not change; it is the human interpretation of those texts that changes; but texts act on realities only through this human interpretation that is obstructed by certain turns of phrase and glides over others without seeing them.

Notes

1 See Buskens (2003) for the various phases of the genesis of the Moudawana. See also the *Code du Statut Personnel et des successions. Dahir de 1957 et 1958* (1968), Casablanca: Sochepresse.
2 The Berber Customary Law was also called *Berber Dahir*, and was introduced by the French colonizers as part of a pluralistic project that aimed to divide and rule Morocco on ethnic grounds.

3 After the independence of the countries of North Africa, each new state chose a specific school of *fiqh* for the crafting of its family law. In the case of Morocco, the Maliki school of *fiqh* suited the country's monarchical type of political and religious ruling.
4 See Harrak (2009) for more details on the provisions of the first Moroccan family law code.
5 See Buskens (2003) for more details.
6 The Plan for Integrating Women in Development contained 214 points, only 8 of which concerned the Personal Status Code. Yet, it was demonized by the conservatives as an import from the West that targeted shari'a.
7 To put pressure on the government, the women's movement organized a march in Rabat; to show their political muscle, the Islamists planned their own march in Casablanca. Attendance estimates for the Rabat march ranged from 40,000 to 100,000 people, but twice as many participated in Casablanca.
8 Women's marriage rights are stated in Article 84 of the Family Law. They include the remainder of the *sadaq* (dower), the *'idda* pension (widowhood), the *mut'a* (consolation donation) and the right to stay in the family house after divorce. Under the previous Moudawana, divorced wives were expelled from the family house.
9 The fact that judges need to take into consideration sources of reference other than the Maliki school when enforcing the Moudawana is corroborated by the Royal speech of 10 October 2003, in which the king made it clear that the text of the Family Law should be approached with realism, wisdom and perspicacity because it is an effort of *ijtihad* that suits today's Morocco, a country that is open to progress.
10 Morocco lifted its reservations on the Convention on the Elimination of Discrimination against Women (CEDAW) in 2011.

Bibliography

Al Monitor (2013) Available online at www.al-monitor.com/pulse/culture/2013/04/morocco-gender-equality-failed.html#ixzz2adAAQfK2 (accessed 30 July 2013).

Arshad, A. (2007) 'Ijtihad as a tool for Islamic legal reform: advancing women's rights in Morocco', *Kansas Journal of Law and Public Policy*, XVI(2): 129–56.

Associated Press (2013) 'Rights groups alarmed over Morocco's underage maids'. Available online at http://finance.yahoo.com/news/rights-group-alarmed-over-moroccos-underage-maids-144255146-finance.html (accessed 30 July 2013).

Austin, J. (1975) *How to Do Things with Words*, Cambridge, MA: Harvard University Press.

Badran, M. (2008) *Feminist Activism and Reform of Muslim Personal Status Laws. A look at Egypt and Morocco*. Available online at www.juragentium.org/topics/women/en/activism.htm (accessed 20 November 2012).

Bourqia, R., Charrad, M. and Gallagh, N. (eds) (1996) *Femmes, culture et société au Maghreb*, Casablanca: AfriqueOrient.

Buskens, L. (2003) 'Recent debates on family law reform in Morocco: Islamic law as politics in an emerging public sphere', *Islamic Law and Society*, 10(1): 70–131.

Charrad, M. (2001) *States and Women's Rights. The Making of Postcolonial Tunisia, Algeria, and Morocco*, Los Angeles: University of California Press.

Coulson, N.J. (1964) *A History of Islamic Law*, Edinburgh: Edinburgh University Press.

Ennaji, M. (2005) *Multilingualism, Cultural Identity, and Education in Morocco*, Boston, MA: Springer.

——(2011) 'The new Muslim personal status law in Morocco: context, proponents, adversaries, and arguments', in G. Di Marco and C. Tabbush (eds), *Feminisms, Democratization, and Radical Democracy*, San Martin, Argentina: UNSAM Edita.

Folbre, N. (1995) *Engendering Economics: New Perspectives on Women, Work, and Demographic Change*, Annual World Bank Conference on Development Economics, World Bank. Available online at http://graduateinstitute.ch/webdav/site/genre/shared/Genre_docs/3534_Actes1998/4-Eco-Folbre.2.pdf (accessed 20 November 2012).

Hallaq, W.B. (1984) 'Was the gate of ijtihad closed?', *International Journal of Middle East Studies*, 16(1): 3–41.

Harrak, F. (2009) 'The history and significance of the new Moroccan family code', Working Paper No. 09 002, Institute for the Study of Islamic Thought in Africa (ISITA). Evanston, IL: The Roberta Buffet Center for International and Comparative Studies, Northwestern University.

IOM (International Organization for Migration) (2013), Available online at www.iom.int/cms/en/ sites/iom/home/where-we-work/africa-and-the-middle-east/middle-east-and-north-africa/morocco. default.html?displayTab=facts-and-figures (accessed 30 July 2013).

Karamali, S., Ali, P. and Dunne, F. (1994) 'The ijtihad controversy', *Arab Law Quarterly*, 9(3): 238–57.

Maalouf, A. (1998) *Les identités meurtrières*, Paris: Editions Grasset & Fasquelle.

Mernissi, F. (1982) 'Virginity and Patriarchy', in A. Al-Hibri (ed.), *Women and Islam*, Oxford: Pergamon.

——(1984) *Beyond the Veil*, Bloomington: Indiana University Press.

Mir-Hosseini, Z. (1993) *Marriage on Trial. Islamic Family Law in Iran and Morocco*, London: I.B. Tauris.

——(2007) 'How the door of ijtihad was opened and closed: a comparative analysis of recent family law reforms in Iran and Morocco', *Washington and Lee Law Review*, 64(4): 1499–1511.

Ratha, D. (2003) *Worker's Remittances: an Important and Stable Source of External Finance*, Washington, DC: World Bank.

Sadiqi, F. (2003) *Women, Gender and Language in Morocco*, Leiden: Brill Academic Publishers.

——(2010–11) 'Domestic Violence in the African North', Al-Raida, 131–32: 17–27.

——(2012) 'Female perceptions of Islam in today's Morocco', in E. Aslan, M. Hermansen and E. Medeni (eds), *The New Voices of Muslim Women Theologians*, Vol. 2, Leiden: Brill Academic Publishers.

Sadiqi, F. and Ennaji, M. (2006) 'The feminization of public space: women's activism, the family law, and social change in Morocco', *Journal of Middle East Women's Studies*, 2(2): 86–110.

Sell, E. (1907) *The Faith in Islamic Law*, Vepery, Madras: S.P.C.K. Press.

Taoufik, A. (1993) *The Code of the Personal Law and the Latest Amendments*, Casablanca: Da Al-Thaqafa.

UNDP (United Nations Development Programme) (1996) *Human Development Report*, New York and Oxford: UNDP.

Zeidguy, R. (2007) 'Analyse de la jurisprudence', in M. Benradi, H.A. M'chichi, A. Ounrir, M. Muqit, F.Z. Boukaissi and R. Zeidguy (eds), *Le code de la famille. Perceptions et pratique judiciaire*, Fez: Friedrich Ebert Stiftung: 217–71.

8 Family Law in Post-Revolutionary Iran

Closing the door of *ijtehad?*

Anna Vanzan

Introduction

With the advent of the Islamic Revolution in 1979 all previous family laws were suspended. The legal system was Islamized, and the Constitution and the shari'a according to the Shi'i Twelver Ja'fari school became the sources of law. In addition, special civil courts (*dadgah-e madani-ye khass*) were established to adjudicate family law matters. However, the Iranian legal system has evolved since the beginning of the Islamic Republic and many norms related to family law have been amended in response to the requirements of a modern society. In addition, women's increasing awareness of their rights and the bottom-up pressure exerted by a young, well-educated and increasingly restive population have prompted legal reforms, and constant negotiations are producing new interpretations of existing laws.

After examining Iranian family law and its changes since the onset of the Islamic Revolution, this chapter shows how civil society engages with the legal system and sometimes successfully changes it.

Before the revolution

Under the Pahlavi dynasty (1925–79), major changes had been introduced in the sphere of family law. In particular, the Family Protection Law of 1967 and its amendments in 1975 had abolished extrajudicial divorce, instituted the wife's right to divorce under certain conditions, limited polygamy (by submitting it to judicial approval) and empowered the courts to rule on arrangements related to the maintenance of a divorced couple's children.

Theoretically, the reforms were positive for women: they made it harder for a man to abandon his wife and prevented him from threatening her with the possibility of a sudden and rapid divorce and the consequent loss of custody of her children. The Family Protection Law remained partially based on the Shi'i Ja'fari school of law, for instance by accepting all the conditions that could entitle either party to obtain a divorce, such as insanity and other disabling illnesses. These conditions were expanded and included an important change: if a husband married a second wife without the consent of the first one, the latter could apply for divorce (Article 11).

However, the scope of the article was partially negated by Article 14, which reads:

> When a man, already having a wife, desires to marry another woman, he shall obtain permission from the court of law. The court shall give the permission only when it has taken the necessary steps, and, if possible, has made an inquiry from the present wife of the man, in order to assure the financial potentiality and ability of the man for doing justice [to both the wives].
>
> In case the man marries [another woman] without obtaining the due permission from the court, he shall be liable for the punishment provided in section 5 of the Marriage Act of 1310–16 [iii] (A.H. 1931–37 A.D.).

Therefore, in practice a man could always marry a second wife, provided he had the financial means to do so, while a woman could only file a petition for a certificate of non-reconciliation. However, without the court's consent, her request was ineffective.

Article 15 also discriminated against women: 'A husband may, with the approval of the court, prevent his wife from an occupation which is repugnant to the interests of his or her family or position.'

Last but not least, the Family Protection Law did not touch the institution of *mut'a*, the temporary marriage codified by the Shi'a. While the Pahlavi regime disdained it, it did not outlaw it (Haeri 1989: 6–7).

While this law constituted an important step toward reducing discrimination against women, its actual impact was modest and restricted to middle- and upper-class urban women (Vatandust 1985: 120). However, at the time, the educational level of Iranian women was very low, especially in the villages and small towns where the majority of the population lived. These women were ignorant (in the etymological sense of the term) of the law and had little possibility of knowing their rights and as a consequence they were not affected either by the Family Protection Law or by the social changes taking place in the major cities. Soon, however, the Revolution would bring all these issues to the fore.

The Islamic Revolution and its impact on family law

With the advent of the Revolution and the establishment of the Islamic Republic, the Family Protection Law was suspended (but never formally repealed) along with other 'un-Islamic' laws. The new Constitution, adopted in December 1979 and based on 'Islamic criteria', decreed that 'All people of Iran, whatever the ethnic group or tribe to which they belong, enjoy equal rights; and color, race, language, and the like, do not bestow any privilege' (Article 19), thereby ignoring gender-based discrimination.

However, Article 21 deals exclusively with women, prescribing, inter alia, that the government must 'create a favorable environment for the ... restoration of [women's] rights'; protect 'mothers, particularly during pregnancy and childbearing'; support widows, aged women and women without support; and award 'guardianship of children to worthy mothers, in order to protect the interests of the children, in the absence of a legal guardian' (Iranian Chamber Society).

Therefore, the constitutional provision seems to be family-oriented and women are protected by it in their main role of wives and mothers, an almost *sine qua non* condition also stressed in the preamble:

> Women were drawn away from the family unit and [put into] the condition of 'being a mere thing', or 'being a mere tool for work' in the service of consumerism and exploitation. Re-assumption of the task of bringing up religiously minded men and women, ready to work and fight together in life's fields of activity, is a serious and precious duty of motherhood.

Furthermore, both the preamble and the first paragraph of Article 21 underline the need to reward women for their active part in the Revolution by granting them their 'intellectual rights'. As a matter of fact, the Islamic Republic embarked on an extensive policy of female education that resulted in one of the highest levels of educational attainment in the region.

In contrast, the new Civil Code enacted in 1979 penalized women because, among other shortcomings, it authorized a minimum marriage age of nine years for girls; the marriage of virgin women required the father's consent; polygamy was reintroduced without restraint; a wife's obedience to her husband as a necessary condition in order to obtain maintenance was reinforced; *mut'a* marriage was recognized (Articles 1075–77); in case of divorce, children were placed in the custody of the father, because '[a]ny child born during married life belongs to the husband' (Article 1158).

However, contradictions emerged immediately. So, while the Civil Code stated that 'A husband can repudiate his wife any time he wishes' (Article 1133), the Special Civil Courts Act Article 3/2 stated that:

> if a husband wishes a divorce in accordance with Article 1133 of the Civil Code, the court must first refer the case to arbitration, in conformity with the Holy verse: 'If you fear a breach between the two, bring forth an arbiter from his people and from her people an arbiter, if they desire to set things right; God will compose their differences; surely God is all-knowing, all-aware'. Permission to divorce shall be granted to the husband, if reconciliation between the spouses has not materialized.

Although men were in any case guaranteed divorce, even without providing any grounds for it, they remained bound by the Qur'anic verse that requires arbitration, i.e. a judicial decision. Nevertheless, the right to divorce became once again a male prerogative: not only was obtaining divorce much more difficult for a woman, but a man, according to Article 1109, could also invoke his wife's disobedience (*nushuz*) in order not to pay her the maintenance due during the *'idda*.

Continuity and change: the first decade after the Revolution

Although the law was harsh on women, the rapid social change that Iran underwent in the aftermath of the Revolution necessitated a gradual but constant modification of some of the Articles of the new laws. A number of factors, including the war against Iraq, forced women to leave the home and seek work outside, and they rapidly re-entered the public sphere to an even greater degree than before the Revolution. In the meantime, the educational institutions began to turn out highly educated women who could compete for better positions in the job market. The quest for education and a good job pushed women to delay marrying and to have fewer children; while the presence of women in the universities rose from 20 per cent in the 1960s to 60 per cent in 2005, the fertility rate decreased from seven children per woman in 1986 to 2.3 in 2001, figures that were confirmed in 2011 by the Statistical Centre of Iran (Statistical Center of Iran 1996, 2006, 2011).

The increasing presence of women in the public sphere immediately created tensions and conflicts, especially in the field of law: many women (and men) resented the contradictions between a legal system that had taken them back to the eighth century and the needs of contemporary life. As a result, civil society, of which women constituted a crucial section, embarked on efforts to amend the family law.

As early as 1982, the parliament (*Majles*) added two provisions to the marriage contract: first, the divorced wife was given the right to claim half of the wealth acquired during marriage, as long as the divorce was not deemed her fault (according to the court's judgment); second, the wife acquired the right to divorce if the husband wished to take a second wife without her consent (Mir-Hosseini 1997: 57).

However, in the first phase of the Revolution a multiplicity of family laws were introduced, resulting in contradictory verdicts and many complaints: the 1979 Civil Code, Ayatollah Khomeini's instructions (*Touzih ol-masa'el* or 'Explanation of Problems') and sections of the Family Protection Law, the Articles of which were still partially in force all coexisted. Among those who complained about the inconsistency of court decisions was Azam Taleghani, an Islamist woman who was elected to the first Parliament.[1]

The process toward the coordination of the civil courts was a long one,[2] but it showed, among other things, that women had become an indispensable and active part of the judiciary. Indeed, another female deputy, Maryam Behruzi, who formed a committee on the family (1984), took charge of discussing family rights with the civil court judges and of searching for new solutions to family problems involving women. The discussion on women's rights soon shifted from the parliament and the courts to the press, i.e. into the public sphere, as the conservative daily *Zan-e ruz* (Today's Woman) became a forum in which the limits of family law and of its practice were openly discussed (Paidar 1995: 275–76). In *Zan-e ruz,* women began to ask for new interpretations of shari'a, a prelude to what would later be labelled as 'Islamic feminism'.

Women's grievances were related to many issues contained in the Civil Code, such as:

a) in case of divorce, legal custody of the child remained with the mother only up to the age of seven (for a girl) and two (for a boy) and thereafter it was determined by the courts (Article 1169);

b) a daughter's inheritance was only half that of a son (Article 907);

c) the fact that, should the father die, guardianship of the children remained with the paternal grandfather, not with the mother (Articles 1181 and 1883);

d) a child's citizenship was based on that of the father (Article 976).[3]

The battle for child custody was one of the first that Iranian women embarked on, not only because the divorce rate had increased (with the consequent drama of mothers deprived of their children's presence), but also because of the situation created by the war between Iran and Iraq. Many men had died defending the country (and therefore deserved the appellation of 'martyrs') and their widows had consequently been deprived of both the husband's maintenance and of their children. Under Article 1181 and 1883 of the Civil Code, the children of martyrs came under the paternal grandfather's custody, and this meant that the payment for the care of orphans made by the Martyrs' Foundation (*Bonyad-e shahid*) also went to them. War widows organized massive protests until in July 1985 the parliament passed a bill transferring the right of guardianship and tutorship of martyrs' minors to their mothers, even after a mother's remarriage. This was an important success for a broad coalition of women's groups extending from the Islamists[4] to secularist currents.

Even so, much remained to be done in order to improve women's custody rights. Female parliamentarians had already championed a bill that was more favourable to women in 1982, but it had been rejected on the basis of its perceived incompatibility with shari'a and its concept of *velayat* (legal guardianship). Therefore, women who had backed the Revolution and were now playing leading roles (in the parliament, in Islamic associations and the like) felt that they had been betrayed. While the Constitution and the new regime claimed to defend women's role as mothers, the law failed to grant women full rights to act as mothers in case of divorce. Given that for the government women's 'maternal' identity was their main identity, women wanted to be fully recognized as mothers and deemed to be fit to raise children even if the father was absent. Women did not deny their Islamic commitment, but started to fight for better rights by using Islamic discourses and frames. Islamic feminism was born.[5]

The second revolution: the 1990s

The war against Iraq had created a new group of women, i.e. widows whose late husbands had acquired the title and status of martyrs.[6] In 1987 the parliament approved better pensions for them (the equivalent of the late husband's last salary) while the Martyr's Foundation provided them and their children with several benefits, such as free housing and free school tuition.

The war widows were not the only women in dire straits: the rate of divorce had risen, mainly as a result of financial hardship, and many women were left without any support. At the same time and for the same reasons (economic problems), marriage rates decreased: this trend forced the government to intervene with measures, the consequences of which were of importance to women, though not all of the measures were to their benefit. Perhaps the most crucial one was the parliamentary bill of July 1989: considering that men had too free a hand in asking for a divorce, the *Majles* established that only the special civil courts had the right to approve a divorce. In order to divorce, a man had to produce good reasons and the court had the prerogative to consider those reasons as insufficient and refuse a divorce. This was good news for women. In addition, the new president of the Islamic Republic, the pragmatic Hojatoleslam Rafsanjani, called for the restriction of polygamy, arguing that 'in Iran the male population is about 5 per cent greater than the female population and therefore there was no social justification for taking more than one wife' (Paidar 1995: 285).

At the same time, however, the Republic's concern about the low rate of marriage, which would inevitably turn into *fitna* (i.e. recourse to sex outside wedlock), led to official endorsement of *mut'a* marriages, considered to be a safety valve to prevent prostitution and other 'un-Islamic' sexual behaviours. In spite of the fact that *mut'a* remained culturally and socially stigmatized, its acceptance in clerical/governmental circles was a blow to women, though some of them entered into a *mut'a* relationship not only out of economic need, but also in pursuit of sexual pleasure.[7]

Post-war Iran had to face a number of problems, including high population growth: during the war, birth control had been abandoned in favour of an 'anti-imperialistic' policy (i.e. the government wished to increase the number of Iranians/Muslims in order to overcome Western control), with the result that in the 1980s the Islamic Republic had 55 million citizens with a yearly growth of 3.2 per cent. In July 1989 the Minister of Health announced a new family planning campaign that included the distribution of free contraceptives and the duty for would-be spouses to attend a course focused on the necessity of birth control. The campaign was widely debated on the pages of *Zan-e ruz* and its success can be seen in the dramatic decrease in the birth rate, which dropped from 6.7 per cent in the 1950s to 1.7 in 2010 (United Nations 2012).

These were positive improvements for women, but they still had to fight against discrimination in a number of areas, including in relation to inheritance rights, alimony and the issue of dower.[8] Inheritance is a fairly complicated area of Iranian jurisprudence. Although this subject is based on Sura 4:11, which dictates a parent's heritage to the male child in a portion equal to that of two females, the Shi'i reading of the Qur'anic verses is slightly different. Shi'i jurisprudence rejects the criterion of the agnatic tie and regards both maternal and paternal connections as equally strong grounds for inheritance. In other words, in Shi'i law the presence of a male heir does not exclude the female.[9] The post-revolutionary Civil Code established that a widow could not inherit land, only moveable property and a share of the value of buildings or trees. However, a bill ratified in 2009 enabled a woman to inherit a share of the entire property of her deceased spouse.

Another crucial issue was (and still is) dower, or *mehr*, often defined as 'bride price', which consists of a sum of money promised by the husband and registered in the marriage contract, to be paid after consummation, but more usually paid by the man upon divorce, though Article 1085 states: 'So long as the marriage portion is not delivered to her, the wife can refuse to fulfill the duties which she has to her husband provided, however, that the marriage portion is payable at once. This refusal does not debar her from right of maintenance expenses.'

Article 1085 also clearly demonstrates the exchange nature of the wedding contract in Iran. Iranian civil law is particularly precise in this respect and Articles 1078–1101 on permanent and temporary marriage are devoted to *mehr*. However, the dower is subject to a variety of socio-economic conditions, for example, depreciation: if in a contract the promised *mehr* has a certain value, it is bound to depreciate tremendously over time because of inflation, especially in a country like Iran. Even worse, *mehr* is subject to a man's discretion, that is to say, to many abuses. However, the most common reason why women renounced *mehr* is in order to regain their freedom: *mehr* has, in fact, become the commodity women offer men in order to obtain a rapid divorce. In other words, they renounce *mehr* in exchange for their husband's consent to divorce or to negotiate custody of the children.[10]

The 1990s were years of deep social and cultural changes, the effects of which inevitably had an impact on the laws. The increasing presence of women in every sphere of Iranian society, in addition to the grievances of many (including some Shi'i clerics) who were disappointed by the evident injustice of rules and institutions applied in the name of Islam, triggered important reforms. In 1994 the parliament decided that women could become legal consultants in the special civil courts and in the administrative justice courts, and in the following year about one hundred women were employed in such positions. This resulted in a more gender-based approach to the administration of the law.

In those years, women participated increasingly in Iranian political life: in November 1995, 176 women were accepted as parliamentary candidates by the Council of Guardians and 14 of them were elected as deputies the following March. In the summer of 1997 the reform-minded Mohammad Khatami was elected president of the Islamic Republic, and one of his first measures was to initiate a reform to improve the conditions of working women and introduce the right to have part-time jobs (Shahidian 2002: 245).

In that fortunate but all too brief period that saw a reform-minded president backed by a sizeable group of like-minded deputies, a number of Articles of the Civil Code were amended, particularly the one about the payment of *mehr*. In February 1998 it was decided *that mehr* should reflect the inflation rate, so that women would receive a fair amount of money. Another important step was the introduction of the obligatory presence of a female legal consultant in court during discussions on child custody. In addition, in the summer of 1998, Meymanat Chubak became the first woman to be appointed as a legal consultant in court by the head of the legislative branch.[11] Iranian women had held senior legislative positions during the last shah's reign, but following the Revolution they had been banned from top judiciary positions.[12] Now, in the 1990s, women were slowly regaining their presence in the courts.

It was not only a matter of having more female legal advocates in the court: 'ordinary' women too had deeply changed and were able to fight for their rights. As the famous documentary shot by Ziba Mir-Hosseini and Kim Longinotto shows (Mir-Hossein-Longinotto 1998), Iranian women have learned how to approach the judges and to negotiate for their rights, even without knowing the law. In the apparently rigid and immutable frame of the shari'a, both female litigants and judges have played an important role in adjusting and modifying the rules.[13] Naturally, the discretionary power enjoyed by the judges does not always favour the applicant women, but it is worth noting that judges (who mostly are the clerics), as well as some 'ulama', have become more flexible and try to respond to contemporary social and cultural realities. This is possible even remaining inside the shari'a framework by calling for *ijtehad*, i.e. the act of independent interpretation of Islamic legal sources, which has always been practised by Shi'i jurists. Although, paradoxically, as has been stated, laws in Iran 'retain the patriarchal provisions of Shi'a law, they are neither justified nor achieved through the exercise of *ijtehad*' (Mir-Hosseini 2007: 1499).

It is women who have proved able to challenge the existing inequalities by adopting diversified strategies, including a new and more aware approach to the shari'a. Even so, as Ziba Mir-Hosseini's acutely aware film proves, it was not only necessary to change the law, but also people's mentalities, including that of many women. In fact, out of the three cases followed by Ziba Mir-Hosseini and Kim Longinotto in a Tehran court, the one related to Maryam is particularly telling. Maryam had obtained divorce from her husband because she had fallen in love with another man and married him. She fought for the custody of her two daughters, but, no matter how desperately she tried, the judge gave custody of the children to their father. When the film-makers asked the court secretary for her opinion, she answered that 'it was a fair decision': Maryam had obtained the divorce because of 'her lust', the secretary explained, as she had taken a fancy to another man, so it was a wise decision to leave her daughters to their legitimate father.

Fiction is another domain that Iranian women consider as a useful arena in which to discuss discrimination issues such as those related to family law. A common technique is to delete any male presence in the tale (particularly significant, in this respect, is the novel *Zanan-e bedun-e mardan* (Women without Men), 1990, by Shahrnush Parsipur). Other writers explicitly narrate stories of unpunished 'honour killing' (for example, Farkhondeh Aqa'i in her short story *Yek zan yek 'eshq* (A woman, a love), 1997), or blame the omnipotence bestowed by laws and society on men's shoulders to the detriment of women (for example, Sofia Mahmudi's ghoulish short story *Sham* (Supper), 1999), in which a woman offers herself in the soup that her husband sips without even taking notice of her.

One step forward, two steps back

Mohammad Khatami's presidency (1997–2005) was characterized by highs and lows. The main accusations against the president came from his supporters, who were dissatisfied with his unfulfilled promises of reforms. However, it should be borne in mind that he and his reform programme were struck a major blow after the elections held in 2004, when the *Majles*, whose majority had until then been pro-Khatami, passed into the hands of hardliners. At that point, Khatami was caught in the conservatives' stronghold and reforms became an impossible dream.

Essentially, the amendments to the Civil Code introduced during Khatami's presidency include: 1) the raising of the minimum age for marriage to 13 years for girls and 15 years for boys (marriage before this age needs the guardians' permission and court's approval); 2) in case of divorce, mothers are entitled to the custody of children up to the age of seven; thereafter it is determined by the court; 3) women can petition for divorce if the marriage causes hardship to them; 4) both spouses inherit the entirety of each other's effects; however, in the case of unmovable property and land, the wife receives the price of them (Koohestani 2011: 1–28).

Although these reforms were positive, at the beginning of the third millennium the Iranian population was too socially and culturally aware to accept them. Women, in particular, had gained social, cultural, economic and political importance: they constituted 65 per cent of university students; they were present in virtually every field of work (except at the top of the judiciary and, of course, of the Shi'i hierarchy). Moreover, they had learned to organize themselves in NGOs and reconstituted the feminist movement, now composed of several groups ranging from the most radical and Western-oriented to the most religious ones. They also demanded judicial reforms and this is how the One Million Signatures (*Yek melyun hemza*) campaign was born.

The One Million Signatures campaign was launched by about 50 activists, who included female lawyers, women's rights advocates and journalists. Particularly active was the group gathered around Noushin Ahmadi Khorasani, a radical feminist who had been active as a writer, publisher and founder of women's magazines (such as *Jens-e dovvom*) and websites (*Zanestan, Madrase-ye feministi*), and her colleagues.[14]

The initiative, which aimed to collect one million signatures to demand changes to discriminatory laws against women, was officially launched on 27 August 2001 during a seminar entitled The Impact of Laws on Women's Lives.[15] The initiative was also promoted by Shirin Ebadi, the lawyer who won the Nobel Peace Prize in 2003. After 2001, Iranian feminists started a series of seminars on women's rights that led to a huge demonstration against gender inequality in front of Tehran University on 12 June 2005.

The activists prepared a booklet, in which they listed the main laws they wanted reformed, such as: the law on marriage (i.e. they wanted to abolish the need for the consent of the woman's father and to raise the minimum age for marriage for girls) and the law on divorce (they objected to the husband's misuse of the *mehr* as retaliation for conceding divorce and custody of the children). They also wanted to abolish polygamy and demanded equal weight for a woman's and a man's testimony in court and the woman's right to pass her citizenship to her children in case of marriage to a foreign man. Their programme also targeted criminal law and general discrimination against women, such as the mandatory use of the *hejab*.

This ambitious platform received an enthusiastic welcome from several prominent Iranians (including men) and was also launched at an international level. However, the promoters knew that they needed to reach ordinary Iranian women (and men), especially in small towns and rural areas. Therefore, female activists started a door-to-door campaign, which increased people's awareness about the need to change the law, but, at the same time, attracted the unwanted attention of the conservatives who felt threatened by this attempt to change the status quo. Many activists were arrested (some of them are still in jail), but the fighters did not stop – quite the opposite, as the battle was destined to be stirred up by some unfortunate events.

The empire strikes back

With the election of Mahmud Ahmadinejad as president of the Islamic Republic in June 2005, power passed into the hands of the hardliners, and women fared poorly on several fronts. Women activists were the specific targets of repression and suffered a series of attacks. A symbol of this harsh battle was the closure (in February 2008) of the monthly *Zanan* (*Women*), the country's leading feminist magazine edited by Shahla Sherkat, which for 16 years had constituted a platform for discussion among women.

As regards the law, in 2008 the government proposed a new so-called family protection law, Article 23 of which was particularly criticized. The proposed article stated: 'Marriage to a subsequent permanent wife shall depend on court authorization upon ascertainment of the man's financial capability and undertaking to uphold justice among his wives.' In other words, the bill aimed to reintroduce indiscriminate polygamy, i.e. the possibility for a man to marry a second wife, provided that he could financially afford both wives.[16]

Women immediately rallied, and in September 2008, a group of 50 well-known female intellectuals and activists, including poet Simin Behbahani, Islamic feminist Azam Taleghani and Noble laureate Shirin Ebadi, met representatives from the parliament to express their worries about what came to be known as the anti-family bill. The activists of the One Million Signatures campaign organized mass protests against the bill that brought together women of different conditions and ideas. But even authoritative ayatollahs, such as Yusuf Sana'i, thundered against Article 23, which they considered anti-Islamic. As a result, the parliament was forced to drop the incriminated article.

Proposals to introduce reforms such at the family protection law constituted the hardliners' response to women's efforts to change discriminatory laws, but were also proof that they feared the women's movement and civil society's anger. As a matter of fact, in the long post-presidential electoral crisis that began in June 2009, the conservatives' assaults on civil society have become more intense and aggressive as they attempt to reintroduce, albeit in a modified form, Article 23 as a challenge to the indomitable Iranian women.

Conclusion

There is no doubt that women's legal status has been worsened by the post-revolutionary law codes. However, the utopian project of a society controlled, from above, thanks (also) to the curbing of women's rights, has failed and human/women's rights have become the core of the daily debate and confrontation between civil society and the state. Although the hardliners keep resorting to intimidation and repression, women activists continue to fight by using the weapon of religious arguments, by publicly stressing how practices based on Islamic jurisprudence can be reformed according to the compassionate spirit of Islam and by inventing new, creative ways of resistance.

Proponents of the first strategy include Faezeh Hashemi Rafsanjani, who belongs to a very conservative family (her father is the cleric 'Ali Akbar Rafsanjani, president of the Islamic Republic in the 1980s) but who has become a staunch fighter for women's rights in light of the shari'a. Faezeh Hashemi belongs to a coalition of Iranian women who have been protesting against the present Family Law by using arguments based on a gender-based interpretation of shari'a.[17]

An example of the second type of attempt to resist repression is the ability shown by Iranian women to get round public order rules. If, for instance, a rally in front of the parliament could be dispersed as 'seditious' and lead to the arrest of participants, women would organize themselves into small groups and talk one-by-one to, and lobby through, progressive parliamentarians. This approach has proved to be efficacious as it has helped to prevent or suspend harsh new measures.

Despite the failure of the reform-minded movements, the ideas of reforms and democracy have taken deep root among Iranians. New strategies must be developed by women and new alliances have to be established among different sections of Iranian society in order to obtain better results.

Notes

1 Azam Taleghani founded the society *Jam'e-e Zanan-e mosalman* and directed its periodical, *Payam-e Hajjar*. She is considered one of the first Iranian Islamic feminists.
2 On the introduction of new laws in post-revolutionary Iran, see Paidar 1995: 272–77.
3 Note that in the field of criminal law too women were/are discriminated against, e.g. a) in the case of a murder, the blood money of a Muslim woman is half that of a Muslim man. In such a case, if the family of the woman insists on *qisas* (retribution), then the woman's family is obliged to pay half of the blood money to either the murderer or his family (Laws of Islamic Punishments, Arts 203, 213, 300); b) the testimony of two women is the same as that of one man (Arts 74, 75 and 137); c) women are considered adults and tried as such after they turn nine, whereas men are tried as adults when they are fifteen (Art. 301).
4 I use the term 'Islamists' to indicate women (and men) who politicize Islam and 'Islamic' for the believers who define themselves by strong religious identification.
5 I want to underline that the so-called Islamic feminism in reality is a variegated discourse that mainly proves how Muslim women, who are aware of their multiple identities, cling to the religious one while striving along the path of justice and equality. Therefore I usually speak of 'Islamic feminisms'. See Vanzan 2010.
6 The term martyrdom is deeply imbued with Shi'i doctrine that confers special status to its martyrs: on the topic see Scott-Aghaie 2004; and Chelkowski and Dabashi 1999.
7 On the multiple sides of *mut'a* in Iran, see Haeri 1989.
8 Forms of discrimination such as the duty to wear the *hejab* in public are deliberately not discussed in this chapter.
9 The equal importance given by Shi's doctrine to matter and paternal connections is because of the importance of the Prophet's daughter Fatima in the line of the imams as it is through her that 'Ali and the other imams inherited their link to the Prophet. See Momen 1985: 183.
10 For many examples see, Mir-Hosseini 1997, *passim*.
11 Art. 162 of the Constitution declaring that women were banned from judgeship was amended in 1995 and women were given the right to hold a judicial position as an advisor in administrative justice in specific civil courts, in legal departments and other similar arenas. Women who enter this career usually have a degree from the faculty of law and/or specific degrees obtained in Qom religious schools.
12 Shirin Ebadi, winner of the Nobel Peace Prize in 2003, is an example. After she was forced to step down from her position as a judge, she devoted herself to private legal practice and activism for human rights in Iran.
13 An enlightening picture of the atmosphere in an Iranian court and of how the judge and the parties interact can be found in the recent film by Asghar Farhadi, *A Separation*, 2011. Other previous cinematic representations of the negotiation between women and the structures of power regarding divorce are in Rahimieh 2009: 97–112.
14 Khorasani has a website, primarily in Persian: http://noushinahmadi.wordpress.com/ (accessed 15 December 2012).
15 See the campaign website: www.we-change.org/english/ (accessed 15 December 2012); original Persian: http://we-change.org (accessed 15 December 2012).
16 Another Article proposed to tax *mehr*.
17 See, among others, her interview with *Madrase-ye Feministi* on May 2010. Available online at www.feministschool.com/spip.php?article4689 (accessed 2 November 2012). One common argument shared by Iranian Islamic feminists is that the Qur'anic verse on polygamy should be interpreted in the light of historical, social, economic and cultural issues envisaged by the essence of shari'a, the ultimate objective is to further the well-being of humanity.

Films

Farhadi, A. (2011) *A Separation*, Iran, 123 minutes.
Mir-Hosseini, Z. and Longinotto, K. (1998) *Divorce Iranian Style*, England, 80 minutes.

Websites

Ahmadi Khorasani, N. http://noushinahmadi.wordpress.com/ (accessed 15 December 2012).

Foundation for Iranian Studies. http://fis-iran.org/en/women/laws/family (accessed 15 December 2012).

Iranian Chamber Society. www.iranchamber.com/government/laws/constitution_ch03.php (accessed 15 December 2012).

One Million Signature Campaign. www.we-change.org/english/ (accessed 15 December 2012). Originally in Persian: http://we-change.org/ (accessed 15 December 2012).

United Nations (2012). http://esa.un.org/unpd/wpp/unpp/panel_population.htm (accessed15 December 2012).

Bibliography

Aqa'i, F. (1997) *Yek zan yek 'eshq* [A woman, a love], Tehran: Nilufar.

Chelkowski, P. and Dabashi, H. (1999) *Staging a Revolution: the Art of Persuasion in the Islamic Republic of Iran*, New York: New York University Press.

Haeri, S. (1989) *Law of Desire, Temporary Marriage in Shi'i Iran*, Syracuse, NY: Syracuse University Press.

Koohestani, A.R. (2011) 'Towards substantive equality in the Iranian constitutional discourse', *Muslim World Journal of Human Rights*, 7(2). Available online at www.bepress.com/mwjhr (accessed 30 December 2011).

Khomeini, R. (1979) *Touzih ol-masa'el* [Explanation of Problems], Tehran: n.p.

Mahmudi, S. (1999) 'Sham' [Supper], in *Zan va kudak ba gonjshek va taraneh* [The Woman and the Child with a Sparrow and a Song], Tehran: Touse'eh.

Mir-Hosseini, Z. (1997) *Marriage on Trial. A Study of Islamic Family Law*, London: I.B. Tauris (1st edn 1993).

——(2007) 'How the door of ijtihad was opened and closed: a comparative analysis of recent family law reforms in Iran and Morocco', *Washington & LEE Review*, 64(4): 1499–1511.

Momen, M. (1985) *An Introduction to Shi'i Islam*, New Haven and London: Yale University Press.

Paidar, P. (1995) *Women and the Political Process in Twentieth-Century Iran*, Cambridge: Cambridge University Press.

Parsipur, S. (1990) *Zanan-e bedun-e mardan* [Women without Men], Tehran: Noqreh.

Rahimieh, R. (2009) 'Divorce seen through women's cinematic lens', *Iranian Studies*, 42(1): 97–112.

Scott-Aghaie, K. (2004) *The Martyrs of Karbala. Shi'i Symbols and Rituals in Modern Iran*, Seattle: University of Washington Press.

Shahidian, H. (2002) *Women in Iran. Gender Politics in the Islamic Republic*, Westport, CT: Greenwood Press.

Statistical Center of Iran (1996, 2006, 2011) *Annual Statistics of the Nation*, Tehran: Iran's Center for Statistics Publications. Available online at www.amar.org.ir/Default.aspx?tabid=1241 (accessed 5 August 2013).

Vanzan, A. (2010) *Le donne di Allah. Viaggio nei femminismi islamici*, Milano: B. Mondadori.

Vatandust, G.R. (1985) 'The Status of Iranian women during the Pahlavi regime', in A. Fathi (ed.), *Women and the Family in Iran*, Leiden: Brill.

9 Islamic Family Law in Secular Turkish Courts

Ihsan Yilmaz

Introduction

Western secular laws were transplanted to Turkey in the Ottoman times, about 100 years before the proclamation of the Turkish Republic in 1923. The secularization of laws in the country reached its peak when the Swiss Civil Code was adopted with some modifications in 1926.[1] With this new law, for the first time in Muslim history, secular laws started governing family issues for Muslims. The Turkish Civil Code is different from the provisions of Muslim law in some respects. Evidence has shown that Muslim Turks have tried to meet the requirements of these two parallel laws. As a result of interaction between these two laws, a new unofficial hybrid Muslim law that amalgamates the rules of unofficial Muslim law, as well as those of the official secular Turkish law, has emerged.[2]

In the following pages, we will analyse if and to what extent this hybrid unofficial Muslim law has interacted with the official law within the Turkish courts, which do not recognize Islamic law. The research draws on my previous work (Yilmaz 2005) and focuses on the decades between 1990 and 2010,[3] looking at some family law issues, i.e. solemnization of marriage, marriage age and polygamy.

Solemnization of marriage

Official law

The Turkish Civil Code only recognizes civil marriages solemnized by authorized marriage officers. Article 134 of the new Civil Code 2001 states that the celebration formalities commence with the parties' submission of the necessary documents to the marriage office in the place where they are residing at that time. Upon submission of these documents, the authorities start enquiries to check if there are any impediments to the marriage. Article 143 of the new Civil Code 2001 establishes that a marriage may be solemnized in accordance with any religion if the parties so desire, but this can only happen after the official marriage registration. Thus, only after the registration of the civil marriage is an unofficial Islamic marriage (*nikah*) permitted and the parties have to present their marriage certificate to an *imam* before the religious marriage.[4] If an official solemnization is followed by a *nikah*, the latter does not supersede or invalidate the official marriage because Turkish law does not recognize a *nikah*.[5] The Turkish Civil Code makes it very clear that the official marriage ceremony conducted by civil servants of municipal governments is the only marriage that the Turkish state recognizes. Mosques cannot be registered as official marriage venues and *imams* are never given authorization to officially solemnize and register marriages. Only secular civil servants of the municipal government can officially solemnize and register marriages, and these marriages do not contain anything religious, in terms of speeches, prayers, wording and oaths. In other words, it is a totally secular ceremony. Men and women who perform a religious marriage ceremony without having a legal marriage certificate are considered punishable.

Article 230 of the new Turkish Criminal Code 2004 states that:

> (5) The couples who marry by arranging a religious ceremony without executing official marriage transactions shall be sentenced to imprisonment from two months to six months. Both the public action and the punishment imposed thereby are abated, as are all their consequences, when the civil marriage ceremony is accomplished.
> (6) Any person who conducts a religious marriage ceremony without seeing the certificate of marriage shall be punished with imprisonment from two months to six months.[6]

In the unofficial realm, however, some people continue to apply the unofficial shari'a law in total contravention of the secular official law, as will be elaborated in the following subsection.

Socio-legal reality

State registration of a marriage is not compulsory in traditional Islamic law. If both parties agree to marry in the presence of two witnesses, this marriage is considered legitimate from an Islamic perspective. According to some Islamic legal schools, parental approval is also a requirement. Even though these are the technical requirements, traditionally, Muslims like their marriage ceremonies to be accompanied by prayers and the like because marriage is one of the important life cycles. Because of these expectations, most Muslim Turks are not satisfied with the official registration and they make sure that they have a *nikah* too. As mentioned in the previous subsection, as long as this *nikah* does not precede the official marriage and only takes place after the official registration, the state does not have a problem with this, despite not recognizing it. However, conducting a *nikah* without a marriage certificate is a criminal offence, even though most Muslims would not treat this unofficial marriage as illegitimate. In newspaper columns written by Islamic scholars who respond to religious questions, unofficial marriage issues are discussed freely as if they were not illegal and punishable offences.[7] It is common to come across news in the media about a celebrity announcing that she/he got married by way of an unofficial *nikah* only, with no accompanying negative comments, despite the fact that the marriage was religious, unofficial and illegal. This state of affairs may bring about some ironic outcomes. In some cases that have involved celebrities, a couple who lived together announced that they were married unofficially by way of a *nikah* only, but when an overactive prosecutor tried to prosecute them, in order to avoid punishment they told him that they did not have a *nikah* but were engaged in fornication, which is not an offence in Turkey.[8]

Not only the media, but also field research and even official documents show that unofficial marriages without official registration are a socio-legal reality in the country. According to research conducted by the State Planning Organization (SPO) that involved a sample of 18,210 households representing the whole population in Turkey, the percentage of civil marriages celebrated without a *nikah* was 9.56 per cent of all marriages, while the percentage celebrated with only a *nikah* and no marriage certificate was 4.89 per cent (SPO 1992: 42). Couples who married twice, i.e. conducted both official marriages and *nikahs*, comprised 84.92 per cent of the entire married population in Turkey (SPO 1992: 42). A survey conducted by the Hacettepe University in 1993 found that in Eastern Turkey, while 22.4 per cent of all married couples had only a *nikah*, 75.9 per cent of all marriages were both religious and civil. The same survey found that in western Turkey the figures were respectively 2.2 per cent and 92.4 per cent (HUNEE 1993, cited in Kümbetoğlu 1997: 122).

A survey in 1998 based on data from interviews conducted with 599 women in 19 settlements in eastern and south-eastern Turkey, within the framework of a broader research study on the impact of official, religious and customary laws on women's lives in Turkey, found that the percentage of only civil marriages was 5.8, only religious marriages was 19.6 and both civil and religious marriages was 74.4 (İlkkaracan 1998: 69). Another survey conducted in 2006 in a village in the southern Turkish city of Mersin interviewed 265 married women and found that only civil marriages accounted for 18.9 per cent of all marriages, only religious marriages for 8.8 per cent and both civil and religious marriages for 74.3 per cent (Karataş *et al.* 2006: 11). In recent quantitative research that surveyed 462 married women aged between 15 and 49 who attended the Central Maternal, Child Health and Family Planning Polyclinic in the eastern Turkish city of Van, it was found that while 95 per cent of monogamous women were both officially and unofficially married, 4.6 per cent of them had only had a religious marriage. As for the polygamists, while those officially married represented 61.5 per cent, 38.5 per cent had only had an unofficial marriage (Gücük *et al.* 2010: 128–29).

Until quite recently, when unofficially married couples had children, their children were regarded as illegitimate by the state (Fişek 1985: 289; Kümbetoğlu 1997: 121). They could not be registered, could not get an ID card that is compulsory in Turkey and thus they did not officially exist. In response to this problem, the state enacted several amnesty laws and made legitimization a simple procedure (Hooker 1975: 367; Fişek 1985: 290; Ansay 1996: 119).[9] The most recent of these laws was dated 8 May 1991 and was valid for five years (Ansay 1996: 113).[10] The state also encourages these unofficially married couples to marry officially. From time to time, the state has organized special marriage ceremonies where thousands of unofficially married couples gather in big squares and are officially married.[11] It should be noted that the state never mentioned the Criminal Code to these couples and their 'crimes' were ignored.[12] With the legal reforms introduced in 2001, in line with the EU membership talks with Turkey, unmarried couples can now register their children; thus, there is neither a need for these special marriage ceremonies nor for amnesty laws.

Unofficial Muslim law and the official law in Turkish courts

As Kruger (1991: 209) highlighted, *imams* would solemnize unofficial and thus illegal marriages but could not be detected and punished as long as there was no dispute or conflict. Alternatively, as has occurred in several cases, judges would be tolerant with the convicted *imams* and with the unofficially married couple and the courts generally would change the punishment from imprisonment to only a light financial punishment.[13]

The secular Turkish courts have dealt with a number of unofficial marriage cases. Many of them have even reached Court of Cassation level. Case law shows that the Court of Cassation accommodates unofficial religious marriages 'when the matter at hand is not related to giving effect to the marriage but, for instance, to the law of obligations where the Court does not have to go into the issue'. Thus, for the sake of justice, the Court of Cassation has 'extended the right to compensation for death in work-related accidents to the unmarried cohabiting woman' (Örücü 2008: 45–46).

In a 1996 case, the childless surviving partner of an unofficial religious marriage asked for material and moral compensation after the death of her husband in a work-related accident. The insurance company refused the request because the law does not cover unmarried people, but the Court of Cassation held that the couple were husband and wife in the eyes of the customs of society and 'decided on a percentage lower than that which would be the due of the married wife' (Örücü 2008: 45).[14] In a similar case in 1997, the Court of Cassation decided on a case that involved a woman who was only unofficially married to a man by way of a *nikah* and held that she was entitled to some financial compensation from her ex-husband who unjustly evicted her from their home.[15] Similarly, in another case in 2001, the Court of Cassation treated an unofficial wife, who had only celebrated a *nikah*, as if she was also officially married. Thus, the Court decided in her favour and judged that she was entitled to compensation. The judge reasoned that because there had been a religious marriage in accordance with local customs and also a wedding had taken place, for the purpose of financial compensation only she could be regarded as married in the eyes of the official law.[16] In a 2003 case related to the return of jewellery given at a *nikah*, the Court referred to the unofficial wife as the unofficial partner and held that she had the right to keep the jewellery that was given to her as a marriage gift even though she did not have any official marriage (Örücü 2008: 46).[17]

In 2008, a woman who was married to a man, by way of a religious marriage only, lost her husband because of a traffic accident caused by an unlicensed driver. She filed a motion to intervene in the case, but the lower court refused her demand saying that she was not an official wife. The Court of Cassation overruled this verdict and stated that 'refusing her demand to intervene without taking into account the damage inflicted on her as a result of the accident is against the law'.[18] In several Court of Cassation cases, women who were only married by way of a religious marriage without any official marriage applied to the lower courts for insurance and/or social security claims after the death of their husbands. The courts have generally treated these unofficially married women as if they were officially married and decided in favour of compensation. Based on the customs (read, unofficial Muslim law) of society, the courts perceived them as married in line with social norms.[19]

In a 2009 case a wife who had only had a religious marriage applied to the court with a complaint about her husband's violence toward her and her children and asked for protection, but the lower court decided that because she was not officially married, she could not benefit from the law. Nevertheless, the Court of Cassation overruled this decision, holding that the union that was established by way of an unofficial religious marriage was also a family union and deserved state protection. The Court held that 'even though they are not officially married, it is apparent that there is a de facto marriage. They have a consistent family life that cannot be discerned from an official marriage in any aspect. Thus, there is no doubt that they have a family life that deserves to be protected by law.'[20]

Case law shows that in the area of solemnization of marriage there is conflict between secular official law and unofficial Muslim law. Even though the overwhelming majority of people have been meeting the requirements of both laws, some inevitable clashes pave the way for an encounter between unofficial and official laws before the secular courts. Even though unofficial religious marriage without an official marriage certificate is a punishable offence, the authorities have generally turned a blind eye to these illegal marriages. Even the higher courts treated these unofficial marriages as official marriages in some cases. It is worth noting that in no case have the courts asked prosecutors to commence lawsuits against illegal marriages.

Marriage age

Official law

The marriage age was taken from Swiss law as being 18 years for males and 17 years for females. However, it was not easy to apply these limits in a society where many people would marry their offspring at earlier ages, especially in rural areas. Thus, the age limit was reduced to 17 for males (15 with the permission of the judge) and 15 for females (14 with the permission of the judge) in 1938 (Lipstein 1956: 17).[21] Article 124 of the new Civil Code of 2001 establishes that the marriage age for both parties is 17. Article 124 further states that that under extraordinary conditions a judge may allow a man or woman who is 16 years old to marry. If possible, he should listen to the parents or guardian. Permission can be granted because of one of the following: elopement and deflowerment, pregnancy, or living together as husband and wife.

Socio-legal reality

In this area too, secular official law is in conflict with traditional unofficial Muslim law. In the eyes of the people and of Muslim law, when a girl or boy reaches puberty he or she can marry whatever his or her age. Quantitative data show that people in many cases do not take into account the provisions of the Civil Code. Parents living in rural areas or who are illiterate at times 'marry' their offspring just after puberty. In these cases, families first use a solemnized marriage with only a *nikah* in accordance with unofficial Muslim law. When the couple reaches the officially permitted age of 17, they register their marriage with the state. In the early 1990s Yıldırak (1992: 21) found that the average marriage age of women was lower than the officially prescribed one.[22] In the early1990s the SPO conducted research on a sample (18,210 households from urban and rural communities) representing the whole of Turkey (SPO 1992).[23] This research showed that the percentage of underage marriages in Turkey was about 9 per cent (SPO 1992: 39). While 3.36 per cent of all subsisting marriages were (unofficially) conducted at or below the age of 14, 5.38 per cent of them were solemnized with only a *nikah* at the age of 15 (SPO 1992: 39).

The official census data also documented underage marriages. The State Institute of Statistics (SIS) showed that in the early 1990s the ratio of marriages in the age group of 12–14 was 0.54 per cent for females and 0.88 per cent for males (SIS 1996: 20). Yıldırak (1992: 21) observed in his field of research that when an underage girl and/or boy and their parents inform an *imam* about their consent to the marriage, the *imam* does not ask to see the official marriage certificate and solemnizes the marriage unofficially. In these cases, the *imam* does not ask the bride and bridegroom about their ages (Yıldırak 1992: 22; see also, Elmacı 1994: 105, confirming this). A 1998 survey based on data from interviews conducted with 599 women in eastern and south-eastern Turkey showed that 16.3 per cent of women living in the region were married under the age of 15 and in a religious ceremony (İlkkaracan 1998: 66, 69). In other research, Gücük *et al.* found in the eastern Turkish city Van that '[t]he percentage with age at first pregnancy of ≤14 years was 11.5 per cent for women in polygamous marriages and 10.2 per cent for women in monogamous marriages' (Gücük *et al.* 2010: 127). Of polygamist women, 17.3 per cent were married at or before the age of 14, and the figure for the monogamist women is 20.3 per cent. About 10 per cent of these women (both monogamists and polygamists) had their first pregnancies at the age of 14 or below (Gücük *et al.* 2010: 129). These data plainly show that in spite of all the efforts by the state, underage marriages, which are punishable offences, although rare, are a part of the socio-legal reality in Turkey.

Unofficial Muslim law and official law in Turkish courts

Case law shows that in some cases people succeeded in registering their illegal underage marriages.[24] In other cases, lower court judges tolerated underage marriages. Nevertheless, the Court of Cassation overruled these decisions.[25]

In a 2003 case the Court of Cassation dealt with an underage marriage. The woman unofficially married a man even though she was not at the legally prescribed age for marriage. They lived for some years as husband and wife with a view to having an official marriage when they reached the legal age. They confirmed before the court that they illegally got married before they reached the legal age limit. Nevertheless, before they could officially register their marriage, they were unable to get along with each other and got divorced. However, the woman asked for financial compensation, which the husband rejected. The Court of Cassation held that since the woman had entered the marriage as a virgin, the man's act was unjust, and she deserved some financial compensation.[26] The Court underlined that 'the petitioner's unofficial marriage does not exist legally but social values that paved the way for this marriage put a burden of loyalty on an unofficial marriage'.[27]

Polygamy

Official law

Articles 92, 113, 114, 115 of the Civil Code 1926 and Article 130 of the Civil Code 2001 establish that no person can marry again unless s/he proves that the earlier marriage has been dissolved by death or by divorce or by a decree of nullity. Article 145 of the Civil Code 2001 establishes that a second marriage is invalid if a person has a spouse at the time of the subsequent marriage. In other words, the second marriage is absolutely void, or void *ab initio*.[28] Furthermore, polygamy is a criminal offence in Turkey.

Article 230 of the new Turkish Criminal Code 2004 states that:

> (1) A person who marries another person although he/she is legally married at that time shall be punished with imprisonment from six months to two years.
>
> (2) Any person who officially gets married to a person known as married to another person although he is bachelor shall be punished according to the provisions of the above subsection.
>
> (3) Any person who attempts to get married by concealing his/her identity shall be sentenced to imprisonment from three months to one year.

In short, there is an obvious conflict between traditional Muslim law, which allows a man to marry up to four wives, and the official law of Turkey, which does not recognize polygamous marriages.

Socio-legal reality

Field research has shown that despite its criminalization, polygamy persists in Turkey (Gök'e 1991: 113; Elmacı 1994: 84; Kümbetoğlu 1997: 121; Güriz 1996: 4). A review of Turkish newspapers shows that polygamous marriages do not take place only in the rural and eastern parts of Turkey (Kümbetoğlu 1997: 123), but also exist in metropolitan areas. As a matter of fact, it is easier to have a polygamous life free from the pressure of a *Gemeinschaft* in urban environments (see Elmacı 1994: 105, 108; Tosun 2001; Kardam 2005). News stories document polygamous marriages by famous people such as politicians, businessmen, singers, actors, members of parliament and even ministers of the cabinet.[29]

A late 1990s survey that included 599 women, aged 14 to 75, living in south-eastern and eastern Turkey showed that while 89.4 per cent of them had monogamous marriages, 10.6 per cent were living in polygamous partnerships (İlkkaracan 1998: 69). In 2010, 410 (88.7 per cent) of the surveyed 462 married women aged between 15 and 49 years who attended Van Central Maternal, Child Health and Family Planning

Polyclinic stated that they 'were in monogamous marriages, while 52 (11.3 per cent) were in polygamous marriages' (Gücük *et al.* 2010: 127).

Unofficial Muslim law and official law in Turkish courts

One polygamy case involved a billionaire who was murdered. Because the matter involved a considerable amount of money, the second wife came forward and commenced a lawsuit to claim part of the inheritance. The billionaire had three unofficial wives and five children from the first two. None of the wives had been officially married. The second wife claimed in court that after the death of her husband she was given only three companies, while the first wife received twenty-three of them. She claimed that she deserved much more and applied for the annulment of the contract left by the husband regarding inheritance. The Court of Cassation treated her with some recognition despite the fact that she was only married unofficially with a *nikah* and several times overturned the decisions by the lower courts that treated her unfavourably.[30]

In another polygamy case, the Court of Cassation held that the second wife should be paid some compensation from the insurance company because of the death of her unofficial husband at work.[31] In another instance, an unofficially married wife petitioned that her husband had not informed her that he already had an official marriage at the time she married him. She asked for some financial compensation and the Court of Cassation decided in her favour.[32] In a similar case, a man married a woman with a religious marriage and promised her that he would divorce his first wife. However, he and his first wife evicted the second wife from their home. She demanded some financial compensation from her ex-husband and the Court of Cassation accepted her claim.[33]

Polygamy is not positively regarded by the Turkish society, which is monogamist to a very great extent. Duben and Behar (1996: 161) show that even at the end of the nineteenth century, when polygamy was legal, the proportion of polygamous marriages in Istanbul was only 2.51 per cent of all subsisting marriages. In 1907 this figure was 2.16 per cent (Duben and Behar 1996: 162). Still today, polygamy is rare in Turkey and is not viewed positively. As a result, the courts are not as tolerant as they are with the *nikah* cases and therefore even fewer polygamy cases have come before the courts.

Conclusion

The hegemonic Kemalist elite in Turkey has attempted to change legal rules concerning family matters in a predominantly Muslim society. This endeavour is seen as one of the most daring experiments for a modernizing Muslim elite. However, Muslim Turks have not jettisoned their unofficial Muslim laws, despite secular legal enforcement. Instead, they have tried to meet the demands of both the secular Turkish legal system and the unofficial Muslim law. This is a remarkable manifestation of Ehrlich's (1913, 1922, 1936) 'living law', Griffith's (1986) strong legal pluralism and Chiba's (1989) theory of the continuous interaction of official and unofficial laws.

As Berkes (1978: 522) points out, the Civil Code was perceived by the Kemalist elite as a social engineering instrument aimed at achieving an ideal society, rather than regulating the existing socio-legal sphere. The Turkish state expected that through societal secularization, urbanization, legal enforcement, the process of consent manufacturing (Gramsci 1971) by employing legal literacy campaigns, education and media (Herman and Chomsky 1988), Muslim Turks would jettison shari'a and would only obey the secular official law.

Muslim Turks have had three alternative routes by which they could conduct themselves in relation to secular law. The first was totally avoiding the official secular law and obeying only the unofficial Muslim law. The second option was following only the secular Turkish state law. The third option was following a combination of the requirements of both unofficial Muslim law and official secular Turkish law. As this chapter underlines, many of them have preferred the third choice: they have developed a new unofficial hybrid Muslim law that combines the rules of unofficial Muslim law as well as those of the official secular Turkish law. However, despite the existence of this new hybrid law, tension between the official and unofficial laws continues, paving the way for disputes. When a dispute arises, the socio-legal reality of unofficial Muslim law interacts with the official law, this time in the courtrooms and not just in the socio-legal sphere.

This chapter has also shown that despite the Turkish state's assertively secularist rhetoric, the judges have largely been tolerant of unofficial Muslim law related to marriage issues. None of the judges has so far expressed the wish to apply uncodified Islamic law or to see shari'a reintroduced in the legal system. However, they have not waged a war against shari'a's unofficial existence in the legally pluralist socio-legal sphere either. Instead of staunchly focusing on secularism, they have endeavoured to smoothly tackle the negative consequences of legal pluralism, especially when women are involved.

Notes

1 On 27 November 2001 the Turkish Parliament enacted a completely new civil code, replacing the former one.
2 In addition to family law, many refer to Muslim law in their dealings in business, finance and insurance matters, despite the non-recognition of this law by the state.
3 For the period between 1926–90, see Yilmaz (2005) in detail.
4 Article 143 of the new Civil Code and Article 237/3 of the Criminal Code. This is today regulated by the new Penal Code 2005's Article 230.
5 Article 143 of the new Civil Code 2001.
6 The previous Criminal Code's relevant Article indicated that: (1) A marriage officer who knowingly solemnizes the marriage of persons who are not legally entitled to marry, parties to such a marriage, and appointed or natural guardians who consent or lead the parties to such a marriage, shall be imprisoned for three months to two years. (2) A public officer issuing marriage certificates without abiding by legal requirements shall be punished by imprisonment for not more than three months. (3) Whoever performs a religious ceremony for a marriage without seeing the certificate indicating that the parties are lawfully married shall be punished by the punishment prescribed in the foregoing paragraph. (4) Men and women who cause a religious ceremony to be performed prior to being married lawfully shall be punished by imprisonment for two to six months.
7 Unofficial marriages are so common that one can find many examples for this, see for instance, *Zaman*, 11 April 1998, p. 11.

8 See for example, *Milliyet*, 6 March 1998, p. 3. I am not arguing for criminalization of fornication, because it is a private matter, as long as it is private and consensual and thus it is a matter between them and God. What I find ironic is that in the secular Turkish law religious cohabitation, i.e. *nikah* without an official marriage certificate, is seen as a crime while cohabitation between people who are not married to each other and who have not performed a *nikah* is not illegal.

9 Between 1933 and 1965, benefiting from five such bills, 2,739,379 unions were registered as marriages and 10,006,452 illegitimate children were legitimized (Fişek 1985: 292).

10 Law no. 3716, promulgated on 16 May 1991. Previous laws nos. 2330, 4727, 5524, 6652, 1826 and 2526.

11 See for example, *Hürriyet*, 9 March 1997.

12 *Hürriyet*, 14 November 1997, p. 11. For another example see, *Milliyet*, 19 November 2000, p. 21, which reports that the governor, military officers and some students bore witness to the official marriage of 130 already married (unofficially) couples.

13 Y2HD E. 983/2664 K. 983/3310 T. 06.06.1983; Y2HD E. 985/5223 K. 985/5310 T. 04.06.1985; Y4CD E. 992/2504 K. 992/3125 T. 28.04.1992.

14 Y2HD E. 96/1606; K. 96/1661 T. 21.3.1996; YKD, 22, 1996, 1291.

15 YHGD E. 1997/4–690 K. 1997/893 T. 5.11.1997, for a similar 2002 case see YHD 4 E. 2001/13026 K. 2002/3866 T. 01.04.2002.

16 Y4HD E. 2001/4849 K. 2001/8843 T. 1.10.2001. For a 2004 case that is also about an unofficial marriage, see Y4HD E. 2004/5370 K. 2004/14142 T. 13.12.2004.

17 Y2HD E. 02/1153 K. 03/2380 T. 6.3.2003; YKD 29, 2003, 1044. The unofficial wives are not always treated as official wives by the superior courts. In a 2005 Council of State case, an unofficial wife applied to the state for financial compensation and social security payments as her unofficial state-employee village-guard husband was killed in a terrorist attack while on duty. The lower administrative court refused the application, arguing that she was not officially his wife and the Council of State upheld the decision of the lower court, D11D E. 2003/121 K. 2005/5372.

18 Reported in *Milliyet*. Available online at www.milliyet.com.tr/default.aspx?aType=SonDakika&ArticleID=1017782 (accessed 9 September 2012).

19 Y4HD E. 2004/15423 K. 2005/13451 T. 13.12.2005, Y21HD E. 2007/289 K. 2007/8718 T. 28.5.2007. For similar previous Court of Cassation cases see Y21HD E. 1996/1604 K. 1996/1661 T. 21.3.1996, Y21HD E. 2000/711 K. 2000/637 T. 03.02.2000, Y21HD E. 2001/4847 K. 2001/6170 T. 25.9.2001 and Y21HD E. 1997/2093 K. 1997/2188 T. 25.3.1997.

20 Reported online at http://haber5.com/guncel/imam-nikahina-yargitay-korumasi (accessed 9 September 2012). For a more recent Court of Cassation case involving only religious marriage, see YHGK E.2010/3–634 K.2010/677 T. 22.12.2010. For different views in the doctrine on religious marriage, see Ayan 2004: 303; Badur 2009: 73; Köseoğlu 2008: 329. See also an ECHR case on the issue: *Şerife Yiğit v. Turkey: Family Life and the Prohibition of Discrimination* (Article 8 in conjunction with Article 14 ECHR). On 20 January 2009 the European Court of Human Rights decided, on the basis of Article 8 ECHR, on the rights that can be derived from a religious marriage. On 14 September 2009 the case was referred to the Grand Chamber. A man and wife entered into a *nikah* in 1976. Six children were born within this marriage. The husband died in 2002. The wife asked for the registration of her marriage in the Turkish register and for the registration of her children as the children of the deceased husband. The registration of the children was accepted, but the registration of the marriage was refused. The Court considered that there was a de facto existing family life that fell within the protection of Article 8 ECHR. However, the wife's claim was eventually dismissed. The Court considered that although there are Member States of the Council of Europe that recognize other stable relationships alongside traditional marriage, Turkey cannot be obliged to do the same (Rutten 2010: 83).

21 Act No. 3453, 1938.

22 The research conducted by Yıldırak (1992: 8) was conducted in 14 different cities of Turkey, in various geographical regions.

23 Cities and regions included are: Istanbul, Izmir, Bursa, Sakarya and Denizli from western Turkey, Gaziantep, Adana, Antalya and Hatay from south Turkey, Ankara, Eskişehir, Konya and Kütahya from central Turkey, Samsun, Zonguldak, Trabzon and Kastamonu from the Black Sea area, and

158   *Ihsan Yilmaz*

Malatya, Erzurum, Diyarbakır, Sivas, Van, Kars, Şanlıurfa, Adıyaman, Siirt and Ağrı from east and south-east Turkey, SPO (1992: 9).
24 Y4CD E. 990/916 K. 990/1435 T. 14.03.1990.
25 See for instance, Y.21.H.D. E. 2000/711 K. 2000/637 T. 03.02.2000. There were several cases of underage marriage decided before 1990s; see, for example, Y2HD E. 8499 K.7437 T. 24.9.1985 and Y2HD E.4496 K. 4385 T. 7.5.1985.
26 YHGD E. 2003/4–55 K. 2003/100 T. 26.02.2003.
27 YHGD E. 2003/4–55 K. 2003/100 T. 26.02.2003.
28 YHGK E. 2/751 K. 287 T. 26.03.1986; Y2HD E. 1729 K. 2054 T. 27.02.1986; Y2HD E. 194 K. 2546 T. 03.06.1990.
29 For a case concerning a minister of the cabinet, as he then was, who was a member of the then-ruling Welfare Party, which became a controversial issue between European and Turkish politicians with regard to human rights issues in Turkey, see *The Independent*, 17 April 1997, p. 14. For another case regarding another former minister of the cabinet who is also former chairman of a very popular football club, see *Hürriyet*, 7 November 1997, p. 27.
30 Daily *Zaman*, 15 March 2007. Available online at www.zaman.com.tr/haber.do?haberno=513245 (accessed 9 September 2012).
31 Y21HD E. 1604 K. 1661 T. 21.03.1996.
32 YGK E. 2006/2–558 K. 2006/568 T. 20.9.2006.
33 Y4HD E.2004/14503 K. 2005/11211 T. 20.10.2005.

Bibliography

Ansay, T. (1996) 'Family law', in T. Ansay and D. Wallace, Jr. (eds), *Introduction to Turkish Law*, The Hague: Kluwer Law International.

Ayan, S. (2004) *Evlilik Birliğinin Korunması*, Ankara: TBB.

Badur, E. (2009) 'Ailenin Korunması Alanındaki Son Gelişmeler', *TBB Dergisi*, 84: 63–92.

Berkes, N. (1978) *Türkiye'de Çağdaşlaşma*, Istanbul: Doğu-Batı Yayınları.

Chiba, M. (1989) *Legal Pluralism: toward a General Theory Through Japanese Legal Culture*, Tokyo: Tokai UP.

Duben, A. and Behar, C. (1996) *Istanbul Haneleri: Evlilik, Aile ve Doğurganlık, 1880–1940*. Istanbul: İletişim.

Ehrlich, E. (1913) *Grundlegung der Soziologie des Rechts*, Berlin: Duncker & Humblot.

——(1922) 'The sociology of law', *Harvard Law Review*, 36(2): 130–45.

——(1936) *Fundamental Principles of the Sociology of Law*, Cambridge, MA: Harvard UP.

Elmacı, N. (1994) 'Polygamy: Çok-eşli Evlilikler', in N. Arat (ed.), *Türkiye'de Kadın Olmak*, Istanbul: Say.

Fişek, H. (1985) 'Introduction', in T. Erder (ed.), *Family in Turkish Society. Sociological and Legal Studies*, Ankara: Turkish Social Science Association.

Gökçe, B. (1991) *Gecekondularda Ailelerarası Geleneksel Dayanışmanın Çağdas Organizasyonlara Dönüşümü*, Istanbul: Sosyoloji Derneği.

Gramsci, A. (1971) *Prison Notebooks*, New York: International Publishers.

Griffiths, J. (1986) 'What is legal pluralism?' *Journal of Legal Pluralism and Unofficial Law*, 24:1–56.

Gücük, S. *et al.* (2010) 'Van İlindeki Çok Eşlilik Oranları ve Etkileyen Faktorler: Kesitsel Çalışma', *J Kartal TR*, 21(3): 127–33.

Güriz, A. (1996) 'Sources of Turkish law', in T. Ansay and D. Wallace, Jr. (eds), *Introduction to Turkish Law*, The Hague: Kluwer Law International.

Herman, E.S. and Chomsky, N. (1988) *Manufacturing Consent: The Political Economy of the Mass Media*, New York: Pantheon Books.

Hooker, M.B. (1975) *Legal Pluralism*, Oxford: Clarendon Press.

HUNEE (Hacettepe Üniversitesi Nüfus Etüdleri Enstitüsü) (1993) *Türkiye Nüfus ve Sağlık Sraştırması*, Ankara: Ministry of Health and HUNEE.

İlkkaracan, P. (1998) 'Exploring the context of women's sexuality in Turkey', *Reproductive Health Matters*, 6(12): 66–75.

Karataş, B., Derebent, E., Yüzer, S., Yiğit, R. and Özcan, A. (2006) 'Kırsal Kesim Kökenli Kadınların Aile İçi Şiddete İlişkin Görüşleri', Second International Conference On Women's Studies, Eastern Mediterranean University Center For Women's Studies, Famagusta, Turkish Republic of Northern Cyprus.

Kardam, F. (2005) 'Dynamics of the honor killings in Turkey. Prospects for action', Ankara: UN Development Program.

Köseoğlu, B. (2008) 'Ailenin Siddetten Korunmasi', *TBB Dergisi*, 77: 307–41.

Kruger, H. (1991) 'Aile Hukuku Sorunları Osmanlı İslam Geleneği', in B. Dikeçligil and A. Çiğdem (eds), *Aile Yazıları*, Ankara: T.C.B. Aile Araştırma Kurumu Başkanlığı.

Kümbetoğlu, B. (1997) 'Aile, Evlilik, Nikah: Farklılaşan Kavramlar', *Toplum ve Bilim*, 73: 111–26.

Lipstein, K. (1956) 'The reception of western law in Turkey', *Annales de la droit d'Istanbul*, 5–6.

Örücü, E. (2008) 'Judicial navigation as official law meets culture in Turkey', *International School of Law in Context*, 4(1): 35–61.

Rutten, S. (2010) 'Protection of spouses in informal marriages by human rights', *Utrecht Law Review*, 6(2): 77–92.

SIS (State Institute of Statistics) (1996) *Marriage Statistics: 1994*, Ankara: SIS.

SPO (State Planning Organization) (1992) *Türk Aile Araştırması*, Ankara: DPT.

Tosun, R. (2001) 'Çok Eşlilik', *Yeni Şafak*, 12 February 2001.

Yilmaz, I. (2005) *Muslim Laws, Politics and Society in Modern Nation States: Dynamic Legal Pluralisms in England, Turkey and Pakistan*, Aldershot: Ashgate.

Yıldırak, N. (1992) *Köy Kadınlarının Sosyo-Ekonomik ve Kültürel Konumları*, Istanbul: Friedrich Ebert Vakfı.

Glossary

ahkam zanniyya	relative rules
'alim	religious scholar
al-'amal bihi	precedent
amir al-mu'minin	Commander of the faithful; title first attributed to the second caliph Umar and used by several leaders in the Muslim world throughout history, including, today, the King of Morocco
aqal darar	the least harm
'aqd	contract, justice
'aqd abadi	eternal contract
'aqd nikah	marriage contract
'aqd 'urfi	customary contract
arkhan	pillars
arkan al-din	pillars of the faith
ashkhas	persons
ayat	verse
bay'	sale
bid'a	innovation
al-bughd	hate
dadgah-e madani-ye khass	special civil courts (Iran)
dahir	royal decree
dalil al-'aql	the evidence of reason
darar	harm, injury; according to some legal schools, it constitutes a valid ground for female-initiated divorce
al-darb wa-l-sabb	ill treatment such as physical and verbal abuse
dar-ul quzat	shari'a courts (India)
darar haqiqi	true harm
darura	necessity; a legal principle allowing a person to set aside a shari'a norm in a particular circumstance if fulfilling it could lead to harm
faqih	an expert in the law
faskh	annulment of marriage if certain conditions exist, which differ from school to school (all recognize impotency and apostasy as valid grounds)

fatwa	authoritative but not binding legal opinion issued by a *mufti*
fiqh	jurisprudence
fitna	disorder; anarchy (also with a sexual meaning)
fuqaha'	pl. of *faqih*
hadana	custody
hadd	lit. limit
hadith	saying of the Prophet
al-hakim	judge
halal makruh	detestable but permissible act
halala	remarriage of a divorced couple after an intervening marriage
haqq	right
hawa'	whim
hijab / hejab	veil
hisba	the practice of supervision of economic and commercial affairs
hizanet see hadana	suspension of commercial and other secular affairs
hudud	pl. of *hadd*
hukm	ruling
huquq shar'iyya	religious rights
'idda / 'iddat	period following divorce or death of the husband during which a woman is entitled to maintenance and cannot marry another man
ijma'	consensus; one of the canonical sources of Islamic law
ijtihad / ijtehad	method of reasoning by which a mujtahid derives law on the basis of the primary sources (Qur'an and Sunna)
ikhtilaf	difference of opinion within *fiqh*
'ilm	knowledge
imam	religious figure who leads worship services and provides religious guidance; also a honorary title for scholars; in the Shi'i context, a successor of the Prophet in his political and spiritual capacity
istabdad	despotism
istikrar	stability
istihsan	lit. preference; a method of inference preferred over qiyas and based on alternative textual evidence if it leads to a more reasonable result that does not involve undue hardship
istislah	a method of inference that does not resort directly to a revealed text but draws on rational arguments that are grounded according to Sunni majority *fiqh* in the protection of life, mind, religion, private property and family
ita'a	obedience
jama'at	committees
jati	caste

jihad	lit. striving, effort
ijma'	consensus of religious scholars; one of the canonical sources of shari'a
jalsa	hearing
kahf amin	trusted cave
kafa'a	equality of status
katib	recorder in a court
khul'/khula	divorce at the initiative of the wife in which she asks the husband to repudiate her in exchange for a sum of money or property or the forfeiture of some or all of her financial rights; in classical Islamic law it required the agreement of the husband
li'an	mutual cursing causing the dissolution of marriage
madhhab	interpretive community; legal school
madrasa	religious school
mahakim shari'yya	shari'a courts (Lebanon)
mahakim ruhiyya	spiritual courts (for Christians in Lebanon)
mahakim madhhabiyya	*madhhab* courts (for Druze in Lebanon)
mahkamat al-tamyiz	Court of Cassation (Lebanon)
mahila	(or *nari adalat*) women's courts (India)
mahr/mehr	dower, one of the requirements for a valid marriage; the sum of money or object owed by a husband to his wife, considered as a binding element of the marriage contract
mahr al-mithl	appropriate dower
mahr al-sirr	secret dower
majlis/majles	assembly, council
maqasid al-shari'a	goals of shari'a
marja' al-taqlid	source of emulation; a high religious figure of Shi'a Islam
al-mashhur	common; majority position within a legal school
maskan shar'i	legal (in the sense of in conformity with shari'a rules) marital home
maslaha	welfare
maslahat al-'amma	general interest
mawadda	amity, love
mithaq	pact
mu'ajjal	prompt dower
mu'ajjal	deferred dower
mu'akhkhar al-sadaq	deferred dower
mubara'	divorce by consent of both spouses; unlike *khul'*, it does not entail the wife's forfeiture of financial rights
mufti	jurist who is entitled to issue *fatwas*
muharram	prohibited
muhtasib	one who holds the office charged to perform *hisba*, markey inspector, moral policeman

mujtahid	a learned jurist capable of *ijtihad*
mukhtasar	abridged manuals
muqaddam al-sadaq	prompt dower
muta'	financial compensation for the wife who has been unjustly divorced
mut'a	(*nikah al-mut'a*) 'pleasure' marriage; temporary marriage allowed by Shiism
mutlaq	absolute
muwazana	equilibrium
nafaqa	maintenance of wives and children by the husband
nari adalat	see *mahila*
nasab	lineage
al-na'ib al-'amm	civil judge
nikah	religious marriage
nikahnama	marriage contract
nizam	order
niyya	intention
nushuz	disobedience
panchayat	village council
qadi / qazi	judge
qanun	positive law
qisas / qesas	retribution
qiwama	maintenance
qiyas	a source of Islamic law; analogy
rahma	mercy
ra'y	reasoning
al-rajih	probable
rajm	stoning
rijal al-din	men of religion
riba	interest
al-sadaq al-musamma	specified dower
sahih	correct, sound, authentic
shahid	martyr
shahna	rancour
shari'a / shariat	lit. path; divine law contained in the Qur'an and Sunna
shaykh	elder; leader; Islamic scholar
shiqaq	discord; one of the bases for women-initiated dissolution of marriage
shurut	conditions
siyasa shari'iyya	regulatory authority of the state as recognized by Islamic law
sulh	reconciliation; agreement
Sunna / Sunnah	tradition; decisions and actions of the Prophet
ta'a	obedience

ta'dil al-muhur	changing the *mahr*
takhayyur	selecting opinions from various schools
talaq	unilateral divorce by the husband
talaq al-ahsan/talaq-e-ahsan	single pronouncement of *talaq*
talaq al-tafwid/talaq-e-tafweez	delegation to the wife of a husband's right to repudiate her
talaq al-bid'a/talaq-ul bida'at	'innovatory repudiation', i.e the triple *talaq*
talaq al-mustabidd	despotic repudiation
talfiq	bringing together different parts of a doctrine or different opinions from various schools on specific legal issues
taqlid	imitation
tasammu'	hearsay
tatliq/tafriq	judicial divorce
thawabit	fixed foundation
'ulama'	religious scholars (sing. *alim*)
'urf	custom
al-usra	family
usul al-fiqh	roots of jurisprudence; a field of study on the sources of law and methods of interpretation
velayat-e faqih	guardianship of the jureconsult (doctrine upholding the Iranian political system that has a supreme *faqih* at its apex)
wakil	agent
wali	male guardian of the bride
wali al-amr	person in authority
waqf	religious endowment
wilaya/velayat	legal guardianship of brides or children
zahir	the exterior or apparent meaning of things
zawaj	marriage
zawaj 'urfi	customary marriage
zawaj al-mut'a	temporary marriage
zawaj munqati	limited marriage
al-zawja al-mushakasa	a quarrelsome wife
zakat	an obligatory tax required of Muslims, levied on specific categories of property and movable goods
zani/zaniya	a man /woman who commits *zina*
zina	illicit sexual intercourse

Index

In classifying entries no account is taken of the letter *'ayn* and the Arabic article *al-*. The countries included are only those which are not the object of specific chapters. Names of individuals are listed only when they appear in the text, and not in the notes and bibliography. Terms that are recurring throughout the book, such as polygamy, dower (*mahr*) and *ijtihad*, are not listed here.

'Abduh, M. 7
Abou El Fadl, K. 2
ADR (alternative dispute resolution) 24, 50
adultery (*zina*) 2, 9, 13, 16, 18, 20–22, 24–25, 28 n. 19, 53, 73–74, 79, 83 n. 2, 128
al-Afghani, J. al-D. 7
Afghanistan xvii, 9, 12, 15, 19
Ahmadinejad, M. 144
Amanullah 9
apostasy 11, 27 n. 10, 41, 53, 107
Arab spring xvii, 25, 100
Arabi, O. xiii
Austin, J. 129
Al-Azhar 14, 101

Bangladesh xix, 12, 22
Behbahani, S. 145
Behruzi, M. 139
Berkes, N. 154
Bogra, M.A. 71

Chiba, M. 154
child custody (*hadana*) 11, 12, 13, 21, 25, 35, 40, 43, 77–78, 82, 84 n. 36, 100–101, 118 n. 63, 124, 137–40, 142–44
Chubak, M. 142
citizenship of children 139, 144
conditions attached to the marriage contract 37, 72, 90–91, 92, 94–95, 125–26
consummation of marriage 10, 74, 93, 103 n. 31, 116 n. 9, 141
Cyprus 33

disobedience (*nushuz*) 39, 138
divorce: by *khul'* xvii, 11, 13–14, 17, 22, 28 n. 14, 35, 41–42, 45 n. 19, 60–61, 75–76, 81, 88–89, 95, 97–101, 104 n. 57, 106, 113, 115; by *mubara'* 11, 103 n. 54; by *talaq* 2, 10–13, 41, 45 n. 18, 52–57, 71, 79, 87–88, 95, 96–97, 100–101, 113, 118 n. 61, 123, 138; *see also talaq-i-tafwid*; for discord (*shiqaq*) xviii, 13, 22, 25, 28 n. 8 and 12, 96–98, 104 n. 57, 122, 124–27, 132; for injury (*darar*) 11, 21, 42, 96, 101, 103 n. 48, 107–11; for polygamy xvii, 20, 58, 111–14.
darura 2

Eaton, M. 82
Ebadi, S. 145
Ehrlich, E. 155

faskh 11, 41, 60

Griffiths, J. 155, 160

hadana *see* child custody
Hallaq, W.B. xii, 4, 5, 8
Hassan II 123–24

Ibn 'Abidin, M. A. 17, 35
'idda 10, 11, 41, 54–56, 61–62, 65 n. 21, 66 n. 24, 76–77
ikhtilaf 3, 5, 13, 26
impotence 10, 11, 41–42, 119 n. 79
Indonesia xix n. 1 and 2, 12, 18, 21
inheritance 72, 141, 144
Iraq 12, 35, 139–40